Married Women's Separate Property
in England, 1660–1833

D1103928

Married Women's Separate Property in England, 1660–1833

Susan Staves

Harvard University Press
Cambridge, Massachusetts
London, England
1990

R00730 32796

Library of Congress Cataloging-in-Publication Data

Staves, Susan, 1942–
    Married women's separate property in England, 1660–1833 / Susan
Staves.
        p.   cm.
    Bibliography: p.
    Includes index.
    ISBN 0-674-55088-9 (alk. paper)
    1. Married women—Great Britain—History.   2. Separate property—
Great Britain—History.   3. Married women—United States—History.
4. Separate property—United States—History.   I. Title.
KD761.S4S73 1990
346.4104—dc20   89-15263
[344.1064]   CIP

To the memory of Irvin Ehrenpreis

Preface

"Speak to me not of settlements," Evelina murmurs to her fiancé, Lord Orville, in Fanny Burney's novel of 1778. She deferentially indicates her trust in his willingness to provide adequately for her and, probably, her ignorance and presumed inability to comprehend the arcane mysteries of married women's property—a subject, like sex, not to be contemplated by a young lady. Given the difficulty of some of the legal concepts in this field, it is no wonder that almost all eighteenth-century women despaired of understanding them. Most historians today, I dare say, would have difficulty understanding a sentence on this subject in a recent monograph published by Cambridge Studies in Legal History: "In attempting to explain the invalidity of a gift over of a remainder for the life of a tenant in tail in the conveyance of an entail, Coke argued that the remainder must be void."

Because many of the important developments in married women's property law are quite technical, the problems of exposition are considerable. In this book I have attempted to explain complex and unfamiliar ideas clearly for a diverse audience of historians, legal scholars, scholars of eighteenth-century culture and literature, and intelligent people concerned with women's issues. I hope that the book both makes an original contribution to legal history and provides more ordinary information about the social history of the period. Readers unfamiliar with legal terms like "jointure," "equity of redemption," and "remainder for the life of a tenant in tail" can be confident that an explanation of such terms will be forthcoming as soon as it is needed to follow the argument. A glossary of technical terms may also be found at the back of the book. I beg the patience and trust of such readers and can promise, on the basis of my experience in giving papers on this subject to audiences of "nonlawyers," that it is not necessary to be a lawyer to understand this history. In the interest of making the subject accessible to a larger audience, I also beg readers already at home with the legal vocabulary to excuse definitions and explanations which may seem to them superfluous or, worse, occasionally incomplete or imprecise. The near-incomprehensibility of the rules of this property system is itself a social fact that deserves—and will get—analysis.

For generous support of this work, I am indebted to the American Council of Learned Societies for a Study Grant which supported me for one year as a Harvard Liberal Arts Fellow in Law. At the Harvard Law School I profited from the—very different—approaches of Frank Michelman to Property, Duncan Kennedy to Torts, Catharine MacKinnon to Sex Discrimination, and Samuel Thorne and Charles Donahue to earlier English Legal History. A John Simon Guggenheim Fellowship also made possible an additional year of the crucial research and thinking for this book.

I am grateful to a variety of audiences to whom I spoke about various aspects of this book for their encouragement and comments: the Northeast Society for British Studies, the Social Science History Association, the American Society for Eighteenth-Century Studies, Boston University Law School, the Law School of the State University of New York at Buffalo, and the University of Minnesota Humanities Center. Like many eighteenth-century scholars in Boston, I feel a special affection for my friends in the Boston Eighteenth-Century Club, whose wide-ranging curiosity about the period has made them a most friendly and encouraging audience for works-in-progress, including this one. I am indebted, too, to my friends in the Cambridge Early Modern History Seminar, especially its organizers, John Brewer and Simon Schama, for acute discussions of parts of this book and for generally contributing to my education in history.

To paraphrase the scholar to whose memory this book is dedicated, I am sure that, compared with the ideal of a definitive treatise, the present volume has more faults than its author has blushes. Nevertheless, for careful reading of the manuscript and for saving me from at least a few of those blushes, as well as for constructive suggestions, I am most grateful to Charles Donahue and to the three readers for Harvard University Press, J. H. Baker, Joanna Innes, and Roy Porter. The errors that remain are, of course, my own.

An earlier version of Chapter 5 appeared as "Separate Maintenance Contracts" in *Eighteenth-Century Life,* 11, n.s., 2 (1987), and an earlier version of Chapter 6 appeared as "Pin Money" in *Studies in Eighteenth-Century Culture,* 14 (1985). I thank the editors and publishers of those journals for permission to make use of that material here.

Contents

Married Women's Separate Property
in England, 1660–1833

1

Introduction

Present and Past

In the 1980s, a book on eighteenth-century marriage law and married women's property may be elegiac. Both Margaret Thatcher and Ronald Reagan have attempted to promote nostalgic family policies—or policies which are supposed to be nostalgic—but it seems clear that in England and in America the traditional obligations and rights of husbands and wives at common law, the traditional incidents of the status of marriage, have been dealt a variety of blows from which they are unlikely to recover.

In England now, the deconstruction of the status of marriage has gone very far in practice and still further in theory. Even establishment legal theory is willing to contemplate radical proposals. Thus, a 1982 article in the respectable *Modern Law Review* argued for the elimination of "marriage as a legal institution and status." The author was quite willing to see citizens indulge themselves in whatever religious or personal ceremonies they liked, but she insisted that—ideally—there was no good reason for the legal system to lend any support to such personal relationships or to regulate them in any way.[1] Given this revolutionary change, "the dependence of children" requires that some public provision be made for them, although that provision ought not be the "marriage" of their parents but rather a legal "institution of Parenthood" which would regulate the ties of mothers to their children and of fathers to theirs. Another recent article in a British law journal evinces some of the current dissatisfaction with results achieved by the major family law statutes of the 1960s and 1970s. Since these statutes, in the writer's view, have failed to produce a system of family law which is either theoretically or practically defensible, the time has come for a state system of no-fault insurance for marriage. All married couples could pay into a state-maintained insurance fund which, if divorce occurred, would pay out "rehabilitation" allowances to spouses who needed them. Perhaps, he suggested, if the state were serious about its purported interest in encouraging secure family units, this fund might also issue rebates in the form of old-age pension bonuses to couples who had stayed married for long periods of time.[2]

Even without the adoption of such theoretical proposals, marriage in England has already been stripped of what were traditionally considered crucial status incidents.[3] For example, marriage no longer gives a husband control over his wife's body. English husbands have lost their rights to confine or corporally to punish disobedient wives, and they now risk civil and criminal actions should they attempt to exercise those old prerogatives. Similarly, husbands have lost their right to have sexual intercourse with their wives in the absence of the wife's consent, and can be criminally convicted of rape as though they were strangers. A husband no longer has the right to an action for civil damages for criminal conversation should another man have intercourse with his wife. Wives have a legal right to abort their fetuses whether their husbands like it or not. The husband's right to determine the domicile of the couple has also been abolished, along with his right to compel his wife to return to him should she abscond, and even his absolute right to refuse to maintain a "deserting" wife.

The property consequences of marriage have also been altered. By statutory changes, husbands no longer automatically acquire use rights to wives' real property or ownership of wives' personal property upon marriage. During marriage, wives can retain considerable "separate property" and the wages they earn are their own, not their husbands'. If the contemporary English wife takes the trouble to register her claim to the "matrimonial home," the husband cannot even sell a house he himself bought unless she consents to the sale.

Marriage is now rather easily dissoluble at the will of either spouse. A husband or wife innocent of any "matrimonial misconduct" is powerless to prevent divorce if a spouse, however "guilty," insists on divorce and can show "irretrievable breakdown" of the relationship. Traditional matrimonial misconduct, including adultery, is no longer even supposed to affect a court's decision unless it bears specifically on the welfare of the children. To live with an adulterous mother is no longer officially thought inimical to the welfare of children.

In both England and America these kinds of changes in the traditional common law have led to organized political resistance from groups like Divorced Fathers United, the National Congress of Men, and Father's Rights of America.[4] Fathers are not now the sole or automatic guardians of their legitimate children; in custody disputes with wives they may lose. Losing custody of minor children most often entails also losing the matrimonial house, which is awarded to the custodial parent in the interest of minimizing the disruption of the children's lives.

Wives, for their part, have lost some of the traditional common law "protections" earlier afforded them and acquired some new obligations. A wife innocent of any matrimonial fault is no longer entitled to automatic life-long maintenance or support from her husband but may find herself divorced and awarded a short-term "rehabilitation" allowance. Moreover, a wife may under certain circumstances be found to have acquired an obligation to maintain her husband.[5] A wife who commits certain criminal offenses in the company of her husband will no longer avoid conviction by being assumed to have acted under his compulsion or constraint. Wives do apparently still owe their husbands traditional "service," although the husband's powers to enforce his entitlement to such service now appear very weak. Should one spouse become disabled and the couple seek state benefits, there is now a movement toward sex-blind benefits so that the nondisabled working spouse—husband or wife—is permitted to go on working and to hire a nurse to care for the disabled partner, despite earlier rulings which presumed nursing care would be provided by wives personally.

Such significant changes in the legal definition of the relationship between husband and wife may prompt an elegy for the death of the old common law "baron and feme," but they also provide an enhanced opportunity for historical analysis. The twentieth-century policy debates and rule changes can help illuminate the less articulated political and ideological implications of the older relationship and can show how much less "natural" or "inevitable" the old relationships were than they were considered to be in the eighteenth century.

Subject, Thesis, and the Claim That the Law of Married Women's Property Is Ideological

My principal subject in this book is the legal regime of married women's property from 1660 to 1833. This is a subject which has heretofore not been seen as having much of a history, although both the common law rules governing married women's property and the different rules of the equity courts have from time to time been described.[6] (Equity, alternatively called Chancery, dealt with trusts. Just as now people with wealth often set up trusts to avoid the consequences of tax laws or common law, so also in the eighteenth century some people created trusts to avoid the consequences of the common law of husband and wife.) I propose to examine several important species of married women's property—dower, jointure, pin money and wife's separate property, and separate maintenance allowances—and to explore how the rules governing them were changed during this period.

In general, I will be arguing that the older common law conception of marriage as a status, the concept that generated the earlier rules, crumbled when challenged by contract ideas and contract ideology, but that efforts to apply contract ideas to the marital relation in the mid-eighteenth century led to results which were found socially intolerable. Thus, by the end of the period the courts retreated from contract ideology in this field and reimposed what I am going to argue were deeper patriarchal structures. A principal feature of these deeper patriarchal structures was that women functioned to transmit wealth from one generation of men to the next generation of men. Patriarchy, I take it, is a form of social organization in which fathers appear as political and legal actors, acting publicly for themselves and as representatives of the women and children subordinated to them and dependent upon them in families. In the property regimes of patriarchy, descent and inheritance are reckoned in the male line; women function as procreators and as transmitters of inheritance from male to male.

In a field like married women's property where the history is significantly continuous, the selection of a terminus a quo and a terminus ad quem is necessarily arbitrary. In English legal history, however, the Restoration does constitute a line of demarcation. The interregnum statutes were burnt by the public hangman and the church courts once again opened for business. The Military Tenures Abolition Act (1660) put the final nail in the coffin of a form of property holding that had its origins in the provision of knights in return for the gift of land.[7] The abolition of military tenures, along with the earlier abolition of the Court of Wards in 1645, may be said to mark the beginning of the modern functioning of equity as the guardian of infants and an important maker of family law. After 1660, equity cases were regularly reported, and in 1728 the first published book on equity appeared.[8] As Sir William Holdsworth makes clear, the development of the new doctrines permitting married women to have separate property at equity occurred slowly and haltingly in the sixteenth and seventeenth centuries, and it is certainly not possible to point to any single year as marking the firm establishment of these principles.[9] I believe, however, that the Restoration cases give adequate insight into this process for our purposes.

As for the terminus ad quem, I have chosen 1833 in part because it is the year of the Dower Act.[10] Lee Holcombe elects this date for the beginning of her survey of the legislative "reform" of the nineteenth century, and, in fact, the act may be said to mark a transition from an earlier period in which married women's property was governed principally by so-called private law rules to a later period in which it was governed by statute. Dower, as we shall see, was a crucial, if peculiar, subject of eighteenth-century legal thought. On the one hand, the Dower Act itself may be seen as a minor bit of legislation, one merely tidying up the system, an act sweeping away a few remaining bits of archaic legal rubbish. It was one of a set of statutes intended to effect "reforms" of real property law and to abolish many crucial "archaic" features of the older system. Better known statutes belonging to this same set are the Real Property Limitation Act (1833), abolishing most of the older real property actions and increasing the importance of ejectment, and the Fines and Recoveries Act (1833), abolishing fines, the classical method of effecting a secure conveyance of land.[11] On the other hand, dower was in an important sense the core of the wife's entitlement under the old common law system, and the legislative abrogation of that entitlement has considerable ideological significance. Moreover, the decades immediately following the French Revolution and before 1833 saw elaborate judicial rethinking of some of the earlier experiments with contract ideology in the field of married women's separate property, rethinking which resulted in repudiations of some earlier eighteenth-century cases and the development of newly refined rules.

The legal regime of married women's property in the eighteenth century was principally created by common law and by a set of private law rules in equity not conventionally seen as political or ideological. Nevertheless, I will maintain that this property regime was political and ideological, that it involved some political choices by individuals based on ideological principles. It will be one aim of the legal analysis in this book to show that judges' decisions in property cases were not simply forced by legal logic, but also involved political choices. Obviously, it would be absurd to claim that Parliament could just as well have adopted the Matrimonial Proceedings and Property Act of 1970 in 1770 or that eighteenth-century equity cases could have been decided following exactly those principles. Yet within the limits of the legal ideas available to them, eighteenth-century judges, I will argue, had much more room to maneuver than they availed themselves of, so that both what they elected to do and what they declined to do are significant and revelatory of their ideological principles.

What do I mean by ideology? Ideology, for my purposes here, is people's various "articulated forms of social self-consciousness," the explicit public ideas they have about human relationships, especially those ideas that serve to justify the power relationships between people, and to explain why it is right and good that different people should have different roles and different entitlements to power, wealth, and other social goods.[12] An ancient ideological statement is to be found in Book XII of the *Iliad* when Sarpedon tells Glaukos that it is because they stand in the forefront in battle and fight that they are "honored before others / with pride of place, the choice meats, and the filled wine cups . . . good land, orchard and vineyard, and ploughland for the planting of wheat."[13]

As ideology represents the relations of classes, so also it represents the relations of gender, including the relations of men and women within marriage. It has never historically been the case and is not now the case that marriage can be regarded as a private relationship not subject to public definition and public control.

Public interests in the control of human sexuality and reproduction and in the socialization of children were asserted in the early modern period and continue to be asserted today. For example, Lord Chancellor Eldon in 1805, considering the validity of separate maintenance contracts between husband and wife, declared:

> It is admitted every where, that by the known law, founded upon policy, for the sake of keeping together individual families, constituting the great family of the public, there shall be no separation *a mensa & thoro,* except *propter saevitiam aut adulterium* [that is, there shall be no separation from bed and hearth except for cruelty or adultery]. . . . Independent of the effect of the contract of marriage itself, the rule upon the policy of the law is, that the contract shall be indissoluble, even by the sentence of the law: . . . upon the principle probably, that people should understand that they should not enter into these fluctuating contracts: and, after that sacred contract they should feel it to be their mutual interest to improve their tempers.[14]

In a similar vein upon a similar subject, Mr. Justice Buller had opined in 1788, "it cannot answer the ends of public policy to permit a separation to take place on too easy terms, or without a very sufficient cause."[15] It was also of consequence that the legally established relationship of husband and wife should seem fair, so it was an important function of the courts to provide legitimation for the dominance of husbands and the subordination of wives in the family. Thus, Lord Chancellor Thurlow bothered to explain that the law gave a husband rights over his wife's property in exchange for the legal obligation to support her which he assumed at marriage.[16]

Two recent cases might be mentioned as among the more startling reminders that sexuality and marriage cannot even now be considered as taking place within a private sphere. A California statutory rape law, which criminalized intercourse between adult males and minor females but ignored intercourse between adult females and minor males, was challenged by a man convicted under it on grounds of sex discrimination.[17] The Supreme Court resisted the challenge, reasoning that the state had an interest in controlling the number of out-of-wedlock births. Furthermore, some justices thought, since women were already deterred from illicit intercourse by having to risk the burden of pregnancy, the California statutory rape law was not sex discrimination, but actually a sort of affirmative action program to provide a symmetrical deterrent for men. Recently, also, a British court was forced to consider in *Corbett v. Corbett* whether a man who had had transsexual surgery and married another man had contracted a valid marriage which could support his claim for alimony.[18] After struggling with various testimony about anatomy, surgery, psychology, hormones, chromosomes, and even a pathetic letter from the plaintiff (a transsexual sailor) to the aristocratic defendant, and after having noted that the Ministry of National Insurance had issued the plaintiff "a woman's insurance card and now treat her as a woman for national insurance purposes," the judge decided that since marriage "is the institution of which the family is built, and in which the capacity for natural hetero-sexual intercourse is an essential element," the plaintiff before him must be considered "not a woman for the purposes of marriage" but "a biological male" from birth to the time of trial.

Insofar as the counters of ideology are—in Marx's phrase—"empty generalities . . . torn away from the facts," ideology is inevitably deceptive, illusory, a mystification.[19] *Corbett* suggests that it is possible to consider even so apparently natural a category as "woman" as an "empty generality" with a problematic relationship to any actual person. Ideologies are, nevertheless, attempts at world-representation, attempts to represent both why things are the way they are and how things are. Characteristically, ideologies idealize existing social relations by clothing them "in an inappropriately attractive guise" and also represent existing social relations as natural or necessary or inevitable.[20]

Critical examination of ideological representations, consequently, entails dissipating this illusion of naturalness and inevitability. One strategy for attacking the illusion is to point to "the facts" left out of the ideological representation. Another strategy, as John McMurtry suggests, is to expose the selectivity with which the generalities are used "so that they validate what promotes the established social order, and invalidate what challenges this order," for example, using the generality of "respect for property" to protect the material interests of the ruling class but not to protect customary rights affecting the material interests of the ruled.[21] With respect to ideologies of marriage, similarly, we might observe, generalities about the importance of conjugal fidelity are selectively applied to protect the perceived interests of men but only weakly applied to protect women. Or, as we shall see in the discussion in Chapters 2 and 3 of the attack on widows' common law right to dower, claims of the public importance of maintaining the alienability of real property were used to defeat widows' dower rights but were not used to prohibit the development of strict settlement in tail male, a development which interfered more seriously with alienability than did dower.

Because legal history has usually been done by judges and law professors involved in a system which society requires to produce articulate defenses of the justice and rightness of current legal institutions, legal history has most often been celebratory, explaining how the law was more and more beautifully adapted to the needs of society, more and more perfectly reflective of absolute justice. Such constructions appear in legal histories given in the eighteenth century by legal intellectuals like Lord Chief Justice Mansfield, Lord Chancellor Hardwicke, and William Blackstone. Thus, in the field of married women's property Lord Hardwicke made one of the more self-conscious early modern statements about the necessity of applying old rules to new species of property. Admitting that the Statute of Uses (1535) required jointures to be of freehold land to bar dower, he explained that at the time of the statute "the chief kind of property then regarded was freehold estate in land, and so the statute applied to that only." But in his own time, he added,

> how many species of property have grown up since by new improvements, commerce, and from the funds. Equity has therefore held, that where such provision has been made before marriage, out of any of these, she shall be bound [that is, barred of dower] by it. Consider how many jointures there are now made on women out of the funds, and not one of them within the statute of 27 *H.* 8. So multitudes of jointures out of trust estates, not one of them within the statute; yet equity has always supported them.[22]

Hardwicke here anticipates what Robert Gordon has plausibly described as the dominant modern explanation of legal history, variously called "adaptation theory" or "evolutionary functionalism." As pithily stated by Gordon, this is the notion "that the natural and proper evolution of a society (or at least of a 'progressive society' . . .) is towards the type of liberal capitalism seen in the advanced Western nations . . . , and that the natural and

proper function of a legal system is to facilitate such an evolution."[23] Legal actors represent themselves as only passively adapting to such changes. Thus Hardwicke simply notes the arrival of
new forms of property like stock and consols, and then moves to
"Equity has therefore held" that stocks and consols shall be treated
as the equivalents of freehold land. It is one of the aims of critical
legal history to show that such "therefores" are not inevitable, that
they instead represent active judicial choice. This celebratory
strain in the legal history written by judges and law professors is
one reason why Christopher Hill has urged historians to rescue
legal history from the hands of the lawyers.

Appropriate Sources

My subject of married women's property law in the eighteenth
century resists analysis, even coyly hides from analysis, in intriguing and significant ways. To construct eighteenth-century married
women's property as a subject of analysis appears to import into
the eighteenth century a category first named and elaborately discussed in the nineteenth century in debates over parliamentary
legislation, debates ultimately leading to the important Married
Women's Property Acts of 1870 and 1882. No such "reform"
agitation and no major parliamentary debates over legislation in
this area existed in the eighteenth century, although there were a
few obscure parliamentary acts of interest to me and, more important, some major equity cases finally debated and decided in
the House of Lords. Not surprisingly, therefore, it has not occurred to historians of eighteenth-century parliaments to discuss
changing public policies concerning married women's property.

Nevertheless, it is conventionally said, and said with considerable truth, that the ideas of married women's separate property
developed in eighteenth-century equity practice provided the conceptual bases for the nineteenth-century Married Women's Property Acts.[24] The eighteenth-century equity practices are seen as
affording advantages to women from wealthy families which, in
the nineteenth century, trickle down to middle- and working-class
women by legislative reform. Thus, Lee Holcombe in her *Wives
and Property: Reform of the Married Women's Property Laws in Nineteenth-Century England* ends a chapter surveying earlier equity
practice by pointing to one source of public sympathy for the

nineteenth-century feminists' demands: "Many . . . people could agree with the feminists about the intolerable injustice of the existence, in fact if not in theory, of 'one law for the rich and another for the poor,' and could accept the plea that poor women who suffered under one body of law [common law] should be granted protection similar to that enjoyed by wealthy women under a completely different body of law [equity]." In the Victorian period, married women's property is clearly seen as a matter of public policy, and historians have a convenient archive of legislation, parliamentary debate, petitions, pamphlet literature, contentious magazine articles, and so on.

What significance should be attached to the absence of such an archive in the eighteenth century? One answer might be to say that, in the eighteenth century, married women's property was a matter of private law rather than public law. But this is unsatisfactory for two reasons. First, this modern antithesis between private law and public law was not usually invoked in the early eighteenth century.[25] Second, as I have already suggested, regulation of the relation between husbands and wives and control of sexuality have been considered of communal importance from the middle ages to the present. At no time, including the present, has the larger community or the state been willing to permit individual family members to deal with each other as they saw fit or to deal with the property of married women as they saw fit. What differs between the eighteenth and the nineteenth centuries is not that married women's property uniquely became a matter of public policy in the nineteenth century, but rather that public policy in this area was more covertly made outside the legislature, principally in the equity and common law courts and in the practices of eighteenth-century lawyers and their clients.

If the nineteenth-century legislative acts are conceptually based on eighteenth-century equity practice, where do the eighteenth-century equity practices come from and why should they have arisen in the seventeenth and eighteenth centuries? Clearly, there are crucial differences between the medieval married women's property regime and the eighteenth-century equity regime. That these equity practices have a history has been appreciated, to some extent, by legal historians, including Holdsworth, A. W. B. Simpson, and Lloyd Bonfield.[26] As parliamentary historians like Holcombe see the nineteenth-century legislation as "reform," so these

legal historians generally characterize the seventeenth- and eighteenth-century equity innovations as "inventions," "accommodations," or "improvements." According to these twentieth-century
legal historians, resourceful and intelligent early modern conveyancers invent ways to secure family property from the depreda-
tions of feckless husbands, inventions unknown to the cruder
common law, and equity judges permit those innovations to be
effective. The equity system nicely adjusts the law to a modern
world in which landed property is no longer the only important
source of wealth.

What sort of an archive do legal historians like Holdsworth,
Bonfield, and Simpson use to write this history? Principally they
use reported equity cases with the addition of a smaller number
of common law cases. (Bonfield also uses settlements and conveyancing books.) Such materials are crucial, and I will also rely
on them heavily, tracing the development of the eighteenth-century legal rules concerning married women's separate property
more fully and, I believe, more analytically than has so far been
done. Nevertheless, as most legal historians realize, reported cases
have significant limitations. First, as Holdsworth pointed out effectively in his sustained account of the law reports in *A History
of English Law,* the early modern reports were quite unofficially
prepared by individual reporters of varying degrees of competence
and industry, selecting cases to report based on their opinions of
what would be especially interesting to legal practitioners at a
particular time. On the one hand, this reporting practice is convenient for historical purposes since it highlights changes in rules,
or at least what some contemporary practitioners thought were
changes or new developments. On the other hand, just as the use
of any legal record is problematic for social history because it is
apt to create skewing toward those atypical instances that produce
litigation, the early modern practices of law reporting are problematic because they downplay cases in which existing rules were
applied in ways that resolved controversy. For these reasons and
others, a number of legal historians have recently argued stren-
uously for more use of primary records.[27]

Furthermore, at the risk of being accused of incompetence by
those with more formal legal education, I will make bold to say
that these reports pose significant problems of intelligibility for
anyone who wishes to analyze the cases with some rigor. This

problem of intelligibility is not terribly serious in criminal or tort cases, which are relatively simple, but in the kind of property cases involving elaborate settlements and future interests which are crucial in married women's property, intelligibility is a serious problem. The principle for which the reporter claims the case stands is usually clear enough, but other elements of the settlement or other issues are often not reported fully or clearly enough to support a confident analysis.

Indeed, eighteenth-century judges sometimes complained about the inadequate reporting of earlier cases, including Restoration and earlier eighteenth-century cases, that one side or another appearing before them was urging the court to adopt as relevant precedent. Thus, in 1756 we find Lord Chancellor Hardwicke complaining about the printed report of *Oxwick v. Brockett* (1698) in the *Abridgement of Equity Cases,* and even declaring that the court's own manuscript records are not adequate to supplement the printed report: "How authentic that report is, I cannot take it on me to say, for the decree is not entered in the register's book, and the minutes are so imperfect that nothing material can be collected from them, except that there was an assignment of a mortgage term to attend the inheritance in the case."[28] Similarly, Sir Richard Arden, Master of the Rolls, in 1789 complained about the report of *Tilly v. Bridges* (1705): "I have some doubt about the authority of that case, for it is more particularly stated in Vernon than in Pre. Ch., and yet, what is said in Vernon as to the injunction not preventing the entry, certainly cannot be right." Later in the same opinion he observed that another case, *Mordaunt v. Thorold* (1690), "has been cited from Salkeld, tit. *Dower,* but it is also reported in 3 Lev. [Levinz] 375, and the result is stated differently in the latter book, though the state of the case seems copied from the other; for in Levinz, it is said the Court *inclined* to that opinion, but . . . no decision was given; and it is to be observed, that Levinz was himself counsel in that case."[29]

Nevertheless, I maintain that the printed cases are best evidence for the species of legal history with which I am here concerned: the history of legal ideology or the history of what the profession publicly represented its rules and their rationales to be. The significance of these rules certainly requires to be understood in some larger context of social and economic history, and I will try to consider that larger context, but the development of the rule system itself and the public ideology for which it stands is my principal focus, so I feel justified in emphasizing the printed cases as much as I do. Robert Gordon rightly says in discussing the use of "mandarin materials" like these appellate cases in critical legal history: "The mandarin materials are among the richest artifacts of a society's legal consciousness. Because they are the most rationalized and elaborated legal products," they contain "an exceptionally refined and concentrated version of legal consciousness."[30]

After the reported cases, my next best evidence comes from less authoritative abridgments and treatises. During this period the role of the treatise changes dramatically with consequences that I do not think have been sufficiently appreciated.[31] The differences between the legal literature of 1660–1700 and that of 1780–1830 are drastic. Restoration lawyers relied considerably on *Coke on Littleton* (1628), a compendium of property law based on the fifteenth-century *New Tenures* of Littleton, in which, in Frederic William Maitland's memorable phrase, "Coke shovelled out his learning in vast disorderly heaps."[32] Supplemented by additional seventeenth- and eighteenth-century notes, *Coke* remained "the principal textbook on property law" throughout this period.[33] Most striking to a modern reader in the Restoration abridgments and treatises is this effect of "jumble," of miscellanies of cases clustered around topics with little discernible rational order or relation. When Henry Rolle's *Abridgment des Plusieurs Cases* appeared in 1668 even one contemporary judge complained that "it contained so many conflicting opinions that it made the law ridiculous."[34] Something of this same effect persists even in the more modern *General Abridgment of Law and Equity* (1741–1753) by Charles Viner.

By 1785–1833, however, legal literature was transformed. Contemporary concern with the inadequacies of the case reports had led to a publishing venture issuing regular reports contemporaneously with the cases reported, beginning with Durnford and East's *Term Reports* (King's Bench, 1785–1800) and *Vesey Junior* (Chancery, 1789–1817). Blackstone had published his *Commentaries* in 1765–1769, a comprehensive work intended to give educated gentlemen an introduction to the legal system of their country.[35] Before the *Commentaries,* as Simpson has pointed out, there had been few English treatises or monographs "of any substance" on particular branches of the law, but after Blackstone such treatises became the dominant form of legal literature in the later part of our period.[36] Like the earlier maxim literature they supplanted, these treatises attempted to state general principles under which large numbers of decided cases could be subsumed. Among those of interest relating to married women's property are Charles Fearne's *Essay on the Learning of Contingent Remainders and Executory Devises* (1772), John Fonblanque's revision of Henry Ballow's *Treatise of Equity* (1793–94), Charles Watkins's *Treatise on Copyholds* (1797–1799), R. S. Donnison Roper's *Revocation and Republication of Wills and Testaments: Together with Tracts upon the Law Concerning Baron and Feme* (1800), and Edmond Gibson Atherley's *Practical Treatise on the Law of Marriage and Other Family Settlements* (1813). An additional very useful source for my purposes, one of an entirely different and novel character, appeared at the end of this period in the *First Report Made to His Majesty by the Commissioners Appointed to Inquire into the Law of England Respecting Real Property* (1829). I believe that the increased publication of reports of cases and other legal literature like abridgments and treatises in this period contributed to an increased awareness of contradictions among cases, not all of which would previously necessarily have been reported or noticed or juxtaposed in a single printed text.

At the same time that more cases were reported in more detail, the seventeenth and eighteenth centuries were periods of some euphoria about the possibilities of systematization and rationalism. When Newton charted the physical world and reduced it to a rational system in a printed book and when John Wilkins thought he could reduce the chaos of natural language to his proposed rational language in his *Essay towards a Real Character of a Philosophical Language* (1668), Locke, Hume, Montesquieu, and Adam Smith were emboldened to create a new "science of man," to borrow Hume's phrase from the *Treatise of Human Nature* (1739–40). This enlightenment spirit also animates Blackstone in the *Commentaries* as he seeks to transform law from a Romish or antiquarian monkish subject into what he calls "a liberal science"—"this most useful and most rational branch of learning"—informed by "the principles of universal jurisprudence."[37] He proposes to replace the old system, in which he alleges the student was "to sequester himself from the world, and by a tedious lonely process to extract the theory of law from a mass of undigested learning,"

with "the novelty" of scientific and theoretical teaching for gentlemen and noblemen sociably studying at the university with their
peers.[38] At the university, these gentlemen will have been instructed to "reason with precision, and separate argument from
fallacy, by the clear simple rules of pure unsophisticated
logic . . . [to] pursue truth through any the most intricate deduction, by the use of mathematical demonstrations." So empowered,
they will be able to follow Blackstone in his project of improving
"the science of the law," particularly in "improving it's method,
retrenching it's superfluities, and reconciling the little contrarieties, which the practice of many centuries will necessarily create
in any human system."[39]

Blackstone and many of the following generation of treatise
writers took this enlightenment project seriously. What the blun-
ter Restoration judge characterized as "conflicting opinions
that . . . make the law ridiculous," Blackstone—with that sub-
limely bland rhetoric which was one of the great strengths of
British liberalism—now characterizes affectionately and diminu-
tively as "the little contrarieties" soon to be reconciled. The task
of reconciling these contrarieties necessarily entailed either ig-
noring or suppressing some conflicting cases or criticizing them
as errors. It would not suffice merely to distinguish cases in apparent contradiction, because while distinguishing cases can remove contradictions, it threatens to produce a unique rule for
each case and so is inimical to system. Some cases were ignored
in the interest of reducing contradictions, but to ignore cases ran
counter to the growing impulse toward publication of a complete
record. Consequently, in the interest of rationality and systematization this late enlightenment legal literature is often also critical.

Post-Blackstone treatises are characterized by novel critical at-
tacks on decided cases which the treatise writer cannot accom-
modate to the general rules he is attempting to articulate. Watkins's
Treatise on Copyholds provides a striking example of this critical
spirit in late eighteenth-century treatise writers. Surveying the
earlier legal literature on his subject—a literature which included
a surprisingly early effort at treatise writing attributed to the re-
vered Coke, a little volume called *The Complete Copyholder*—only
prompts Watkins to describe the earlier literature as a "crude mass
of matter." For his own part, he tells the reader in a preface,

He has . . . endeavoured to reconcile the jarring and discordant cases on several points which he had to consider; but this, he must confess, sometimes appeared to be rather out of the reach of the powers usually allotted to humanity; and which he, consequently, could only lament. He has endeavoured also to reduce some cases to acknowledged principles, and to rescue others from the clouds of mystery in which they had been so long enrapped. And if he has been *guilty* of unusual *freedom* in so doing, in calling in question the doctrines consecrated by time or by *authority* (as it is too frequently termed; as if anything could be an authority against truth!) but which, perhaps, had nothing but time or such authority to consecrate them, he can only say that he is sorry that such freedom had not been executed by others before him, rather than left unexecuted 'till so late a day.

True to his promises not to be cowed by authoritative assertions of rules of law which do not appear logical to him, Watkins does proceed to identify some rules of law as established by authority and then to denounce them. Thus, in describing the rule of no dower of a trust (which I will explain and discuss at length in Chapter 2), a rule he considered erroneous, Watkins exclaims: "But, in the name of wonder, if the matter be wrong, why not set it right? If dower be a *moral* claim, and the *favourite of equity,* why should *equity* suffer '*some hasty precedents*' to come in its way?"[40] Judges clearly read this literature (or wrote it themselves) and at least some judges in the period 1785–1833 also were in sufficient sympathy with the general project of rationalization that their decisions reflect the influence of these critical arguments.

Despite the various defects, limitations, and difficulties here surveyed of this body of mandarin materials concerning married women's property between 1660 and 1833, they nevertheless constitute a knowable set of texts that repay analysis. These printed materials, moreover, have not yet been worked on sufficiently even to provide a descriptive history, as Marylynn Salmon, an Americanist necessarily interested in English sources and comparisons, has rightly complained: "Because no historian has attempted a study of English law on married women's separate estates in the seventeenth and eighteenth centuries, our knowledge of the development of various principles and precedents is slight. . . . We need a detailed study of English precedent law on separate estates before we can be precise on the chronological development of this area of the law."[41] But beyond simple description, we shall see that the mandarin materials reveal much about the legal ideology of marriage in this period.

Plurality of Laws

My usual focus throughout is on equity decisions because the equity judges and conveyancers principally created the eighteenth-century doctrines of married women's separate property. Yet the common historiographical tactic of selecting a unitary archive of materials—here decisions of equity judges—would be misleading and too limiting in dealing with this subject. Between 1660 and 1833 England had a remarkable plurality of laws. For our purposes, one useful way of analyzing this plurality would be to say that there were three radically different coexisting legal systems, each with separate and distinct subsystems, that could potentially come to bear on any particular dispute involving husband and wife: first, the ecclesiastical court system, based on the pre-Reformation canon law, which, in turn, had some Roman legal roots; second, the traditional system of customary English law administered throughout the country in manorial courts by lords of the manor; and, third, the London-based national system of common law and equity. Although the church courts progressively lost power and jurisdiction throughout our period, they still did considerable matrimonial business into the nineteenth century.[42] They had jurisdiction over questions such as the validity of marriages, heard claims for the restitution of conjugal rights, and could grant what we now would call annulments and separations, then called, respectively, divorces *a vinculo matrimonii* and divorces *a mensa et thoro*. Divorces *a mensa et thoro* were granted only for cruelty or for adultery, but, in this system derived from Roman law, wives had standing to sue their husbands, and either spouse could complain of the other's cruelty or adultery and be granted a divorce. While the determinations of the church courts had the full force of law, their armamentarium of enforcement powers was weak. In particular, their sanction of excommunication failed to impress many secularized eighteenth-century defendants. The training, intellectual culture, and procedures of the lawyers in these courts were quite different from those of their common law brethren.

They were civilians trained at the universities rather than in the Inns of Court and likely to practice exclusively in one or several of the Roman law courts: Admiralty, the ecclesiastical courts, or to work in England on Scottish appeals. A common though not universal judicial style in these courts was to give opinions deciding cases one way or another without articulating rules of law or offering reasoned defenses of them. Thus, although the ecclesiastical divorce trials offer a rich source to the social historian, they are less useful and interesting as sources of intellectual history. I have written earlier about the ecclesiastical courts,[43] but I will not focus on them in this book because their jurisdiction was over the person rather than over property, because the opinions are not as rich ideological sources as the common law opinions, and—last but certainly not least—because I understand that both Randolph Trumbach and Lawrence Stone are currently writing books about matrimonial litigation in the ecclesiastical courts.

Nevertheless, it is important to be aware of the ecclesiastical courts as a competing and parallel jurisdiction. For example, a widow's claim to her husband's property might be challenged by a counterclaim from his heir that she was not legitimately married, and the case would then have to be sent to the ecclesiastical courts to have that issue tried. Jurisdictional struggles back and forth between the ecclesiastical courts and the common law courts were fairly frequent and significant. It was entirely possible to weave complex and protracted webs of litigation in essentially the same case back and forth between the ecclesiastical courts and the common law courts. Thus, even toward the end of our period when the church courts were weakest, the Earl of Westmeath and the Countess of Westmeath's quarreling provided steady work for both canon and common lawyers from 1817 to 1831. Along the way, he entered into a separate maintenance contract including a provision not to sue her for the restitution of conjugal rights in the ecclesiastical courts, but then did sue her there for a restitution of conjugal rights; she replied by suing him in the same place for a divorce on the grounds of cruelty and adultery; he sued her in Chancery challenging the validity of the separate maintenance agreement; he sued her at Common Pleas on a writ of *habeas corpus* demanding the return to him of their daughter (who was living with her mother according to the separation agreement)—with copious appeals all-round. In deciding the ecclesiastical appeal for

Lady Westmeath in the ecclesiastical Court of Arches in 1827, Sir
John Nicholl commented:

> the parties have been engaged in litigation with each other from the
> moment of separation to the present time; not in one court only,
> but in all courts—in equity, common law, and ecclesiastical courts;
> and in those several jurisdictions Lord Westmeath has been the party
> commencing the proceedings. These circumstances are not likely to
> engender more good-will and cordiality. They do not operate as
> sweeteners to prepare the parties for the performance of matri-
> monial duties with affection and consideration.[44]

Yet Sir John's assertion that Lord Westmeath pursued his wife
in "all courts" was a rhetorical exaggeration. In fact, among other
possibilities, he missed out on the manorial courts. Manorial
courts, run by the lord of the manor or his appointed bailiff, were
still important in our period. They administered a customary law
which varied significantly from locality to locality, and thus, as the
Enlightenment developed, became increasingly controversial. On
one side, it was claimed that they represented the bad old days of
feudalism, in which the arbitrary will of the lord was the rule of
right, and that their essentially oral and local procedures were
hopelessly antiquated, superstitious, and irrational. On the other,
it was claimed that they represented the sacred traditional rights
of Englishmen. Just how normal a feature of country life the manorial court was in the mid-eighteenth century may be glimpsed in
the diary of Thomas Turner, a shopkeeper and churchwarden,
who went to the "court-leet and baron" of the Duke of Newcastle
to transact various mortgage business concerning land on the
manor.[45] By the seventeenth century, manorial courts were not
simply the private courts of the lord. Their decisions could be
challenged in the king's courts, and the king's judges thought hard
about what balance to strike between deference to local custom
and insistence on national and rational justice. Although it might
seem that humble tenants on a manor were not likely to generate
much fancy appellate business in London, many quite substantial
and even wealthy people had pieces of land held subject to customary tenure or copyhold land (land held by virtue of copy of
the manorial court roll) in what we may think of as their "land
portfolios." Thus, not only do we find some apparently humble
people appealing decisions of manorial courts to the king's courts

or asking the king's courts for decisions on lands held in one customary tenure or another, but many obviously wealthy people did so too. Among the tests of manorial customs applied by the king's courts perhaps the most ideologically rich was the rule that a custom must be reasonable.

Ecclesiastical law and customary and manorial law were present but diminishing in importance throughout our period. The third system, the London-based national system of common law and equity, grew at their expense. The common law courts of Common Pleas and King's Bench based their judgments on common law as revealed in past cases and on statutes. With respect to property, they handled a wide variety of litigation based on claims of legal estates or interests in both real and personal property, claims including trespass, ejectment, widows' claims of dower in their husbands' lands, debt, conversion, and so on. Among the armamentarium of remedies at the disposal of the common law courts were the award of monetary damages and imprisonment.

The other branch of the London-based national system was Chancery or the equity courts. Originally, the Chancellor had received complaints of injustice presented to the king in council and had provided ad hoc remedies based on conscience in particular cases. In the period 1660–1833 the Lord Chancellor was a member of the king's cabinet and a very important and powerful political figure. But also at this time, although still a court of conscience, equity had its own set of general rules which were further developed and elaborated by important Chancellors like North, Hardwicke, Kenyon, and Eldon. A crucial and virtually exclusive area of equity's jurisdiction was the trust. Procedures in equity were quite different from procedures at law, in some respects more like those of the courts based on Roman law. Available remedies were also different, most notably the power to decree specific performance—for example, the power to direct a man who had promised in a marriage settlement to convey certain land actually to convey that land. Chancery's procedures and remedies were sufficiently popular in the eighteenth century that Chancery business grew exponentially. By the early nineteenth century the amount of its business was vastly in excess of its resources, delays were intolerable, and many "reforms" were proposed—almost all of which were successfully resisted by Lord Chancellor Eldon during his long tenure from 1801 to 1827 (with one brief intermission). Just as there were important jurisdictional rivalries between the ecclesiastical courts and the king's courts, so there were similar rivalries between the common law courts and equity. Some rule changes in each court were motivated by changed social realities created by another court's actions or by unwillingness to acquiesce in another court's "stealing" jurisdiction. Yet neither the ecclesiastical courts nor the common law courts were as assertive as they might have been in hanging on to jurisdiction they had, while the equity courts were notably successful in gaining more.

The ultimate appellate judges for the ecclesiastical courts were the Archbishops of Canterbury and York, each for his respective province. Appeals from Chancery decisions went to the Lord Chancellor. The Lord Chancellor's power and political importance are worth emphasizing. If his decisions were appealed to the House of Lords, the appeals were in practice often enough decided by himself, although, as I shall explain, he could be outvoted in the House of Lords even by lay lords.

Almost all Lords Chancellor in our period began as commoners and were promoted up the legal ladder after displaying both legal competence and political ability.[46] Almost all had served the government as members of the House of Commons, drafting legislation and helping to marshal majorities for government policies. Subsequently, in climbing the professional ladder, almost all also served as Solicitors General or Attorneys General prosecuting both unpolitical and political criminals and generally making legal defenses of government policy when it was challenged in the courts. For example, Edward Thurlow, before becoming Lord Chancellor Thurlow, in 1770 as Solicitor General prosecuted Almon for publishing Junius's *Letter to the King* and then Millar and Baldwin for printing it; in Parliament he opposed a bill to prevent the Attorney General from filing *ex officio* informations (in order to bypass grand juries reluctant to indict), declaring that if the opposition bill were passed: "Nothing will be published but libels and lampoons. The Press will teem with scurrility, abuse and falsehood. The minds of the people will be poisoned with vile aspersions and misled by scandalous misrepresentations. The many-headed beast will swallow the poison and the land will be one scene of anarchy and confusion."[47] Similarly, in an earlier phase of his career as Attorney General, John Scott, later Lord Eldon, prosecuted Horne Tooke, Thomas Hardy, and John Thelwall; he also worked on drafting and passing the Habeas Corpus Suspension Act of 1794 and the Treasonable Practices and Seditious Meetings Act of 1795.[48] Promotion to the Lord Chancellorship was, in part, a reward for such services.

The Lord Chancellor was the only judge who served at the pleasure of the king, and also the only judge who was by virtue of his particular judicial office a member of the cabinet. He was also Speaker of the House of Lords. To imagine something of the extent and political nature of his power, imagine that the American Chief Justice of the Supreme Court served at the pleasure of the President but was also the Attorney General and the Speaker of the Senate. The Lord Chancellor was appointed by the Prime Minister, with the consent of the king, and in turn, with their consent, appointed the Lord Chief Baron and various puisne common law judges. Vast legal and ecclesiastical patronage belonged to his office. Lord Hardwicke, for example, in 1736 had 1,276 clerical livings in his gift.[49] Political ability a man had demonstrated in the House of Commons was supposed to be available for governmental purposes when he was promoted to the Lord Chancellorship and made Speaker of the House of Lords. As Michael McCahill has pointed out in a study of the House of Lords between 1783 and 1806, peers holding legal offices, led by the Lord Chancellor, "were the most powerful conservative forces in the upper house and repeatedly gave direction and focus to their less articulate and brilliant colleagues."[50] Until the office of Vice-Chancellor was created in 1813 in hopes of diminishing the backlog of equity cases, the second equity judge immediately under the Lord Chancellor was the Master of the Rolls. David Duman correctly notes that Masters of the Rolls were "frequently important politicians whom the government wanted to keep in the Commons but at the same time honour with a judicial appointment."[51]

Ultimate appeal in Chancery decisions lay from the Lord Chancellor to the House of Lords.[52] Although English law had already been professionalized in many senses in the Renaissance and became professionalized in additional ways between 1660 and 1833, it was not yet so fully professionalized as to have banished lay control. Most members of the House of Lords, of course, were not lawyers, but in theory all members had an equal right to vote on appeals. Normally, appellate business in the House was handled by the Lord Chancellor with other available legally trained peers holding legal offices, often with advice from judges who were not peers. Because of the character of record-keeping and reporting in the House of Lords, we know less than we would like about procedures there, yet it is clear that even on ordinary and fairly boring—to most laymen—occasions, a few lay lords might turn up to vote on an appeal, and that on more controversial occasions many more might exercise their right. The lay lords usually listened to professional advice, but professional advice was often divided on appeals and the lay lords could in any case ignore advice if they chose. What few and relatively feeble efforts there were to get the lay lords to yield this ultimate appellate jurisdiction were effectively resisted throughout our period. We shall see a number of cases involving married women's property in which rules articulated by professional judges were overturned on appeal to the House of Lords and replaced by new rules more to the liking of the lords.

A final, marginal set of courts might be mentioned briefly, namely the courts of other parts of the Empire. Although the king in parliament deferred in varying degrees to the local customs and local law of these courts, different kinds of appeals to England might be allowed from various parts of the Empire, and some decisions and even some legislation in the colonies was sufficiently politically or ideologically abhorrent to London that it was overruled in London.[53] Colonial charters required that colonial laws not be "repugnant to the laws of England"; the Privy Council or the Board of Trade disallowed laws discovered to be repugnant.

Most revelatory for our purposes are certain decisions made in London about the Irish and the American law of property and of the family. For example, in 1773 the Privy Council disallowed a divorce bill that had been enacted by the Pennsylvania legislature.[54] Ireland had its own common law courts and its own parliament, but the English Parliament in this period also enacted legislation specific to Ireland, including legislation affecting property rights. Until Poynings' Law was modified in 1782, the Irish Parliament itself could pass no bill that had not been approved by the king and Council in England.[55] During most of our period, appeals lay from Ireland to the English King's Bench and then to the English House of Lords.[56] In an English attempt to quell Irish agitation in the 1780s, Ireland got back appellate jurisdiction on its own cases, but then on the occasion of the Act of Union in

1800, appellate jurisdiction went back to the English House of Lords again.[57] Both Irish and American property rules and their fates reveal how conscious legal intellectuals and politicians of the day were of the intimate relations between such things as the laws of inheritance of real property, social structure, ideology, and political power. Legislation for Ireland, for instance, was carefully designed to keep Protestant property from coming into Roman Catholic hands by marriage; thus, a statute of 1697 criminalized any attempt to perform a marriage between a Protestant woman with an estate of £500 or more and any man who had not obtained legal certification that he was a Protestant.[58] The American material has additional interest because some of the American colonists were law reformers who succeeded in enacting what they considered reforms—a number of which were then struck down by the Privy Council as repugnant to the laws of England. The Irish and the American legal materials also provide useful comparative evidence of what could be considered possible within the conceptual world of eighteenth-century common law thought.

Theory and Practice

The set of mandarin materials constituted by the printed cases from these various courts, particularly the appellate cases, is principally revelatory of the elite legal ideology of this period. But, used along with other sources, it can also tell us something of the social history of married women, especially if we are careful to remember that there may be vast distances between the official rules under which women are supposed to live and the actual conditions of their lives. In these materials we see official ideology, important for its own sake as ideology, and important as it provides and articulates a code according to which at least some people in English society tried to live.

But even among the well-to-do, who are my principal focus, many people, especially many women, were relatively ignorant of the content of the official law of married women's property; others, who knew quite well what the code was, did not necessarily conform their conduct to it. The code was essentially a patriarchal one that justified the dominance and privilege of men by reference to their superior abilities to create good order in families and their duty to provide protection and support for subordinated women and children in their families. Yet the code did not prevent Sir Edward Coke, the author, as we have noted, of the most important general text used in our period, from advancing his own fortunes by forcibly marrying his fourteen-year-old daughter, Frances, to a man most unsuited to protect her. Coke had Frances tied to bedposts and whipped until she consented to marry Sir John Villars, who suffered from periodic fits of insanity that caused him to smash glass and bloody himself and who after his marriage had to be confined as mad.[59] Nor, in the late eighteenth century, did Lord Chancellor Thurlow's particularly intense fulminations from the bench about the importance of families to society and the importance of virtuous conduct in families seem to interfere with his own practice of living openly for many years with a barmaid from Nando's coffee house, by whom he had a son and three daughters.

2

Dower and the Rule of
No Dower of a Trust

Four Possible Histories of Dower

Once upon a time widows had dower rights. Whether this was in the halcyon days of yore or in the bad old days of feudalism or patriarchy remains to be seen. At common law a widow was entitled to a life estate amounting to one-third of all the real property of which her husband had been the legal owner at any time during the marriage.[1] In other words and to give a simple hypothetical example, at the death of a farmer whose entire real estate had consisted of thirty acres of hop fields, his widow would be entitled to a life estate in ten acres of the hop fields, entitled, that is, to control them and to enjoy the revenues from them for the duration of her own life. In this system of property law, estates could be carved up spatially (the ten acres north of the river for X) and temporally (a term for the length of her life for Y or a term for ninety-nine years for Z). Ownership of land entails possession in terms of space and time; temporal terms for the life of an individual—life estates—were common.

Sometimes wives were actually endowed with specific land, land set out by metes and bounds, at the church door immediately before their marriages. In the absence of such a specific assignment of dower to his mother (or stepmother or other widow of the previous owner), the heir had forty days after his father's death to assign particular lands to her. Should the heir fail to make the assignment of dower lands, the widow had a writ of dower to compel him to do so. Should the heir assign poor land or not enough land, the widow could invoke the assistance of the sheriff to guarantee herself an assignment. In well-to-do families the widow might expect land with a traditional dower house on it. Among copyholders and holders by certain customary tenures there was an analogous widow's right called by the more humble name "free bench," suggesting that among smaller land holders where there was only one house the widow would be entitled to particular space within it.

Dower rights have now, for the most part, disappeared. In England they were finally abolished in 1925. In 1833 the Dower Act made them largely defeasible at the will of the husband.[2] An extensive and historically valuable survey of the legal profession by the Commissioners of Real Property preparatory to the passage of the Dower Act led to the conclusion that by the early nineteenth century women no longer married with expectations of enjoying dower rights. How, we may ask, did dower rights disappear? What does their disappearance mean?

While the legal profession devoted considerable thought to the development of the law of dower between 1660 and 1833, an important object of its activity was to ensure that at least among the classes who married only after taking good legal advice, women could not claim dower. Some of the legal devices by which this was accomplished were capable of arousing the highest degrees of professional enthusiasm as "extremely ingenious," "skillful contrivances," and "masterstrokes of ingenuity."[3] Toward the end of the period, when claims of dower were made they were frequently thought to be the unfortunate result either of drafting mistakes in settlements or deeds to real property or of women being misled by unscrupulous advice. Dower was even in 1700 barrable in so many different ways and was apparently so often successfully barred (that is, the right of dower was prevented from attaching to the property) that it seems symptomatic of the general archaism of eighteenth-century legal learning that so much is said about dower attaching.

The changes in the law of dower are nevertheless worth study because they reveal much about the contemporary ideology of marriage and the family. Moreover, since jointure in an important sense was developed as a substitute for dower, developments in the law of jointure in this period cannot be thoroughly understood without a prior understanding of the law of dower. The changes in dower law also illustrate how a traditional right could be lost in a judicial system which claimed to operate upon precedent and which, for the most part, denied that its rules were affected by changing economic considerations or considerations of social welfare.

Here, very briefly, it may be useful to explain a few underlying ideas and terms of English property law as they relate to dower. Property could be divided into two kinds: real property (land and buildings) and chattel property (movable things). Since property law developed as land law, a variety of rights which may not look to modern eyes very much like rights to land were understood as issuing from land and treated as real property. One example is an advowson, the right to appoint a clergyman to a benefice. There is sufficient room for ambiguity to sustain the oxymoronic intermediate category of "chattels real." Dower only attaches to what is considered real property. Historically, some forms of property were conceptualized at one time as chattel and at another as real. In the eighteenth century, whether certain leases, terms of years, mortgages, or annuities were considered real or chattel property affected the results in dower.

Common law courts were prepared to deal with disputes over both real and chattel property, but they did not recognize trusts or the earlier Renaissance form of trust, the use. If in 1500 property was held by A in trust for (or "to the use" of) B, as far as common law was concerned A was the owner. If B wanted to enforce any rights, he had to go to the equity courts. Uses set up groups of trustees which were self-replenishing, did not die, and thus offered ways of avoiding feudal dues at the beneficial owner's death or escheat if he died without an heir. Uses also afforded unique ways of restricting alienation of property from the male line of the family, ways of devising real property when common law did not allow it, and ways of barring dower.

Uses were considered to have led to abuses, so in 1535 the Statute of Uses provided, roughly, that at law the beneficiary of a use was to be regarded as the legal owner; it followed that his estate was subject to escheat or to feudal dues. [4] The preamble to the statute included a complaint that uses were barring women of their dowers. Some families who had opted out of the dower system had substituted jointures, guaranteed annual revenue from land payable to a wife should she survive her husband, often provided in a clause of the prenuptial marriage settlement. Since by 1535 some women had already had jointures settled on them in the expectation that dower would be barred, the statute provided that a jointure might bar dower if it gave the woman a freehold estate at least as great as a life estate which she could enter immediately upon her husband's death.[5] Thus, Parliament seems to have been concerned that the jointure estates substituted for dower estates be roughly equivalent in quality (that is, that they be freehold rather than of so-called baser tenure like copyhold) and security. For reasons I will consider later, Parliament does not seem to have focused on what may appear to us a more obvious and important kind of equivalency: equivalency of quantity measurable as annual cash income produced by the estate. Women whose jointures were settled on them only after marriage might elect either their jointure or dower, it being presumed that during coverture they could not give valid consent to waive dower (except through the mechanism of the fine). The preamble to the statute also voiced a complaint that through uses men had lost their curtesy, namely, the widower's right to a life estate in all, not one-third, of the land his wife brought into the marriage. Unlike dower, curtesy was contingent upon the birth of a child to the couple.

Both dower and curtesy are what would now be called "forced shares," that is, neither the husband nor wife, once seised of land during coverture, could alone do anything to defeat or to lessen the survivor's entitlement to his or her life estate, no matter how much he or she might wish to. Forced share systems seem to have reflected status ideas, whereas jointure came to be thought a contract. In the eighteenth century the equity courts through their dealings with trust estates, the successors to uses, and family settlements involving trusts did much to remove some status elements from the marital relationship and to replace them with contract ideas.

To discover how and why dower disappeared we must look into eighteenth-century equity litigation. It is frequently said that equity accomplished progressive changes in the field of married women's property. Maria Lynn Cioni in a study of the Elizabethan equity courts argues that these courts were especially attentive to the needs of women and asserts: "The unquestioned improvements in the status of propertied women, which are so marked a feature of the social scene of the seventeenth and eighteenth centuries, rested ultimately upon the consideration given to their needs by the Elizabethan Chancery."[6] Janelle Greenberg has also argued for the early modern period that "equity mitigated the harshness of the common law's treatment of women" and that "when equity is taken into account, the legal status of the English woman appears less distressing than it does when one assumes she had to rely only on common law protections."[7] It was equity that recognized settlements to the separate use of married women and equity that was prepared to enforce the famous or infamous agreements to pay pin money. Some have supposed that these equity doctrines, by meeting the needs of the property-owning classes for reform of the common law, removed pressures for more general legislative reform in the eighteenth century, so that it was only after the extensions of the franchise provided by the various Reform Bills of the nineteenth century that humbler people who ordinarily did not resort to equity courts secured the benefits of equity doctrines for themselves through the Married Women's Property Acts.[8] It is undoubtedly true that these equity doctrines of married women's separate property broke the hegemony of the common law rules giving husbands control over wives' property and in some sense prepared the way for the greater degree of autonomy married women appear to enjoy today.

Nevertheless, equity played a role in the loss of women's dower rights. Equity's role is at least initially puzzling in light of the court's self-consciousness about its function as protector and guardian of the weak, especially women and children. Furthermore, it was part of the eighteenth-century equity judges' self-image that they had got beyond the harshness and rigor of the old common law and were functioning not to strip people of their common law rights but to mitigate archaic features of common law so that the law might better reflect the progress and refinements, including the refinement of feeling, of modern society. How can it be, then, that this court, self-consciously protective of women and children, and apparently progressive in their interests, appears to strip widows of their dowers?

Even taking equity rules and common law rules together, considering their effects on the forms of contemporary property, and limiting our attention to the propertied classes, it is by no means clear whether the position of married women with respect to property improved, deteriorated, or remained about the same between

1660 and 1833. Dower rights were certainly eroded, but one might reply that dower rights were in any case an inappropriate way to secure provision for widows in early modern society, that they should have been replaced by other forms of entitlement, as indeed they were in part replaced by jointure. Married women also newly able to acquire and to hold property to their own separate uses while their husbands were alive could, of course, also retain this property when their husbands died. One might, in fact, tell four very different stories of married women's property during the eighteenth century: one in which things became better for women, one in which they became worse, and two in which they stayed essentially the same, but for different reasons.

The first story we may call the liberal story. In this, the law is seen as happily, albeit with some awkwardnesses, adapting to changing and better times, while also increasing the autonomy of women. A world of stable, landed property gives way to a world in which land is a commodity like others. New commodities like stock and bank annuities replace land as major ingredients of wealth, and the law of dower changes to reflect this, limiting widows' rights to land but giving them equivalents in newer forms of wealth. Customary dower rights interfered with the alienability, the marketability of land, because the wife of an owner had a potential dower right which attached to her husband's land, no matter how often the land might be sold during the husband's life. No one would want to purchase land if he were exposed to the risk of a widow of some remote prior owner suddenly, at that prior owner's death, demanding her dower of the subsequent purchaser. Dower thus made it difficult to achieve the highest economic use of the resource of land; erosion of dower rights increased wealth generally. The forms of widows' wealth substituted for dower were preferable. Older customary and humiliating restrictions on widows' freedom were eliminated, such as the lord's power to compel the remarriage of a widowed heiress or free bench customs that made forfeiture of land the penalty for a widow's fornication or subsequent remarriage.

This liberal story, it is worth observing, appears to dominate the history of dower law changes developed in the early modern period and even now seems to dominate the received history. It is, moreover, a fragment of the larger "evolutionary functionalist" account of legal history Robert Gordon describes as so pervasive in modern legal history generally that it has become "deeply embedded in standard legal speech." This larger evolutionary functionalist story (as briefly noted in Chapter 1) recounts "the gradual liberation of the individual from the shackles of feudalism and superstition—from restraints on trade, on free alienation of land, and on free movement of labor; from the oppressions of feudal dues and tithes and of perpetual subordination to customary hierarchies of ecclesiastical and noble orders; and from established religions."[9] According to this view, it can be argued that the substitution of jointure for dower meant, most crucially, more freedom of alienation of land, and also more freedom for women from the customary status constraints that required dower to be forfeited for adultery and elopement and free bench to be forfeited, in some customary usages, for the widow's fornication.

Early modern treatise writers themselves advanced various versions of this liberal story, especially stressing the importance of the free alienation of land. According to Blackstone in the 1760s, "Upon preconcerted marriages, and in estates of considerable consequence, tenancy in dower happens very seldom: for, the claim of the wife to her dower at the common law diffusing itself so extensively, it became a great clog to alienations, and was otherwise inconvenient to families."[10] Another treatise writer of 1819 agreed that dower had been disfavored because of "the increased expense occasioned by the attachment of the title of Dower in all cases where real property is to be pledged, or converted into money, in the way of sale or mortgage. In the multifarious transactions of modern times, this becomes an object of no slight consideration; and in small purchases, the expense of levying a fine has often been very severely felt."[11] In outline, this liberal view may also be said to be that of the Real Property Commissioners in the early nineteenth century; they saw themselves as recognizing and facilitating the widow's essential entitlement to support, wishing to perfect and regularize by statute what had already been imperfectly accomplished by conveyancers and equity. Their report lay behind the passage of the Dower Act in 1833.

Alternatively, one may tell a story, probably one that sounds truer to neo-Marxist ears, of the worsening position of women during early capitalism. In this story, under color of the necessities of legal logic, law as the agent of the propertied classes strips widows of their customary entitlements as those are perceived to block the interests of capitalism, including agricultural capitalism.[12] Just as in *Whigs and Hunters* E. P. Thompson's worthy but humble denizens of the forest lose their traditional entitlements to game, lops and tops, and so on to the new moneyed men, so widows lose their dower and free bench—by a process which, if anything, is even more insidious because it occurs primarily not through legislation but rather through judicial interpretation of what are supposed to be common law and equitable rights.[13] Because the cases in which this is done are actually taking away traditional rights, they depart from precedent and are in that sense bad law. Because to a significant extent the judges explicitly deny the legal authority of policy arguments even as they respond to changing social pressures, their reasoning in such cases is particularly strained. Judges, conscious of their own bad faith, attempt to rationalize what they are doing with specious reasoning. Married women as a class without power are subjected to rules which the dominant class has no intention of applying to itself. Newer contract ideas behind jointure and married women's separate estates, far from giving women greater security, as the liberal view maintains, rob women of the security attached to status rights and falsely pretend that women have the power to negotiate in their own best interests. According to this view, once women gained control over separate property, they were merely easier to exploit; as even contemporaries realized, women with property settled to their separate use were likely to be "kissed or kicked" out of it by their husbands.

The third story, that despite apparent changes in the rules of married women's property basically the position of women neither improved nor worsened, has a sociological and a feminist version. In the sociological story, all societies make some provision for widows and the particular provision each makes is one that fits into its larger structures. Each provision is "appropriate" in that sense, and one is not to be preferred to another. Thus, George Caspar Homans notes a medieval custom: "On some manors, if a [widowed] villein heiress did not get herself a husband, the lord exercised the right of ordering her to marry, amercing her if she did not, and even picking out the man she was to marry." Then, with sociological sympathy for medieval ways, he remarks: this "may have seemed a necessity of the successful management of property in land."[14] Eighteenth-century judges were also capable of understanding a sociological point of view and of justifying their own decisions as necessary accommodations of women's property rights to changed social structures, particularly the changed forms of property and property holding. In an opinion of Lord Hardwicke's noted in Chapter 1, he observed that the Renaissance freehold estate in land was no longer the dominant form of property in the mid-eighteenth century: "As property stood at the time of the statute [of Uses], personal estate was then of little or trifling value . . . trusts of estates in land did not arise till many years after. . . . But the chief kind of property then regarded was freehold estate in land, and so the statute applied to that only. But how many species of property have grown up since by new improvements, commerce, and from the funds."[15] He then uses this observation to justify allowing jointures of personal property to bar dower rights. Here there is no claim of making things better or worse for women (except in so far as they somehow participate in a world with "new improvements") but merely a desire to "adjust" the legal rules of dower to make them fit better with modern society and the forms of property which characterize it.

A feminist variant on this view would agree that basically nothing changed—not because English society as it changed continued to find appropriate forms of married women's property, but rather because the deeper structures of male domination and female subordination persisted from the Anglo-Saxons right through to the Family Provision Act of 1975 and beyond. Rules concerning married women's property have always functioned to facilitate the transmission of significant property from male to male; entitlements of women have been to provide them with subsistence for themselves and minor children who are dependent upon them. Men want women to have enough to survive, indeed, to survive at a level appropriate to a woman (not man) of their husband's rank, but not enough to exercise the power that comes with a significant accumulation of property. In any case, women are considered incompetent to exercise control over property or the power it brings. Thus when John Humphries, author of a treatise on real property, was asked by the Real Property Commissioners what he thought of changing dower so that the widow became a tenant in common of one-third of all her husband's estates, instead of having one-third assigned to her in severalty, he replied that that would not be objectionable, although it would be better still to assign a rent: "I think women are unfit to manage real estate; they ruin estates; and they are themselves cheated and beggared. . . . my great object would be to prevent the widow from meddling with the soil."[16] Much more recently—in 1960—W. D. MacDonald in *Fraud on the Widow's Share* expressed a similar idea when criticizing forced share schemes that give widows lump sum payments: "No thought is given to the possibility—indeed, the probability—that the widow will be inexperienced in money matters and that the lump sum will soon be dissipated."[17]

From this feminist point of view, it appears that when forced shares of a husband's property afford subsistence and not much more, patriarchy is content with forced shares; when individuals accumulate sufficient property that a forced share is significantly more than subsistence for a woman of that rank, then forced share schemes are criticized, evaded, or repealed. Dower might be all well and good among thirteenth-century manor folk or eighteenth-century Massachusetts farmers, but one could hardly expect an eighteenth-century English magnate to sacrifice a potential life estate in a third of his family's lands to a woman. The critical aspect of jointure was not so much that an equitable jointure could be made in such things as bank annuities rather than land but that— if the wife's family's bargaining position were not strengthened by her ability to bring substantial assets into the marriage—the jointure could be for much less than the value of a life estate in a third of the husband's lands. Among the freemen of London, whose property was characteristically chattel property rather than real property, the custom was that widows should have a forced share of a third of the husband's chattels. By 1584 wealthy men were already evading the custom by "deeds of gifts and cautelous [crafty] conveyances to strangers."[18] By 1724 so many men "of wealth and ability, who exercise the business of merchandize, and other laudable employments" in London were allegedly refusing to become freemen of the city because of the customary forced shares that Parliament abolished the custom.[19]

Furthermore, although men can see the necessity of supporting the women who belong to them so long as the women do belong to them, they dislike seeing what they regard as their assets going to support another man's woman. Hence, the medieval widow would lose her free bench if she remarried or even committed fornication; by Westminster 2 (1285) a wife was mandated to lose her entitlement to dower if she eloped and committed adultery; eighteenth-century jointures defeasible upon remarriage could bar dower; and twentieth-century divorced wives and widows are apt to lose things like alimony, trust fund payments, or social security benefits if they remarry. Complainers about widows' entitlements under the custom of London in the sixteenth century apparently lamented, "She will marrie, and enrich some other with the fruite of my travaile. Wherefore I thinke it necessarie to abridge her of that libertie which the custome doth extende."[20] Wealthy men today, like men in the early modern period, are also capable of seeing to it that their assets are dealt with in ways that keep their wives and widows from "wasting" them, accumulating "too much," or spending them on some other man; inter vivos conveyances and trusts continue to be popular instruments useful to this end. Anthony R. Mellows has observed that before 1975 there were no anti-avoidance sections in the family provision legislation, and that even the 1975 act leaves "a determined testator in a position in which he can take a number of steps to defeat the claims of his dependents."[21]

The Rule in Chaplin: No Dower of a Trust

The history of a leading dower case, *Chaplin v. Chaplin* (1733), allows us to understand how equity supported the elimination of dower rights, and to begin to consider whether a liberal, neo-Marxist, sociological, or feminist account of the process is the most plausible. In *Chaplin* it was settled that there should be no dower of property held in trust for the beneficiary's wife. Since so much land was held in trust and since it had also been established that the wife of the trustee was not to have dower either, *Chaplin* meant that there would be no dower at all of this land.[22] It had, however, also been settled and continued to be the rule that there was curtesy of a trust. For the hundred years between *Chaplin* and the Dower Act of 1833 this different treatment of dower and curtesy was generally perceived to be an awkward anomaly, indeed, an embarrassment. The commentary provoked gives insight into the principles upon which the equity courts acted and into their conceptions of the different rights of men and women in marriage. It will become evident that the rule in *Chaplin* was not established without considerable misgiving and struggle.

Some thought there should be both dower and curtesy of a trust; some thought there should be neither. But almost all agreed that it would be logical to have the same rule for dower and for curtesy. Lord Chancellor Talbot, who decided *Chaplin,* himself disagreed with giving curtesy of a trust. Though he did not propose to overturn that rule, he presumably was emboldened to resist the argument for Lady Chaplin that dower was a favorite right at law and that it could not be "pretended that there were less stronger reasons to be observed in favour of a dowress" than in favor of a tenant by the curtesy by his wish not to extend the mistake already made with respect to curtesy: "He took it to be settled, that the husband should be tenant by the curtesy of a trust, though the wife could not have dower thereof . . . for which diversity, as he could see no reason, so neither should he have made it; but since it had prevailed, he would not alter it."[23] Similar remarks, as we shall see, are frequent in subsequent eighteenth-century cases. Extensive testimony taken by the Real Property Commissioners in the 1830s also fully supported their conclusion that most members of the bench and bar then believed that the dower and curtesy rules were contrary to the general principles that governed equitable estates.

These general principles were extensively considered in *Burgess v. Wheate* (1759) by Lord Keeper Henley (later Earl of Northington), Chief Justice of the King's Bench, Lord Mansfield, and Sir Thomas Clarke, Master of the Rolls. The specific issue in *Burgess* was whether a trust estate was to escheat to the crown after all the beneficiaries disappeared or whether there was a legal estate existing in the trustees which enabled them to take beneficially. Henley, who with Clarke prevailed in ruling that such a trust was not liable to escheat, found the case of a tenant by the curtesy an exception to what he understood to be the general rules of uses and trusts. "But this instance of deviation is not to be argued upon to consequences," he said. "It seems to have prevailed unaccountably and against the opinion of the Judges themselves. . . . It is, I own, almost a reproach to a Court of Equity; but shall not equity therefore follow the rules of uses? shall it make another rule deviating from that? I think that there ought to be a conformity in trusts and uses, and that this case of tenancy per curtesy, which is different, ought to be the only one, and that there the bounds are fixed."[24] Mansfield, who was in the minority in this case, agreed that the dower and curtesy rules were unjustifiably anomalous, but maintained that the mistake had been made with respect to dower: "The case of dower is the only exception [to the principle that a trust in Chancery is the estate at law], and not on law and reason; but because that wrong determination has misled in too many instances to be now altered and set right. . . . And, if an alteration was to be introduced, the best way to set it right would be to allow the wife dower of the trust estate."[25] In 1783 in a later case extending the principle of *Chaplin,* Lord Loughborough, having listened to arguments citing cases where curtesy had been given of trusts, replied, "The case of an estate by the curtesy in a trust, is the anomalous case, not the rule that the wife shall not have dower."[26] The view of Mansfield that the dower rule was a mistake finally prevailed in the Dower Act of 1833 when Parliament provided that a widow was to have dower from an equitable estate to which her husband at his death was beneficially entitled. By 1833, though, dower was in its death throes, and Parliament simultaneously in the act gave husbands new alternate ways to avoid dower.

Why, we may ask, should a rule that was perceived as anomalous at the moment of its inception and for one hundred years thereafter have prevailed? Weight must be given to one reason Lord Talbot mentions in his opinion, namely, that "it had been the common practice of conveyancers . . . to place the real estate in trustees on purpose to prevent dower; wherefore it would be of the most dangerous consequence to titles, to throw things into confusion, contrary to former opinions, and the advice of so many eminent and learned men, to let in the claim of dower upon trust estates." In other words, for some time people had been buying property which they believed upon good legal advice was not liable to claims of dower from some prior owner's wife; to upset these expectations would "throw things into confusion." Lord Eldon in a case decided in 1805, believing that dower ought to have been given of a trust, explained how the opposite result had been reached: "It was found, however, that in cases of dower, this principle, if pursued to the utmost, would affect the titles to a large proportion of the estates in the country, for that parties had been acting . . . upon a contrary principle."[27] The practice of conveyancers had its authority not only because to go against it would upset expectation in a world where great importance was attached to the stability of property rules, but also because conveyancers were learned in the law and—in the case of the dower rule—had been acting upon the widely accepted principle that trusts were analogous to uses, concluding that since there had been no dower of a use there would necessarily be no dower of a trust.

Yet the practice of conveyancers is hardly a sufficient explanation. Conveyancers, like modern tax lawyers, were engaged in a seemingly interminable war with the state: the conveyancers worked as agents of members of the propertied classes who sought to maximize their control over their property both during life and long after their deaths; the state attempted to achieve various social welfare goals and to prevent owners from tying up their property in perpetuity. Sometimes the judiciary helped out the conveyancers, sometimes it assisted Parliament. The conveyancers could argue that as there was no dower of a use, so there should be no dower of a trust, but alternatively it might have been said that as one purpose of the Statute of Uses was clearly to prevent the defeat of dower by uses, so dower should not be defeated by a trust.[28] As some wealthy people have learned to their chagrin, the mere fact that lawyers can invent things like evasions of forced share rules or tax shelters does not necessarily mean that the courts will uphold them.

One cannot help suspecting that the rights of women have been especially vulnerable to the sort of "legal accidents" that lie behind the maxim *communis error facit jus* (common error makes law). Practices that are errors can only become common and established when they are not effectively challenged close to their inception, and women have not been in the best position to make such challenges. Describing another dower rule which he believed unjust, Courtney Stanhope Kenny noted, "unfortunately no dowress disputed the efficacy of these·assignments until the practice of making them had become so universal that to insist on their invalidity would have shaken innumerable titles."[29] Again, an apparent accident; *communis error facit jus* to the detriment of doweresses. Of course, even though the technicalities of marriage settlements and property law generally were quite beyond the learning of almost all, if not all, eighteenth-century women, the male relatives of doweresses frequently saw to it that their legal rights were enforced. Yet it does seem to have happened that protectors of widows were not as effective in asserting their interests as widowers were in asserting their own. Another great maxim of equity, *aequitas erroribus medetur* (equity corrects errors), never seems to have occurred to anyone in this connection.

The anomaly of dower and curtesy rules was also a result of an underlying paradox in eighteenth-century trust doctrine. Equity used contradictory principles in defining the nature of trust estates. On the one hand, there was the maxim *aequitas sequitur legem,* equity follows the law. This meant that the same rules that applied to legal estates at common law ought to be applied to ostensibly analogous equitable estates by the Chancery judges. Since what was owned at law and what was owned at equity—the whole spectrum of estates expressed in a common vocabulary of fee simple, fee tail, remainders, reversions, and so on—were basically the same, it seemed reasonable that the two modes of ownership should be governed by the same rules. Given that there was an existing set of exceedingly elaborate but known rules governing the various forms of legal estates, it made sense that the rules of these legal estates should be the rules of the corresponding equitable estates, that if you could create a legal fee tail special by saying, "to A and the heirs of his body by his wife W," you could create an equitable fee tail special by saying "to T and his heirs to the use of A and the heirs of his body by his wife W"—and have confidence that you knew what rules would apply. Coke said of uses that they should be governed by common law rules "which are certain and well known to the professors of the law, and should not be made so extravagant that no one will know any rule to decide the questions that will arise upon them."[30]

The maxim *aequitas sequitur legem* and its rationale were repeatedly invoked in eighteenth-century cases dealing with trusts. It was this maxim that helped Lord Cowper draw the conclusion that there should be curtesy of a trust in *Watts v. Ball* (1708): "Trust estates were to be governed by the same rules, and were within the same reason, as legal estates . . . and as the husband should have been tenant by the curtesy, had it been a legal estate, so should he be of this trust-estate; and if there were not the same rules of property in all courts, all things would be, as it were, *at sea,* and under the greatest incertainty."[31] Following this same logic, Mansfield opined in *Burgess v. Wheate* that when all the beneficiaries of a trust were exhausted, the trust estate escheated to the king, just as a legal estate would have escheated upon the failure of heirs: "What ever would be the rule of law, if it was a legal estate," said Mansfield, "is applied in equity to a trust estate": "the trust must be co-extensive with the legal estate of the land."[32]

On the other hand, trusts were said to be like uses, and uses and trusts, as the creatures of equity, might be molded as seemed appropriate to the equity courts. Had the rules of legal estates given men what they wanted, uses would not have been invented to evade them. Early uses, as already noted, were employed to avoid feudal dues which the common law would have exacted and to gain powers to dispose of land by will when the common law did not allow the devise of land. Trusts similarly were designed as ways of avoiding common law rules, just as they are now used to avoid inheritance and tax rules. In the eighteenth century, trusts to the separate use of married women gave them powers over land the common law denied, and family settlements allowed restraints on alienation of land from the male line when the common law rules had made it relatively easy to bar entails. If equity were to follow the law exactly, if equitable estates were to be exactly like legal estates, then there would have been little point in having uses and trusts. Thus, to the maxim *aequitas sequitur legem* are counterposed the principles "trusts are now what uses were" and equity "can act upon its own creature."[33]

The logic of uses was followed in *Burgess* by Henley and Clarke when they ruled that there was no escheat of a trust: "The law was, that the lord could not have the escheat of an use."[34] Uses and trusts prevented what would have been an escheat if the estate had been held as a legal estate by the beneficiaries. The logic of Mansfield's minority position in this case was open to the criticism that it annihilated trust estates altogether. Strictly within the context of the eighteenth-century doctrine of trusts, Henley and Clarke's position was probably the more correct, in deciding both that the trust should not escheat and that the dower rule was right and the curtesy rule wrong.

Equity can clearly be seen to "act upon its own creature" in the field of trusts to the separate use of married women, a notable creation of equity courts. When the restraint upon anticipation— that is, a restraint upon alienation made part of the settlement of property to the use of a married woman preventing her from alienating the property during the marriage—was invented toward the end of the century, it was at first doubted that these married women, "owners" of property, could be denied the rights of alienation thought to be intrinsic to legal ownership. But Lord Chancellor Cottenham decided that without a restraint upon anticipation much of the benefit of the rules that had been developed governing married women's separate property would be lost: "Why then should not equity in this case also interfere; and if it cannot protect the wife consistently with the ordinary rules of property, extend its own rules with respect to the separate estate, so as to secure to her the enjoyment of that estate which has been so invented for her benefit?"[35]

This underlying paradox of trust doctrine allowed the courts to employ now one principle, now the other, as seemed appropriate for reasons outside the constraints of legal logic. Some policy considerations made curtesy more tolerable than dower. A major objection to dower was that a purchaser would be subjected at an indefinite future time to the appearance of some prior owner's wife claiming her life estate. A husband could not release his wife's dower rights, and the wife herself could only do so, if she were willing, by the process of a fine. (A fine was a fictitious suit by the party to whom the land was to be conveyed, the buyer, claiming that the possessor of the land had promised to convey it; the object was to produce a public record of the new owner's title. The process required the court to conduct a "separate examination" of the seller's wife apart from her husband, an examination supposed to prevent her agreement from being coerced by her husband.) It was sometimes claimed that fines were cumbersome and expensive. A husband, however, could release or sell his right to curtesy any time he pleased. Lord Eldon claimed in 1805, "no person would purchase an estate subject to tenancy by the curtesy, without the concurrence of the person in whom it was vested": "It was necessary for the security of purchasers, of mortgagees, and of other persons taking the legal estates, to depart from the general principle in case of dower; but it was not necessary in the case of tenancy by the courtesy."[36] Also, given that so much property was held in trusts, it may well have been that men simply would not have tolerated the loss of curtesy as the price of enjoying the benefits of trusts, whereas women were not able to protest. One of the equity lawyers who was questioned by the Commissioners for Real Property said that the difference between curtesy and dower arose "merely because the ladies were not the judges who settled the law."[37]

Holdsworth attempted to reconcile the opposing principles of trusts by saying: "Equity recognized the same estates as the common law, and gave to these estates some of the same incidents as they possessed at common law. . . . though equity faithfully followed the law in the variety of estates which it recognized, it retained considerable power to mould the incidents of these estates in accordance with its ideas of justice and public policy."[38] This distinction between "variety of estates" and their "incidents," however, is not very meaningful: if an "estate" is anything beyond a mere name, it is the sum of its "incidents." To say that equity "faithfully followed" the law in recognizing the incident of curtesy while denying the incident of dower is to say that the equitable estate tail was a different estate than the estate tail at common law. Estates differ from each other by virtue of their incidents.

Extension of the Rule in Chaplin

Chaplin continued to stand for the principle that there was no dower of a trust. But the particular trust estate involved in *Chaplin* was a rent charge to the use of the husband's father in tail male, and, as I have explained, the entire variety of legal estates was echoed by the variety of trust estates. After deciding *Chaplin,* the courts could have proceeded to understand it narrowly, limiting it to the kind of trust estate in *Chaplin.* Such a narrow construction would have kept the dower/curtesy anomaly limited to one kind of trust estate. Moreover, the impact of earlier cases in which curtesy had been allowed of various kinds of trusts could have been broadened by finding curtesy and dower sufficiently analogous that dower would be allowed of those kinds of trusts; this would also have reduced the dower/curtesy anomaly. Indeed, at the time of *Chaplin* there were cases in which dower had been allowed of a trust and in which curtesy of a trust had been accepted as a relevant precedent. *Fletcher v. Robinson* (1653), *Dudley v. Dudley* (1705), and *Otway v. Hudson* (1706) were cited for the widow; *Ambrose v. Ambrose* (1716) and *Banks v. Sutton* (1732) might have been.[39] Lord Chancellor Talbot in *Chaplin,* however, elected to distinguish *Otway, Dudley,* and *Fletcher* as cases involving more limited issues than trusts generally, as it was not difficult to do.

Banks v. Sutton (1732), not discussed in *Chaplin* and not in the printed reports at that time, was a case involving an equity of redemption, but Sir Joseph Jekyll, Master of the Rolls, in deciding *Banks* gave an elaborate statement of his understanding of the general nature of dower and curtesy and a general argument that there was dower of a trust. In *Banks* it was decided that a widow was endowed of an equity of redemption in a mortgage which came to her husband as tenant in tail of a trust. (An equity of redemption is the right of a mortgagor, after a nonpayment or breach of the condition of the mortgage, to redeem property from the forfeiture by discharging the obligation within a reasonable period.)[40] To Jekyll, *Fletcher, Dudley,* and *Otway*—cases urged for the widow in *Chaplin*—all seemed appropriate precedents for dower of a trust. Furthermore, he thought, "as dower is more favoured in law, reason, and equity, than curtesy, therefore every precedent for tenant by the curtesy of a trust, is an authority for dower of a trust."[41] Jekyll ventured to say that a wife had not only a legal and equitable right to dower but also a moral right:

> The relation of husband and wife, as it is the nearest, so it is the earliest, and therefore the wife is the proper object of the care and kindness of the husband; the husband is bound by the law of God and man, to provide for her during his life, and after his death, the *moral obligation* is not at an end, but he ought to take care of her provision during her own life. This is the more reasonable, as during the coverture, the wife can acquire no property of her own . . . her personal estate becomes his absolutely, or at least is subject to his control. . . . As to the husband's personal estate . . . he may give it all away from her; so that his real estate (if he had any) is the only *plank* she can lay hold of, to prevent her sinking under her distress; thus is the wife said to have a *moral right* to a dower.[42]

Jekyll thought a distinction might be made between trusts created by the husband or of a purchase he made, on the one hand, and trusts created by another person, the ancestor or donor of an estate to the husband, on the other. He allowed that dower might be denied from the first kind of trust, "since it may be presumed to be done with intent to bar dower, and every man may do as he pleases with his own."[43] (The moral right of the wife to dower would here be lost.) Where the trust was created by someone other than the husband, as was the case in *Banks,* Jekyll thought, dower ought to be allowed. The facts of *Banks* allow it to be said that the case turned on equity's assuming that a trustee had acted as he was supposed to act under a will ("Equity regards as done that which ought to be done"), and both Jekyll's distinction between husband-created and donor-created trusts and his general statements about dower and curtesy were later explicitly rejected. *Banks,* however, does illustrate the real possibility that *Chaplin* might have gone the other way, and that *Chaplin* afterward might have been narrowed as *Fletcher, Otway,* and *Dudley* were.

What actually happened after *Chaplin* was that the issue of whether there should be dower or curtesy of a trust was presented again and again in a variety of different sorts of trust estates, thus giving the judges an opportunity to lessen or to increase the dower/curtesy anomaly. They elected to increase it by giving curtesy of other forms of trust and denying dower. Perhaps the most interesting and significant example of how the rule in *Chaplin* was extended is the judges' development of a rule that there should be no free bench of a copyhold held in trust. Copyhold begins as an unfree tenure in which a villein holds of the lord of the manor by virtue of an entry on the rolls of the lord's manorial court; thus, he is a tenant by copy of the court roll or a "copyholder." By 1660, however, copyholding had become a more attractive tenure in various ways; as noted in Chapter 1, many estates of the nobility and gentry included some parcels of land they themselves held as copyholders.

Unlike dower, free bench was only an entitlement to a fixed share of the lands of which the husband died seised, so the objection to free bench as a clog on alienability should be less. In *Otway* (1706) the court had allowed free bench of a trust, noting that curtesy had been allowed of trusts, and saying, "The widow of the *cestuy que trust* [the beneficiary] of a copyhold estate, ought to have her *free bench* or widow's estate, as well as if the husband had had the legal estate in him: there it may be said, that *equitas sequitur legem*."[44]

After *Chaplin,* however, Lord Chancellor Hardwicke decided in *Godwin v. Winsmore* (1742) that there was no customary dower of a trust. Jekyll's opinion in *Banks* was explicitly rejected, and *Otway* was said to turn on the fact that the husband had tried to acquire the legal estate but the trustees had refused to assist.[45] *Foder v. Wade* (1794) finally came to stand for the rule that there was no free bench of a trust.[46] Counsel for the losing side in *Foder* made some interesting arguments distinguishing free bench from dower and urged, "The rule as to a woman's not having dower of a trust, is a harsh rule, and ought not to be extended to copyholds." There had not been uses of copyholds, so the argument that since there was no dower of a use there ought not to be dower of a trust should not apply to free bench. Lord Chancellor Loughborough rejected counsel's invocation of *Otway,* noting in passing that "about the time of that decision, the Courts were fluctuating upon the wife's right to dower in equitable estates." Instead he decided to follow *Godwin,* concluding, "to determine otherwise would be to raise an anomaly upon an anomaly"—meaning that the no dower of a trust rule was already an anomaly, and to decree free bench of a trust would create an anomaly upon that anomaly.[47]

There were, as we have seen, substantive technical arguments to support the position that there should be no dower of a trust. But in the early nineteenth century the dominant view of legal intellectuals had come to be that the anomaly in the dower/curtesy rules was an embarrassment, and that, technically, dower should probably have been given of a trust. Contemporaries explicitly offered two major reasons to explain why the opposite result had, in fact, been reached. First, they said, conveyancers had established such an expectation that there would be no dower of a trust that for the judges to have ruled otherwise would have too much shaken titles to land. Second, they said, to have given dower of a trust would have been too much of a clog on alienability and would have interfered with the interests of purchasers and mortgagees. There had also been a shift from some of the earlier judicial rhetoric in which dower was described as "a moral right" that equity ought to defend against legal evasion to an early nineteenth-century view according to which Lord Chancellor Eldon could speak of dower as a "mere legal right."[48]

The policy arguments about alienability offered by contemporaries cannot explain why the judges determined that there was to be no free bench of a trust, since the husband could freely alienate copyhold land during the marriage, and his wife was entitled only to free bench in the lands of which he died seised. Nor can these arguments explain why legal intellectuals did not solve their problem of the dower/curtesy anomaly by recommending a statute which modified dower so that it conformed to free bench in giving the widow an entitlement only to land of which her husband died seised. That this would have been a fairly obvious solution is shown by the fact that the Connecticut legislature passed such a statute in the seventeenth century.[49]

The English Parliament was, no doubt, less inclined to enact real property statutes than American legislatures were, but they certainly did enact such statutes from time to time. Reading only appellate cases can sometimes give the impression that contemporary legal intellectuals treated all the classic common law real property categories as sacrosanct fetishes. But this is a false impression. When they liked, contemporary legal intellectuals tinkered quite happily with particular features of the common law of real property that seemed to them unfair or inconvenient. For example, in 1706 they invented a procedural remedy for reversioners or remaindermen who believed that they were kept out by the beneficiary of a trust entitled only to a term based on the life of someone whose death the beneficiary concealed. Or, for another example, in 1769 they elected to protect minor or feme covert heirs of copyhold who were entitled by descent or surrender to the use of a last will from forfeiture of their inheritance by reason of nonpayment of fines. Moreover, they felt capable of transforming one of the most basic real property relationships, that of landlord and tenant, by a series of statutes which treated rents less like real property and more like chattel property. In 1660 landlords who were owed rent had common law distress as a summary remedy. They were entitled to seize goods and chattels on the tenant's premises and to hold them as pledges for payment. The Sale of Distress Act (1689), however, gave landlords the right to sell the items so taken. This statute, and subsequent statutes, including the Landlord and Tenant Act (1709), and the Distress for Rent Act (1737), as F. A. Enever has pointed out, "to a very large extent, destroyed the fundamental legal principles of distress at common law."[50] Hence some statutory modification of common law dower was not inconceivable at any point during this period.

Finally, in the 1830s, Sir John Campbell, as Solicitor General, did bring in a bill with precisely this feature of limiting dower entitlement to land of which the husband had died seised. Campbell had been one of the lawyers appointed in 1829 to the Commission to Inquire into the Law of England Respecting Real Property. He introduced his bill at a historical moment when he could also claim, plausibly, that the forced share of a third in all the real property of which the husband had been seised at any time during the marriage had been "constantly rendered useless by the modern practice of settlements."[51] When in 1832, as Mr. Campbell, M.P., he had brought in his dower bill, some members had objected that it did not sufficiently protect the rights of married women. One Mr. Blamire, for instance, had complained that the provision allowing the husband to take away the wife's dower by will was "very unjust." Campbell met such objections by pointing out that conveyancing techniques had virtually defeated women's dower rights anyway, and by claiming that his bill, which became the Dower Act of 1833, offered women a fair exchange. In exchange for bestowing on husbands increased power to defeat dower by alienation in their lifetimes or by testamentary devise, Campbell proposed to correct the dower/curtesy anomaly and to give wives a new right of dower out of husbands' equitable estates, an advantage, he claimed, that would more than compensate for the disadvantages of the other clauses in the bill.[52] Had the problem of dower as a clog on alienability been the only objection to dower, the provision of Campbell's bill limiting dower entitlement to land of which the husband had died seised could have been enacted much earlier, as it had been enacted in seventeenth-century Connecticut. Instead, in England such a provision was enacted only at a much later time when there was general agreement that the dower system as a forced share system was a dead letter. Its enactment allowed legal intellectuals to feel that they had corrected an error but preserved for individual women no socially enforced rights; an individual woman got nothing except what her own husband privately elected to bestow.

Fraud against the Spouse's Rights

As we have seen, contemporaries did frequently perceive the differences between the rules for dower and curtesy of trusts as anomalous and asymmetrical. Yet there seems to have been almost no similar consciousness of what from a modern point of view is an even more striking asymmetry. Men in contemplation of marriage could and did convey their property to trustees in order to, as they said, avoid the inconvenience of dower attaching and for other purposes. Such conveyances were not necessarily part of the settlement documents signed by the bride to be. It barely seems to have occurred to anyone in the seventeenth century that a prospective groom ought to be required to obtain the consent of his prospective bride for such conveyances to trustees to be valid. I have found only one moment of awareness that such conveyances by grooms might be regarded as fraud. In the argument reported in *Radnor v. Vandebendy* (1697), counsel observed: "Perhaps it must be agreed, That if the Husband had just before Marriage made a long Lease on Purpose to prevent Dower, and the Woman expecting the Privileges which the Common Law gives to Women married and survived him, Equity might have interposed. And yet even this was practised by a Reverend Judge of Equity, Mr. Serjeant *Maynard,* who made such Lease to his Man *Bradford* the day before his last Marriage."[53] But prospective brides' attempts to convey to trustees in contemplation of their marriages provoked husbands to allege fraud.

Widows with property and prior experience of marriage were particularly likely to try to protect themselves and children of prior marriages by conveying to trustees before a second marriage. Such conveyances could have had the effects of depriving the new husband of his common law rights to curtesy and also of the use for his own benefit of the wife's property during the marriage. Significantly, Restoration courts held that a widow's attempts to convey to trustees before marriage were fraud against the marital rights of the husband and void. In the leading case of *Howard v. Hooker* (1672–73), the court found that the new husband had not been privy to the settlement, that he had married "in Confidence of having the Interest she had in the Estate," and so set her deed aside as fraudulent.[54] This case thus anticipates the plot of Congreve's *Way of the World* (1700) in which the hero, Mirabell, helps his former mistress, the widow Arabella, protect herself by having her convey all her property to him as trustee before she marries the comic villain, Fainall. When Fainall, who certainly married Arabella "in confidence of having the Interest she had in the Estate," behaves badly, Mirabell and Arabella produce the trust deed and send Fainall, gnashing his teeth in frustration, from the stage. Fainall would have gotten more sympathy from the equity judges in 1700 than he gets from Congreve.

There was no theoretical reason why the complaints made in the ordinary language of contemporaries that men's conveying their property to uses or trusts in contemplation of marriage was a "crafty," "cautelous," or "devious" derogation of women's dower rights could not have been translated into a legal rule that a conveyance by a man to trustees in contemplation of marriage to defeat his wife's dower right was fraudulent and void. The legal concept of fraud is a particularly rich and labile one, especially in the field of uses and trusts. Lord Hardwicke in a letter to Lord Kames observed: "Fraud is infinite, and were a Court of Equity once to lay down rules, how far they would go, and no further, in extending their relief against it, . . . the jurisdiction would be cramped, and perpetually eluded by new schemes which the fertility of man's invention would contrive."[55] Under the rubric of fraud, judges work to project their most fundamental ideas of fairness.

Clearly, all conveyances ever made by a feme sole who later married could not be considered frauds as against the marital rights of the after-acquired husband. It may be the destiny of every young girl to marry, but she has to be allowed to buy a loaf of bread, tea cakes, or a simple frock while she is waiting, without having such transactions viewed as thefts from a man she has not yet even seen. Hence the judges subsequently developed rules about when such conveyances by women would be effective, rules which embodied their notions of how men and women ought to behave and what kinds of marriages they ought to make. In particular, they determined that widows, in contemplation of remarriage, could convey their property to trustees for the benefit of children of prior marriages without the consent of the new husband-to-be or even, apparently, notice to him.[56] This exception permitted women to make an "unselfish" disposition, helped prevent the children from the prior marriage from becoming public charges, and—significantly—acknowledged that a woman might rationally mistrust the protection and support a husband was supposed to provide to his wife and children when those children were not his biological children. Lady Cotton, in one of the cases which established this rule, had nine children by her first husband, Sir Thomas Cotton, children who were said to be "very slenderly provided for."

Conveyances by the woman for her own benefit were less tolerated. Since a husband had a common law obligation to maintain his wife, the situations of husband and wife were not exactly symmetrical. One might say that it would be unfair for a woman to convey away all her assets and then come into a marriage expecting to be supported. Lord Thurlow, indeed, expressed this idea in 1789: "The rights of the husband over the property of his wife are given him in consequence of the burthens which on the marriage are imposed on the husband in respect to his wife. The law therefore certainly has said, that these are rights against which frauds *may* be committed."[57] But one response to this argument might be that since a woman was obliged to provide service for her husband, that service was sufficient recompense for his support; the idea of the equity of such an exchange is fundamental to the common law reciprocity of support and service in marriage.[58] Alternately, and with more practical relevance to the marriages of the wealthy, one might respond that it was fair for the woman to convey away from a prospective husband property she owned in excess of what would be required for her support and maintenance. In the case of Lady Cotton, the court attached some significance to the fact that, even if they allowed her settlement on her children to be valid, the second husband, King, still had "had a considerable sum of money with Lady *Cotton.*" Also, he himself had been "in very mean circumstances" and "did not so much as pretend he could make any settlement or jointure on Lady *Cotton.*"[59] No one, however, appears to have suggested a rule that a woman's conveyances in excess of what was required for her support should be valid. Such a rule would have conflicted with the idea that the husband alone should be judge of what level of support and maintenance his wife should have.[60] Thus it was generally held that conveyances by a woman in contemplation of marriage to trustees for herself were fraudulent.

Difficulties were caused by conveyances by third parties to the woman for her benefit. A widow possessed of a trust term conveyed to her by her former husband married Lord Chief Baron Edward Turner, who sold the term. Lord Chancellor Nottingham decreed that Turner had had no right to the term, but was reversed in the House of Lords. Shortly thereafter, feeling himself bound by the precedent of Turner's case, Lord Chancellor Nottingham worried in *Pitt v. Hunt* (1681): "People made provisions for their children according to what the law was then taken to be; and now those provisions are defeated by this new resolution; so that now it is almost impossible for a man to provide for his child but it shall be subject to the disposal of an extravagant husband."[61]

As settlements to women for their separate use independent of the control of their husbands (as though they were feme sole) were made with increasing explicitness and were given effect, this difficulty Nottingham complained of in *Pitt* was ameliorated, and the equity of a married woman's having beneficial enjoyment of separate property was accepted. Patriarchal judges became comfortable with such trust provisions made by fathers for daughters, even though they were based on some mistrust of the future husband's ability or willingness to provide and protect, but judges were less comfortable with a similar lack of confidence expressed by a woman's creating a trust for herself.

Yet the judges were not prepared to formulate a rule that trusts made in contemplation of marriage for the separate use of a woman were fraudulent if made by the woman but not fraudulent if made by her father or some other male relative. To have done so would have too much compromised the fair and gender-blind appearance of the rule system itself. Usually, special property rules were formulated not to discriminate between men and women but rather to distinguish between normative legal individuals (men and single women) and those women who had presumably elected to alter their own legal status by entering into the special legal status of married women.

The tension between the fraud cases stemming from *Howard v. Hooker* and the increased acceptance of settlements to the separate use of a wife is evident in *The Countess of Strathmore v. Bowes* (1789). Bowes claimed that a settlement made by his wife, the Countess of Strathmore, for her own benefit less than a week before their marriage deprived him of his marital rights and was fraudulent. Lord Thurlow, a quite conservative and patriarchal judge, observed that he personally did not think much of permitting married women to have separate property and agreed with Bowes that a husband had rights in his wife's property against which fraud could be committed. Nevertheless, Thurlow was compelled to observe, "but as our law now stands, it is impossible to argue that it is fraud on the husband, whenever he is deprived of the dominion over the wife's property. It is in every day's experience that such dominion is intercepted by some previous act;

therefore there must be something beyond the mere deprivation of the husband from these rights to constitute a case of fraud."[62] Mr. Justice Buller suggested that that "something beyond" which constituted fraud must be the woman's "falsely holding out" that she has an estate unfettered"; Lord Thurlow thought it would be "if any thing appears to be done by the wife *animo celandi*." The facts in *The Countess of Strathmore* indicate that Bowes had no notice of the trust and also seem to support his contention that the Countess appeared to be the legal owner of the estates, though perhaps not that she explicitly said that she was. Nevertheless, the judges thought Bowes was a terrible person, "not entitled to much consideration in a court of justice." He was notoriously a bankrupt lieutenant on half-pay who had wasted the fortune of a previous wife, fought a sham duel to influence the Countess to marry him, then treated her with cruelty, extorted a deed from her by duress, and had her kidnapped by ruffians when she tried to escape from him.[63] The Countess got an ecclesiastical divorce from Bowes on March 2, 1789, and the following day the Lord Chancellor pronounced her prenuptial settlement on herself valid. Buller had optimistically said, "the circumstances of this case are such as probably never happened before, and may never happen again."

The rule that a woman's conveyances in contemplation of marriage could be struck down for fraud against the marital right of her husband survived Bowes. The judges did not quite go to the length of deciding that any settlement a woman made on herself in contemplation of marriage with any man was void, although some seem to have been tempted to do so. What they did say was that any settlement a woman made on herself in contemplation of marriage with a particular man was void as against that particular man. The Countess of Strathmore's case could be said to fall outside this rule because she made her settlement in contemplation of a marriage with Mr. Grey and with his assent, then days later married Bowes instead, Bowes claiming ignorance of the settlement. The precise moment at which a given woman began to contemplate marriage with a given man could be difficult to establish. In *Goddard v. Snow* (1826), in which Lord Gifford, Master of the Rolls, surveyed the earlier cases and articulated the rule I have just described, Lord Gifford was able to satisfy himself on the basis of rather diffuse oral evidence from acquaintances that the wife in question had had her marriage with the plaintiff in contemplation ten months before it had been celebrated, and thus to decide that her settlement on herself dated ten months before the wedding was void as a fraud on the husband's marital rights.[64]

In theory, the judges might have developed rules making husbands' conveyances to trustees in order to avoid wives' dower void as frauds on wives' marital rights, using the principles they invoked in this line of cases from *Howard* through *Goddard*. In practice, as we have seen, they elected not to do so and permitted husbands' conveyances to trustees to defeat dower. Contemporary explanations for changes in the dower rules that claim they were motivated by the importance of honoring conveyancing practices and by the importance of promoting alienability require more critical scrutiny. But conveying to trustees was only one way that dower was avoided in the eighteenth century. Before we can look at this contemporary history more critically, we need to understand how dower was avoided by other conveyancing tactics, which is the subject of the following chapter.

3

Avoidance of Dower by More Complex Conveyancing Techniques

Conveyancers

We have seen that in *Chaplin* weight had been given to the practices of conveyancers, who were said to have assured their clients that there would be no dower of a trust. The judges professed reluctance to upset expectations conveyancers had created and fear of throwing titles "into confusion" by deciding against what was said to be dominant conveyancing opinion. Holdsworth, indeed, correctly observed that in the early modern period the "practice and opinions of the conveyancers gradually came to be regarded almost as a secondary source of law."[1] In Holdsworth's view, given "the highly technical and complicated state of the land law," such judicial respect for the practice of conveyancers is "very desirable": "for it affords a strong guarantee to land-owners that the instruments drawn up by their advisors will have the effect which they desire."[2]

Within the ethos of the legal profession, conveyancing work has enjoyed a peculiar and high prestige. Conveyancers, removed from the sordid and material worlds of criminal law or tort law, manipulate highly abstracted interests in land or other valuable resources for the benefit of those eminently respectable clients most able to reward the best lawyers. What conveyancers do is, to laymen, so boring as to be virtually invisible, but, to the rarefied and superior intelligence of the better legal minds, appears the dazzling epitome of professional expertise. Thus, in the recent book *The Law of Property* (1982), written by two professors of law at Oxford and designed in part to initiate neophyte law students into the mysteries of the profession, we read: "The Law of Property has the reputation of being one of the most difficult branches of English law, and its reputation is not undeserved."[3] "A large part of the work of property lawyers with wealthy clients," the neophyte is told, "consists of creating complicated arrangements known as settlements. . . . This part of the law of property . . . is the most intellectually rewarding for the student."[4] Later, by way of a warm-up to their discussion of the doctrine of estates as abstract entities, the professors confide:

> Now [the student] will find himself brought face to face with a new activity of the conveyancer and with a type of conveyancer whom he probably never knew to exist, the expert barrister who sits in his chambers in Lincoln's Inn and hardly . . . [ever] goes into court, who spends his time like a spider, weaving webs of legal gossamer in which to tie up corporeal things and the incorporeal things which are the immediate objects of commerce. The purpose of all his activity, is to ensure, as far as the law can ensure it, that the property he is dealing with shall move from one person to another for an appreciable time in the future in a perfectly predictable way and that they shall be managed in the cheapest and most efficient way, attracting the lightest possible burden of taxation.[5]

Even the authors of general textbooks on property celebrate the "brilliance" of early modern conveyancers, especially of Orlando Bridgeman, "the father of modern conveyancing." An amusing example of the characteristic treatment of early modern conveyancing at the level of the property textbook is to be found in *Cases and Text on Property,* by A. James Casner and W. Barton Leach, then professors at Harvard Law School and more enthusiastic about the history of their subject than many. Discussing what they describe as Bridgeman's "slick device of trustees to preserve contingent remainders," they comment: "In the old days the law was thought of as essentially a logical system. If an ingenious fellow like Bridgman could turn the logic of the law against itself—as a judo wrestler throws his opponent by using his own weight against him—the courts acknowledged defeat in a sportsmanlike fashion and left it at that."[6]

Within the legal profession, peculiar pride has also been taken in the way that conveyancing has become so technically difficult as to be unintelligible and mysterious, not only to ordinary laymen and clients but also to ordinary lawyers, judges, and legislators. According to Holdsworth, as conveyancing grew more complex, by the end of the eighteenth century conveyancers became "a class very much apart from other legal practitioners," and, at the beginning of the nineteenth century, "an intimate knowledge of the law of real property was almost confined to a comparatively small number of eminent conveyancers."[7] Law professors quote with delight the estimate one King's Counsel gave to the Real Property Commissioners "that there were not above six persons who understood the laws of real property" and only one "barrister of eminence practicing in any of the courts who has a perfect knowledge of their practical effects."[8] In the history given by our modern Oxford professors of law, we find that while in the early days conveyancers acted "as the servants of the propertied classes, and originally very much under their instruction," "later the law became so technical that only the conveyancers know where it was defective and how to reform it. Even now, when it has been greatly simplified, it is still something of a mystery and largely under their control."[9]

An important fact about the legal history of this period is that legal professionals invented complex and difficult conveyancing tactics which satisfied the desires of male clients and, consequently, also both enriched these legal professionals and became a source of their professional prestige. Holdsworth wrote that "the growth of the complexity of land law, during the sixteenth and seventeenth centuries, caused the growth of a class of professional conveyancers."[10] But the complexity of the land law did not just grow like Topsy and in consequence cause an increase in conveyancing business. Conveyancers themselves were important causes of this increased complexity as they experimented with new technical innovations and urged the judicial acceptance of their validity. Conveyances grew longer, more complex, and hence more expensive. At the highest level of the profession, an eminent barrister like William Murray, Lord Mansfield, could see a fee of as much as £4,726.19s.6d for work on a settlement for a single noble client.[11] Demand was too great to be met by barristers alone, and, according to Michael Miles's study of attorneys, for the ordinary country attorney conveyancing "was by far the most profitable single source of business."[12] The Beverley family attorney of Sir Mark Masterman Sykes, who had an estate in East Yorkshire, prepared a settlement on Sir Mark's second marriage, went to London to consult with two conveyancing counsel, and submitted a bill for £133.10s.[13] According to Miles, the attorneys' acquisition of the nonelite conveyancing work "must be the major factor in accounting for the rapid growth in size of the profession [of attorney] between 1660–1730." One of the country attorneys whose practice Miles has been able to study in great detail from sources including day books, ledgers, and cash books, an attorney in practice from 1748 to 1780, derived only 29 percent of his profits from litigation of all kinds, but 47 percent from conveyancing.[14]

An important and growing "product line" of these conveyancing professionals involved ways to avoid traditional common law rules that their male clients considered "inconvenient." Praising the "skill" of early modern conveyancers, Holdsworth cites as notable examples of that skill "the manner in which technical doctrines were used to evade the consequence of inconvenient rules . . . , firstly the mechanism of conveyance to uses to bar dower, and secondly the manner in which the machinery of terms of years was used to prevent merger when merger was inexpedient, or as a security against claims to dower, or against mesne incumbrances."[15] We have seen in the preceding chapter that dower could be prevented from attaching by conveying land to trustees, but conveying to trustees was not a panacea for all possible "inconveniences" landowners might face and brought some new inconveniences of its own. For example, George Haskins has observed that some landowners were reluctant to convey to trustees because they would lose the power to break the trust "to sell in a rising market for profit or to meet current financial needs."[16] In order to appreciate a fuller range of the conveyancer's "skill" in avoiding dower, it is necessary to have a deeper and more theoretical understanding of early modern settlements, mortgages, and terms of years. This chapter aims both to provide such an understanding and to suggest a critique of the judicial acquiescence in certain of the conveyancing tactics in this field.

Strict Settlement

Recall the first plate of Hogarth's *Marriage à la Mode* in which the apparently cash-poor Earl and the rich merchant are about to agree to a settlement or prenuptial agreement between their bored children. We cannot see what the terms of the particular settlement in Hogarth are, and, since these marriage settlements were private contracts, their terms varied widely according to the individual situations and desires of the parties. In general, however, eighteenth-century marriage settlements often had three important objects: to entail land on the groom and his male descendants so that it could not be sold away from the family, to bar dower for the bride and give her a jointure instead, and to arrange portions for daughters and younger sons born of the marriage. Although it is sometimes said that only the very privileged married with settlements, in fact, settlements were common among substantial country freeholders and among city business or professional people.[17] An intriguing Samuel Richardson manuscript records the novelist's private thoughts concerning the marriage settlement to be made for his oldest daughter and a Bath surgeon; it shows Richardson to have been reasonably well informed about the legal issues involved.[18]

"Strict" settlements were "strict" in preventing alienation of the land away from the male line. The idea was not merely to see that successive elder sons inherited. At common law elder sons were the preferred heirs anyway. At common law, also, should a father not wish to risk the possibility of a daughter's inheriting in a subsequent generation when there were no sons, he could give land to his son not in fee simple but in fee tail male, making it descend to sons alone. (Since the Bennet estate in Jane Austen's *Pride and Prejudice* is entailed in fee tail male, all the Bennet daughters are to be skipped over in favor of their rather distant and absurd male relation, Mr. Collins.) But many wealthy eighteenth-century settlors of estates were not satisfied with the ordinary common law fee tail male. Its simplicity risked escheat or reversion to remote reversioners in the event of a failure of male heirs. Moreover, a common law fee tail male permitted a son in a successive generation to sell the estate and leave his own sons and grandsons with nothing, or nothing but a title which they would lack the material resources to support. Ordinary common law estates in fee simple or fee tail are freehold estates, which include the right to alienate as well as the right to enjoy.

Conveyancers invented a "solution" from within their doctrine of estates to this "problem" of the limitations of the common law fee tail male. The key was to settle the land in such a way that the son in each generation had a "lesser estate" than a freehold, an entitlement to enjoy the proceeds of the estate during his life but not the right to sell it away from successive sons. Suppose on the occasion of the marriage of Tom Jones and Sophia Western we are not absolutely sure that Tom will never again fall into his scapegrace ways and therefore want to protect the family by settling Paradise Hall on him in strict settlement. Suppose also that Squire Allworthy owns the Paradise Hall estate in fee simple. We can advise Squire Allworthy to give Paradise Hall "to Tom for Tom's life, remainder to trustees and their heirs for the life of Tom to preserve contingent remainders, remainder to the heirs male of the body of Tom in tail male, remainder to trustees and their heirs for four hundred years from the death of Tom to raise portions for daughters and younger sons of the body of Tom." In the same instrument, we also settle a jointure on Sophia, and so defeat her claims to dower by following the elaborate rules to be discussed in Chapter 4. By the mid-eighteenth century, it was clear that this tactic would work to defeat attempts by Tom to alienate the estate away from his son.

A key technical innovation by conveyancers was the insertion into settlements of the remainder to trustees to preserve contingent remainders, the clause mentioned above as "remainder to trustees and their heirs for the life of Tom to preserve contingent remainders." (In actual settlements, the phrase "to preserve contingent remainders" does not always appear, but the trustees are given a remainder which comes into play if the estate of the life tenant ends before his natural life, as, for example, if Tom forfeits his life estate by trying to alienate it in fee simple.) My argument that this was a highly debatable experiment—rather than a straightforward technical "improvement," as is frequently claimed—requires explanation for all readers except a few specialists in classical property law, but the reasons are worth understanding and are also necessary parts of the argument.

Consider, first, that a fundamental purpose of the law of real property is to tell us who "owns" any particular piece of property, say Paradise Hall, at any time, either now or at any future time when that time comes. "Ownership" itself is not an undifferentiated entity but rather, as the lawyers say, a "bundle of rights." So the law of real property also wants to tell us who owns which pieces or sticks of that bundle. In the case of landlord and tenant, for example, some sticks of the bundle of rights belong to the landlord, others, including important possessory rights, belong to the tenant. Similarly, in the case of mortgagors and mortgagees, some rights in the given piece of land belong to the mortgagor and others to the mortgagee. And, as noted above, how these rights were distributed between the two has varied considerably historically. In order to regulate the relations of persons with respect to things, the law of real property has tended to divide up these various interests into known "packages": fee simple, estate tail, rights of mortgagees, and so on.

Ownership of a particular piece of land is thus conceptualized as a totality, a sum of rights, which can be fragmented or, as they used to say, "carved up," with respect to time and also with respect to "interests" in the land. Fielding describes Paradise Hall as a building commodious within and venerable without, situated on the southeast side of a hill, sheltered by a grove of old oaks, enjoying a charming prospect of the valley beneath. But to the conveyancer, it appears as a much more abstracted set of interests. In the most technical sense of the word "estate," a particular person's estate is the degree, quantity, nature, and extent of the interest which he has in real property. If we were to ask an eighteenth-century conveyancer, "What estate will Tom have under Allworthy's settlement?" the conveyancer would reply, "Tom will have a life estate."

Thus, from the conveyancer's point of view we might crudely represent the carving up of the rights to Paradise Hall as Squire Allworthy proposes to settle it on Tom and Sophia as in Figure 1 (leaving out, for the moment, the remainder to trustees to preserve contingent remainders). The "largest" estate, we see in the diagram, is the fee simple in Allworthy; the fee simple contains the totality of interests, including right of possession and the right to use without impeachment of waste. If Allworthy owns the estate in fee simple, he can cut down the trees or even tear down Paradise Hall if he likes, whereas if he were only a tenant for a term of years such acts would be "waste" for which the landlord could proceed against him. The fee simple is also an "estate of inheritance," that is, an estate which will descend to the owner's heirs, and descend infinitely so long as heirs can be found, unless he exercises another right of fee simple ownership, the right of al-

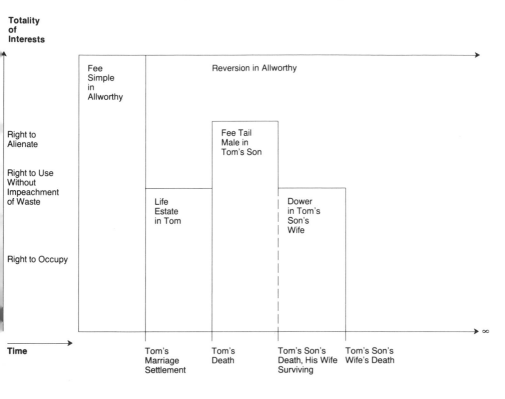

Figure 1. A conveyancer's carving up of the interests in Paradise Hall

ienation. In this example Allworthy has exercised the right of alienation by settling the estate on Tom at Tom's marriage.

The life estate which Tom acquires at the time of the settlement is thought of as "smaller" than a fee simple because it does not include some of the fee simple rights, which are held back and remain in Allworthy as the "reversioner." The life estate is not an estate of inheritance. Tom is entitled to use the land but not to waste it or to alienate it in fee simple; if he attempts either of these, Allworthy has remedies against him and may be able to reenter. At Tom's death, according to this settlement, Tom's son will get a "greater" estate than Tom has had. The son will have a fee tail male, which, unlike Tom's life estate, is an estate of inheritance and an estate that can be alienated in fee simple. As time passes, should Tom's son die before Tom's son's wife dies, then Tom's son's wife will acquire a life estate in one-third of Paradise

Hall as her dower (unless we have prevented this by settling a jointure on her or by some other means). So long as there is no failure of male heirs in the line of Tom's sons, then they will continue in possession with their fee tail male. Should there be a failure of Tom's heirs male, then Squire Allworthy or, if he is dead, his heirs will come into possession as the reversioners.

When Tom wakes up on a morning after his marriage and after the settlement deeds have all been signed, he has a present interest in the land, his life estate. Other persons, yet to be born, have remainders, which are future interests in the land. Remainders are of two kinds: vested and contingent. A remainder is said to be vested if it will become possessory at the termination of the prior particular estate and is subject to no condition precedent other than the termination of the prior particular estate. Thus, to vary our example a little for the purposes of illustration, if Allworthy had settled Paradise Hall "to Tom for life, remainder to Blifil in fee tail male," then Blifil would have had a vested remainder. The estate preceding his, the "precedent estate," would be Tom's life estate, and as soon as Tom's estate terminated at Tom's death, Blifil could enter and take possession of Paradise Hall. Although remainders were future rather than present interests, they could be and were bought and sold. For example, in 1741 when the Duke of Newcastle needed to sell settled lands in which his relation Henry Vane had future interests, the Duke agreed to pay Vane £60,000 for those interests preparatory to having those lands sold to pay interest on the Duke's debts and to pay some of the debts themselves.[19]

In our original settlement, in which Blifil had no interest, the remainders which follow Tom's are all contingent, in this case contingent on the birth of a son to Tom. Contingent remainders are defined as remainders which to become possessory are subject to some additional condition precedent other than the termination of the prior particular estate. If Tom does have a son, called, say, Frederick, at that son's birth the previously contingent remainder to Tom's son in fee tail male will become a vested remainder in fee tail male, a vested remainder belonging to Frederick. In earlier times contingent remainders were not recognized. When they were first recognized in the mid-fifteenth century, the only ones so recognized were remainders to the heir of a living person, like the remainder in our settlement to Tom's son.

An early, failed effort at strict settlement was made by Rickhill, J., who conveyed land to his first, second, and third sons successively in tail male with the condition that if the son in possession aliened in fee or fee tail, then his estate should cease or be void, the next son to take. If this had been allowed, and the first son took his estate in fee tail male, the second son would have had a contingent remainder depending on the condition precedent of the first son's attempting to alienate. Littleton, however, said that such a contingent remainder would be void because it was "repugnant to the nature of the estate granted," that is, that it depended on construing the precedent fee tail estate as not including the right to alienate, which such an estate by its "nature" included.[20] As Holdsworth pointed out, "the idea of repugnancy supplied a technical reason for new applications of the old principle that restrictions on the freedom of alienation are contrary to public policy."[21] Nevertheless, by the end of the sixteenth century a variety of contingent remainders dependent on conditions besides the death of a living person had been recognized.

Contingent remainders could be "destroyed" in several ways. In the first place, contingent remainders required a precedent freehold estate to "support" them; if the precedent estate "failed" or terminated before the contingent remainder could vest, then the contingent remainder was destroyed. The reason for this requirement was supposed to be that seisin had to be continuous; it could not flicker on and off or leave "gaps" in between possessions. Given the medieval requirements for livery of seisin, the formal and actual passing of ownership on the land, this made a certain amount of sense: the next recipient of seisin had to be physically present to take at the moment ownership passed from the preceding owner. (It was also socially desirable that owners of land be publicly known to be so.) The requirement of support produced the controversial case of *Reeve v. Long* (1695).[22] Land had been given to A for life, remainder to his son, remainder over. When A died and had a posthumous son, all the judges agreed that the contingent remainder to the son had been destroyed; they reasoned that since the son had not been born before his father's death, the remainder had failed to vest before or at the time of the death of the father, which was the time of the termination of the precedent estate. (This bit of legal logic was reversed as socially intolerable by the House of Lords and further repudiated by a statute of 1699.)[23]

Contingent remainders could also be destroyed by "merger," either merger at the will of the parties or merger operating independently of the will of the parties. In the eighteenth century remaindermen and reversioners could surrender or sell their interests to those in possession to bring about a merger of interests which could create in the person in possession an estate sufficiently large to defeat or bar the interests of intervening contingent remaindermen. In *Purefoy v. Rogers* (1671) a life tenant bought the reversion in fee from the heir before the birth of a son who was to have a remainder. The life tenant's estate was ruled to have merged in the reversion and so to have destroyed the contingent remainder to the son.[24]

But merger was also crucially important to settlements when it operated "automatically" without any buying or selling of interests by the parties. At common law, according to the Rule in Shelley's Case, a rule articulated in the Renaissance but older than that, whenever a person, either by deed or will, took an estate for life and, in the same instrument, there was a remainder limited, either immediately or otherwise, to his heirs in fee, that person took the whole estate in fee.[25] (A purpose of this rule was to increase the number of times land passed by descent and so to increase reliefs, wardships, and marriages to lords.) According to the Rule in Shelley's Case, if we settle Allworthy's estate "to Tom for life, remainder to the heirs male of Tom in fee tail male," we may not have accomplished what we wished to accomplish. Since in our settlement deed, in a single instrument, we gave a life estate to Tom and a remainder in fee tail male to his heirs, merger operates to give Tom the estate in fee tail. There is a kind of arithmetical addition at work: a life estate to Tom + a fee tail to his son = a fee tail to Tom. If we meant to give Tom only a life estate to prevent him from alienating or in order to prevent dower from attaching, it would appear that our intention has been defeated by the Rule in Shelley's Case and that we have failed to achieve our ends. Most, though certainly not all, settlors in the eighteenth century knew enough not to make so simple a mistake as we have made. Nevertheless, important "accidents" could happen, especially when a life tenant, despite the interposition of other remainders in the settlement, had a remote reversion in fee "descend" on him at the death of the grantor, whose heir at law he turned out to be. Tom, for instance, although only Allworthy's nephew, might eventually turn out to be Allworthy's heir at law (were it not for the fact that Tom is a bastard and by common law a bastard can be no man's heir). As Holdsworth acknowledges, the courts in this period did not follow the strictly logical consequences of their original legal principles with respect to contingent remainders and merger. Had they done so, he admits, "the whole system of settling land by way of contingent remainders would have been rendered impossible."[26]

What the conveyancers and judges did instead of following the strictly logical consequences of their original understanding of contingent remainder and merger was to invent new subrules by way of exception, just those subrules which, to add a bit to Holdsworth's phrase, would allow the whole system of settling land *in fee tail male* by way of contingent remainders. In theory, the same system would equally have permitted land to be settled in fee tail female, and, in practice, some small pieces of land, especially those which came into the hands of women, were actually settled in fee tail female, but I believe no one could quarrel with the observation that the system was intended to settle the vast majority of settled land owned by men on other men, and that it, in fact, operated to do just that. The system also, in so far as it was concerned to keep the current possessor a life tenant only, kept dower from attaching since a life tenant did not have an estate of inheritance to which dower could attach. The new prosettlement subrules were established only after more of a struggle than is usually appreciated.

When conveyancers began to experiment with the elements of strict settlement in the seventeenth century, it was by no means obvious that their experiments would produce the desired results. Indeed, given the repeated historical insistence on the paramount importance of security in titles to real property, it can come as something of a surprise to find that conveyancers were apparently so willing to experiment. After all, a fundamental justification for having a law of real property is the social usefulness of a system that determines title to particular land, rather than leaving people to fight it out with force and violence, and a system that gives possessors sufficient security of title that they can enjoy quiet possession and confidently make improvements. Nevertheless, in a recent careful study of the evolution of the strict settlement between 1601 and 1740 Lloyd Bonfield concludes, I believe correctly, that "conveyancing was carried out by a body of practitioners who were highly responsive to advances in conveyancing technique, and that they were not reluctant to employ them before judicial sanction."[27] The drafting experiments of seventeenth-century conveyancers created real—and sometimes realized—risks that titles to property would go where neither the settlor nor the conveyancer intended or that titles would become so complex and confused that confident determination among competing claimants became virtually impossible. (I will have more to say about the failure to produce secure titles later in this chapter.) In fact, as we have seen, despite these difficulties, between 1660 and 1833 the experiments of the conveyancers succeeded in fulfilling the wishes of their clients to the extent that the demand for the services of conveyancers rose and conveyancing advanced as a profession.

We are now in a position to understand how the conveyancers and judges produced new prosettlement subrules regarding contingent remainders and how those affected the results in dower. One extraordinarily elaborate set of subrules limited the operation of merger. On the one hand, these subrules permitted some mergers that made possible voluntary sales and surrenders between life tenants in possession and remaindermen or reversioners. On the other hand, the subrules limited the operation of merger so as to prevent "accidental" mergers that suddenly bestowed estates of inheritance, alienable estates to which dower attached, on tenants in possession. To achieve these ends, conveyancers and judges treated remainders differently in different contexts, arriving at a law concerning remainders, reversions, and merger which its few friends have admired as abstruse and most who have studied it consider hopelessly overelaborated and confused. A fundamental problem was that according to the classical theory of estates no matter how many smaller estates we carve out for the chain of estates in our settlement, what is left of the fee simple has to be owned by somebody. If we fragment our estate into a series of smaller estates, either we are apt to add at the end of the chain an ultimate remainder in fee simple to the heirs of the life tenant, or—if we do not use such a remainder—the life tenant as heir of the grantor will likely acquire a reversion in fee simple anyway. In either case, merger of the life estate and the remainder or reversion threatens. In order to avoid merger, conveyancers and judges developed an account of the nature of the intervening estates on the chain that supposed they could alter their natures, like chameleons, according to which other estates surrounded them. They thus wandered far from the concept of an estate as a reified fixed entity which was supposed to give the calculus of estates its pleasing mathematical quality and to make the law of real property certain.

The Restoration case of *Plunket v. Holmes* (1662) provides a relatively simple example of how these new subrules limiting merger and new, more fluid conceptions of estates helped settlors who wanted to prefer sons, to restrict alienation, and to avoid dower. Land was devised to Thomas for life, and if he died without issue living at the time of his death, to his brother Leonard and his heirs, but if Thomas did have issue living at the time of his death, then in fee to the right heirs of Thomas. The grantor died and the reversion in fee descended on Thomas. Thomas invoked the Rule in Shelley's Case, claiming that his life estate plus the reversion in fee gave him a fee simple (to which dower would attach), which he promptly sold. Leonard protested. The court did not deny that Thomas had acquired both a life estate and a reversion in fee, but they found for Leonard anyway, declining to let merger operate. Thomas's reversion, they said, "shall not drown the estate for life contrary to the express devise and intent of the will, but shall leave an opening as they termed it, for the interposing of the remainders when they shall happen to interpose between the estate for life and the fee."[28]

Another crucial exception was made to the earlier logic of contingent remainders and merger with respect to the treatment of settlements giving remainders "to trustees to preserve contingent remainders." I have already indicated that this remainder to trustees has been considered a particularly brilliant stroke of the conveyancer's art and that its efficacy depended on the judges' willingness to make new prosettlement rules. We can now see why. The purpose of a remainder to trustees to preserve contingent remainders was to secure the interests of remaindermen should the life tenant's estate terminate before his death. Let us go back to our settlement of the Allworthy estate, now revised to include these trustees: "to Tom for life, remainder to Squire Allworthy, Mrs. Miller, and Lawyer Dowling and their heirs as trust-

ees to preserve contingent remainders, remainder to the heirs of
Tom in fee tail male. . . ." Now, if Tom attempts to alienate Paradise Hall in fee simple (to pay his gambling debts, for instance)
or in the event of other unfortunate contingencies (his being
hanged, drawn, and quartered as a Jacobite traitor and so forfeiting
his estate, say), then the trustees will have a right to enter and to
preserve Paradise Hall for Tom's heirs male.

A principal problem with this tactic was that, as I have explained
in the discussion of contingent remainders, the destruction of the
"precedent estate" was supposed to destroy subsequent contingent
remainders dependent upon it. The trustees have no estate unless
Tom's life estate terminates before his death, and—especially
given the sincerity of Tom's reformation, the positive influence
of Sophia, and his solid Hanoverian principles—what could be
more contingent than the premature termination of his life estate?
But if the trustees' remainder is contingent it will be destroyed
by the premature termination of Tom's life estate, the very event
we want to activate it, not to destroy it.

The "solution" to this problem, which will allow us to achieve
our settlement objectives, is for the courts to rule that the remainder to trustees to preserve contingent remainders is not contingent but vested, which is precisely what they did in *Duncomb
v. Duncomb* (1695).[29] In so doing, as we shall see, they also provided
further security against dower attaching. The settlement in *Duncomb* was to William Duncomb for life, remainder to J. S. and his
heirs for the life of William (the remainder to a trustee to preserve
contingent remainders), remainder to the heirs of William in tail
male, remainder to George Duncomb. When William died without
issue, his wife demanded dower. Her argument was that since
William had been given in the same instrument a life estate and
a remainder in tail male to his heirs, under the Rule in Shelley's
Case, "the whole estate is executed in [William] as in *Lewis Bowles's
case* the whole estate-tail was executed in the father 'till the birth
of the first son," and that William had had a sufficient estate of
inheritance to entitle her to dower. The court, however, ruled
that the remainder to the trustees was "such an interposing estate"
that William had been merely a life tenant. The argument for the
widow occupies most of the short report; the judgment for George
Duncomb, the remainderman, is merely recorded in a final sub-
ordinate clause: "but the Court upon the first argument hastily

gave judgment for the tenant." Although the court did not explicitly declare the trustees' remainder vested rather than contingent, the decision in *Duncomb* was subsequently said to establish this principle.

The issue of whether the remainder to trustees was vested rather than contingent was still alive enough in 1740 to produce the leading case of *Parkhurst v. Dormer,* a case finally decided in the House of Lords. In *Parkhurst* trustees to preserve contingent remainders were found to have a vested interest sufficient to defeat an attempt by a tenant with a term of ninety-nine years and the next remainderman, his son, to alienate the land to the detriment of a more remote remainderman. Several of the principals in this case were lawyers: the original settlor in 1662 was a barrister, one would-be alienator was a judge in Common Pleas, and one claimant was also a judge in Common Pleas. The case represents real debate within the legal establishment about what the rules were and how strict settlements were to be, not accidents or problems arising from amateurish legal advice. The original settlement of 1662 had been to the use of J. Dormer for life, to the use of Robert Dormer for ninety-nine years, to trustees for the life of Robert to support contingent remainders, to the use of the first son and issue male of Robert in fee tail male, remainder to Euseby Dormer in tail male. No one could have seriously doubted counsel's representation as to the intent of the settlor: "that it was the intention of him who made the settlement, to preserve and continue this estate in the male line of the family, was most manifest from this; that he limited it to the male line in a remote degree, in preference to the daughters of his eldest son, Sir John Dormer, who were his heirs at law."[30] But Sir Robert Dormer (one of the judges in Common Pleas), came into possession and joined together with his son Fleetwood in 1726 to levy a fine and suffer a common recovery. This set up a contest between the Parkhursts, who claimed the land had been conveyed to them by the fine and common recovery, and John Dormer, who claimed as the remainderman entitled to the remainder limited to his father, Euseby Dormer, in tail male. John argued that the fine and common recovery were not capable of breaking the settlement. When the title was tried by ejectment at King's Bench, King's Bench found for the remainderman, and the judgment was affirmed in the House of Lords. The interest in the trustees to preserve contingent remainders was found to be sufficiently vested to prevent the breaking of the settlement attempted by father and son and to preserve the interest of the remainderman.

Some quite rarefied and refined reasoning was required to reach this result in *Parkhurst*. Bonfield observes that the path by which Chief Justice Willes reached his conclusion that the remainder to trustees was vested "was quite novel."[31] Willis determined that the trustees' estate was vested "because it emanated from the reversion which the grantor retained in the conveyance of a term" (to borrow Bonfield's useful paraphrase).[32] M. R. Chesterman argues, and I agree, that "there is no doubt that the technical arguments in favor" of reaching the opposite result, that these remainders were themselves contingent, "were strong ones"; "their coming into operation clearly depended on a specific contingency which might never occur," that is, on some act of the tenant in possession or some other event which threatened to destroy the remainderman's interest.[33] In deciding to allow settlements to be this resistant to alienation, the judges were clearly influenced by arguments about the extent to which landowners had already employed such settlements and were relying on their efficacy.

Here, again, the maxim *communis error facit jus* was invoked—although Willis at the same moment he invoked it denied the necessity of doing so: "Surely, it is a much less evil to make a construction, even contrary to the common rules of law (though I think this is not so) than to overthrow I may say 100,000 settlements; for it is a maxim in law, as well as reason, *communis error facit jus*."[34] Moreover, as both Bonfield and Chesterman show, in order for these remainders to trustees to preserve contingent remainders to have their full effect, it was also necessary for the equity judges to confer some positive obligations on the trustees, most importantly, a new obligation to buy equivalent lands with their own money for a remainderman should the tenant in possession manage to sell off the settled land to a purchaser without notice of the settlement.

The rulings in *Duncomb* and *Parkhurst* allowed conveyancers to provide that a man could have an estate that was technically not an estate of inheritance to which dower attached but that would nevertheless be his to enjoy during his life and his heirs' to enjoy afterward. Conveyancers gave the husband a life estate that yielded no dower, and the heir got a remainder in fee, which, since it was not an estate in possession, yielded no dower either. Merger of these two interests and destruction of the heir's contingent remainder was prevented by interposing a remainder to trustees which itself was, on the authority of *Duncomb* and *Parkhurst,* declared vested and indestructible.

Questions of whether or not merger had resulted in tenants for life having larger estates to which dower or curtesy attached or larger estates which they could alienate provoked some very complex cases in the eighteenth century. On the one hand, the courts still had considerable commitment to the older idea of estates as reified entities brought into being by certain formulaic words and subject to the operation of what were often referred to fondly as "known rules of law." The policy reasons supporting such a view were obvious: these seem to be objective standards which allow all to know who owns what. On the other hand, the "accidental" mergers brought about by the operation of these known rules of law interfered with the fulfillment of settlors' intentions when settlors had intended to confine tenants in possession to life estates.

Increasingly, although still not without considerable deference to the older common law rules, the courts formulated exceptions which seemed to give more weight to the will of the grantor. One of the most spectacular and most public legal explosions of the entire period occurred over the application of the Rule in Shelley's Case in *Perrin v. Blake* (1772). Lord Chief Justice Mansfield declined to apply the rule and found the testator's son a tenant for life, which was obviously what the testator had intended him to be. He was then reversed by Blackstone in the Exchequer Chamber when Blackstone applied the rule and found the son a tenant in tail and the jointure settled on his wife valid. In a famous opinion, Blackstone characterized the Rule in Shelley's Case as "a maxim of positive law deduced by legal reasoning from . . . great fundamental principles" and argued that if courts "should indulge an unlimited latitude of forming *conjectures* upon wills, instead of attending to their *grammatical* or *legal* construction, the consequence must be endless litigation." Blackstone was also perfectly aware that application of the rule interfered with the intentions of settlors and made a policy argument on behalf of such interference:

I own myself of opinion, that those constructions of law, which tend to facilitate the sale and circulation of property in a free and commercial country, and which make it more liable to the debts of the visible owner, who derives a greater credit from that ownership;—such constructions, I say, are founded upon principles of public policy altogether as open and as enlarged, as those which favour the accumulation of estates in private families, by fettering inheritances till the full age of posterity now unborn, and which may not be born for half a century.[35]

Considering the technical character of the arguments in this case, a surprisingly heated pamphlet controversy erupted over it, culminating in the publication by conveyancer Charles Fearne of his treatise *An Essay on the Learning of Contingent Remainders and Executory Devices* (1772), in which he defended Blackstone's position.

The complexity and logical difficulties of the evolving rules of merger and the tensions between permitting the application of older common law rules and deferring to the apparent will of the grantor produced a variety of very difficult dower cases. For our purposes, the difficulties may be briefly and adequately illustrated by a pair of companion cases, *Boothby v. Vernon* (1725) and *Hooker v. Hooker* (1733). In *Boothby* a widower claiming curtesy was denied; in *Hooker* a widow claiming dower was granted dower. Both cases turned on whether life tenants in possession who had acquired reversions in fee, by what might be called accidents, had been seised of estates of inheritance to which dower or curtesy had attached. In *Boothby* the land in question had been devised by Sir Harry Boothby to his sister, Anne Boothby, for her life, and if she married and had issue male of her body living at the time of her death, then to such issue male, but if she died leaving no issue male at the time of her death, then to George Boothby and his heirs. Sir Harry died, Anne married Vernon, had a son, died, and then the son died. Vernon claimed curtesy, arguing that Anne's life estate plus the reversion she had as heir to Sir Harry entitled him to curtesy. In *Hooker* the land in question was conveyed to the use of William Hooker the Elder for life, and to his wife for life if she survived him, then to William Hooker the Younger for life, remainder to his first and other sons in tail male, remainder to William Hooker the Elder in fee. William Hooker the Elder and his wife died in the life of William Hooker the Younger, whose wife also died. He had two other wives, the last of whom survived when he died without issue. His third wife demanded dower, claiming that his life estate plus the reversion in fee he had as heir to his father entitled her to dower.

Merger was found in *Hooker,* but not in *Boothby.* Distinguishing these cases from each other required elaborate learning and ingenuity. Some weight seems to have been given to the imputed intent of the testator in *Boothby,* the court commenting, "the intention of the testator is to be considered. Now it doth not appear, that he had any manner of intention that his sister should have any benefit of the inheritance." The distinguishing principle suggested by Fearne in his contingent remainder treatise also seems to give some weight to the intent of the grantor. According to the subrule Fearne constructed, when the immediate grantor of an estate has limited the contingent remainders, the inheritance descending on the heir should not destroy the contingency by merger *(Boothby),* whereas when the descent is only mediate from the person whose will has created the particular estates and remainders, the contingent remainders could be destroyed by merger *(Hooker).* In the former case, Fearne contended, to give the descent "the force and effect of an absolute and perfect descent, would render the *will* originally and totally abortive." Another kind of distinction was ventured by Serjeant John Williams in his notes on Saunders reports: the wife in *Hooker* was dowable "because there was nothing but a possibility which never happened, nor could under the circumstances possibly happen, to distinguish that [her estate] from an estate in fee: for it was impossible the contingent remainders should ever happen, in as much as W. H. the younger was dead without issue; and the case . . . [of *Boothby*] was distinguishable, because there the wife was a bare tenant for life, with a possibility to her issue."[36]

The juxtaposition of *Boothby* and *Hooker* shows that the courts were not prepared to go to any length to bar dower, as Morton Horwitz has claimed the nineteenth-century American courts were. But at both law and equity the forced share nature of dower was being increasingly attenuated by deference to the will of the grantor of property, a deference very much in the spirit of liberalism. Conveyancers were increasingly drawing up wills and family settlements manipulating series of life estates and contingent remainders in ways that prevented dower from attaching initially or even in later generations by merger, or, as contemporaries put it, by reversions in fee falling on or drowning estates for life. Conveyancers certainly exhibited much ingenuity in creating new forms of settlement, but our examination of what they did does not permit us to congratulate them, as Casner and Leach did, on serving their clients by cleanly turning "the logic of the law against itself." Had the judges merely followed the logic of the law and the precedents they had inherited in 1660, it might well not have been the "courts" who had to acknowledge "defeat in a sportsmanlike fashion," but the conveyancers themselves.

Mortgages and Terms of Years

Of particular importance to the development of dower rules were mortgages and terms of years. Dower cases involving mortgages were complicated by the fact that the conception of mortgage was in flux in the seventeenth and early eighteenth centuries.[37] Now we are apt to think of the mortgagor as both the occupier and the owner of the mortgaged property. In the middle ages, however, mortgaged land was actually handed over to the creditor; the land was a pledge rather like a violin would be today if it were pawned. In the Restoration and early eighteenth century the courts were coming closer to the modern view. They expressed their conception by saying that the mortgagee had the legal estate and the mortgagor the equitable estate. The mortgage deed looked rather like a bill of sale, and upon the mortgagor's failure to pay at the stipulated time, the mortgagee could appeal to the common law courts to give him possession. The mortgagor, however, had his equitable title to invoke. Even after he had forfeited the legal estate by a breach of the condition of the mortgage, he still had the right to redeem, called an equity of redemption. One logical consequence of considering the mortgagee possessor of the legal estate was that the estate became subject to the mortgagee's wife's claim of dower. In the early seventeenth century the courts held that her right took precedence over the mortgagor's right to redeem if he had failed to pay on time. This result could be avoided by having a mortgage for a long term of years instead of a mortgage in fee, since there was no dower of a leasehold. But in 1678 Lord Northington changed the rule to eliminate the mortgagee's wife's dower.[38] In *Roscarrick v. Baton* (1673) it was held that an equity of redemption could be entailed, and during the eighteenth century an equity of redemption was increasingly treated in equity not as a mere chose in action but as an estate in land.[39]

In *Casborne v. Scarfe* (1737) the court had to decide whether there was to be curtesy of an equity of redemption. The plaintiffs argued that the wife had only a chose in action, that she was not seised of any real property, and quoted Littleton on the requirement of actual seisin for curtesy. Their position was consonant with the older view of mortgages in which the mortgagee was understood to have seisin and the mortgagor to have a mere chattel interest. They also argued that since it had been held that there was no dower of an equity of redemption because an equity of redemption was a trust estate, so there should be no curtesy. Lord Chancellor Hardwicke replied that an equity of redemption was to be treated as an estate in land, that the wife's possession was equivalent to an actual seisin of freehold at common law, and that the objection concerning dower and curtesy proved "too much, if any thing"; "if any innovations were to be made, I am of opinion the nearest way to right would be, to let in the wife to dower of a trust estate, and not to exclude the husband from being tenant by the curtesy of it."[40] Thus, Hardwicke decided that there was to be curtesy of an equity of redemption.

Casborne was offered as a precedent in *Dixon v. Saville* (1783), where the issue was whether a widow should have dower in an equity of redemption, the estate having been mortgaged from before her marriage until her husband's death. Lord Chancellor Loughborough found against the widow, remarking tersely, "the case of an estate by the curtesy in a trust, is the anomalous case, not the rule that the wife shall not have dower. I confess I think it would be wrong to discuss it much."[41] Therefore, since dower to the mortgagee's wife from an equity of redemption had already been eliminated on the ground that the mortgagee was only a trustee with no beneficial interest in the land, and now dower to the mortgagor's wife was eliminated on the ground that the mortgagor's estate was a trust estate from which there could be no dower, dower in mortgaged land disappeared. Given the vast amount of land that was mortgaged in the eighteenth century, this was not a trivial result. Hardwicke's idea that an equity of redemption was to be treated as an estate in land equivalent to an estate at law, praised as the modern conception, was "inconvenient" with respect to dower and was not applied in *Dixon*.

A more complicated form of trust estate of great importance in the development of the dower rules was the trust in or for a term of years. Since the late fifteenth century, terms of years had been attractive to landowners interested in trying to create inalienable inheritances because by that point the previously popular unbarrable fee tail as a means of securing inalienability had been defeated. From 1472 a tenant in tail could suffer a common recovery (a fictitious suit rather like the fine explained above) and transform his estate into an alienable fee simple. But the owner of a term of years did not own a freehold estate and, consequently, could not avail himself of the common recovery.[42] Suppose that James Harlowe has Blackacre conveyed "to him and the heirs of his body for 499 years, but if during the term the line of lineal descendants of James Harlowe shall cease to remain in exclusive possession of Blackacre, then in that event the term hereby given shall shift over to and belong absolutely to Clarissa Harlowe and the heirs of her body for the enjoyment of the unexpired balance of such term." Then, James Harlowe cannot cut off Clarissa's interest by common recovery, and, if he tries to sell his term out of the line of his descendants, buyers will not want to risk the intervention of Clarissa's interest.

In the eighteenth century it was common for conveyancers to employ long terms of years in mortgages and settlements. These terms, as Blackstone put it with apparent satisfaction, "may be moulded to a thousand useful purposes by the ingenuity of an able artist."[43] Among the purposes to which terms of years were molded were barring dower and, it was said, increasing the security of purchaser's titles.

In the leading case of *The Countess Radnor v. Vandebendy* (1697) the issue was whether the Countess was entitled to dower in a trust term attending the inheritance; during her marriage her husband had sold the land, and the purchaser had had the term assigned to him. Jeffreys ruled in favor of the doweress in 1685, Somers reversed in favor of the purchaser in 1697, and on appeal to lords the reversal was affirmed. Thus the courts sanctioned what became a widespread conveyancing practice used to promote alienability and defeat dower. Let me explain how it worked. Suppose Dr. Slop wants to buy Blackacre from Walter Shandy and knows Walter Shandy is married. Dr. Slop does not want the land subjected to the dower claims of Mrs. Shandy in the event she survives Mr. Shandy. Dr. Slop's lawyer will search the title to Blackacre to see if he can find an old trust term in it created prior to the marriage of Walter Shandy and Mrs. Shandy, say an old trust term of five hundred years in the settlement made on the marriage of Walter Shandy's father and mother for the purpose of raising portions for Walter's sisters, a purpose which has now been "satisfied." Such terms were common enough to make the assignment of them a widespread practice. Dr. Slop's lawyer arranges for this old term to be assigned to trustees for Dr. Slop and tells him that his title to Blackacre will be secure from any claims of dower by Mrs. Shandy—who thus loses her dower without having consented to the loss. By the operation of the Statute of Uses, which converts Dr. Slop's equitable interest into a legal interest, Dr. Slop has acquired a legal estate in Blackacre which postpones Mrs. Shandy's estate to his during the term and which equity will not disturb should Mrs. Shandy come claiming her dower.

But it was by no means inevitable that the courts would roll over and play dead merely because conveyancers dreamed up this tactic of assigning terms to promote alienability. In fact, when the issue first arose in 1685 Lord Chancellor Jeffreys actually said he "could not imagine why" a doweress should not be relieved against such a purchaser. He observed that the purchaser in the case before him "could not but have Notice that" the seller was married, and found for the doweress.[44] Marriage itself was on some occasions considered a purchase for valuable consideration, and there is no theoretical reason why the wife's title to dower could not have been said to be based on a purchase for valuable consideration prior to that of the buyer, and the ordinary rule of *qui prior est tempore potior est jure* (he who is first in time is first in right) applied. However, when Somers succeeded Jeffreys he reversed Jeffreys's decree, the reversal was affirmed in the House of Lords in *Radnor v. Vandebendy,* and the practice established.[45] Lord Chancellor Hardwicke in a later similar case tells us that *Radnor* occasioned great doubt and discussion both in the courts and then in lords, but that when it was asked of counsel in lords, "whether it was usual for conveyancers to convey terms for years to attend the inheritance to prevent dower," counsel, "with great candor," said it was.[46] Basically the same argument seems to have prevailed in *Radnor* that had in *Chaplin:* the practice of conveyancers had given expectations which it would be intolerable to upset, despite the claims of doweresses. Hardwicke explained:

> The point that weighed in judgment was, that this was the case of a purchase for valuable consideration; that, in making conveyances, purchasers relied on that method of taking a conveyance of the inheritance to themselves, and an assignment of the term standing out to a trustee, to attend it; that the outstanding term was prior to the title of dower in the wife, and therefore, purchasers have relied on that, as a bar to dower; so that this court and house of lords were of opinion, that, if they were not to permit it to be so, it would be to overturn the general rule, which had been established and practiced by many titles to estates, and tend to make such titles precarious for the future.

Since ninety-nine years was about the lower limit of these terms and one thousand the upper, a doweress who had to wait upon such a term would probably be dead before it expired. The rules which developed regarding terms were, as contemporaries put it, involved "in many points of great nicety"—too much nicety to be elaborated here.[47] Despite the establishment of this practice, so weak was its claim to legitimacy that even as late as 1829 William Wood, subsequently Baron Hatherley, could pronounce it "an absurd inconsistency in the doctrine as to the assignment of terms."[48] It is not exaggerating to say that the judges simply privileged the interests of commercial purchasers and mortgagees over those of doweresses.

A few years after *Radnor,* in *Lord Dudley and Ward v. The Lady Dowager Dudley* (1705) it was decided that the doweress was to have the benefit of a trust term as against the heir. The ninety-nine-year term in *Dudley* was the sort that was common in eighteenth-century family settlements—there is a similar one in the model settlement printed in Blackstone—basically a trust term for raising portions and annuities for daughters and younger sons. In *Dudley* the court showed some fervor on behalf of the "natural," "legal," and "moral" rights of doweresses. Doweresses prevented by terms could go to the common law courts and obtain judgments in their favor as to dower, but those judgments would be accompanied by stays for the length of the term. In this case Lady Diana

Dudley had gotten such a judgment at law in her favor, but the stay was so long that she would no doubt have died before enjoying any benefit, prompting the equity judge to declare, "all the remedy at law is vain and illusory." In *Radnor* the reasoning was that dower was in essence a right "by operation of law," not equity, and not "by agreement of the Parties": so "where is the Equity that should improve or mend this Right?"[49] In *Dudley,* on the contrary, dower was said to be considerably more than a right at law. There it was represented as the mission of equity to come to the defense of the doweress's "moral right": "Now equity is no part of the law, but a moral virtue, which qualifies, moderates, and reforms the rigour, hardness, and edge of the law, and is an universal truth; it does also assist the law where it is defective and weak in the constitution . . . and defends the law from crafty evasions, delusions, and new subtilties, invented and contrived to evade and delude the common law, whereby such as have undoubted right are made remediless."[50] In *Radnor* and afterward it was agreed that a jointress might be relieved against a term because her right arose by agreement of the parties. In *Radnor* the situation of a doweress was distinguished from that of a jointress, but in *Dudley* the doweress's right was said also to arise by the agreement of the parties in the marriage contract. Indeed, in *Dudley* the doweress was also said to be a purchaser for valuable consideration, namely, the marriage itself. Nevertheless, even in *Dudley* the court did not wish to overturn *Radnor* by preferring the doweress to a commercial purchaser.

The divergent views of dower in trust terms in *Radnor* and *Dudley,* the complexities of the law of terms, and continuing malaise over the anomalies of the dower and curtesy rules as they pertained to trusts combined to produce an intricate set of rules about when doweresses could or could not redeem or set aside terms which were extremely difficult to rationalize and which were vulnerable to criticism.[51] Hardwicke himself in a case he was deciding against the doweress admitted that the decision at the Rolls which he was about to reverse "is absolutely consistent with the mere reason of the thing" if it were to be considered independently of the practices of conveyancers and the equity of precedents concerning them.[52] Fundamentally, conveyancers and their clients wanted terms that prevented alienation of property from the male line upon which it was settled, but they did not want these same terms to prevent alienation from the doweress. Not surprisingly, a schizoid and sex-linked law of terms developed. The Real Property Commissioners concluded that the practice of assigning terms to secure purchasers' titles "occasioned a considerable part of the expense, delay, and difficulties attending alienation" but failed to achieve reliable protection. They also declared that the decisions allowing the assignments of terms ("in reality, a mere fictitious estate") to bar dower were "scarcely reconcilable with principles of justice (as they make the rights of the parties liable to be affected by technical rules and fictions)."[53]

Provisional Conclusions

The degree of choice within the terms of legal reasoning that the courts had in *Chaplin, Godwin, Radnor, Dixon,* and subsequent dower cases is now apparent. There is a sense in which it is fair to say that they chose to allow the expectations of dower to be defeated. What, though, does this initial account of developments in dower allow us to say at this point about the relative merits of the four possible stories of married women's property suggested at the beginning of Chapter 2: the liberal, the neo-Marxist, the sociological, and the feminist? There is apparently some truth in all of them.

In favor of a sociological view, it is certainly the case that the social world was changing in ways which eventually would render dower rights in land a dysfunctional entitlement for most women and for society at large, and that the security provided by dower was being replaced by other forms of security. Furthermore, in comparing medieval and modern society there is absurdity in abstracting one relatively small feature—dower versus jointure or social security for widows, for instance—and trying to say that the medieval or the modern form, each unimaginable as a feature of the other society, is better for women. Yet over a shorter period of time, particularly from 1660 to 1833, when there actually were rival forms of providing security for widows, it is not necessarily absurd to suppose that one or some of them were more advantageous to women than others. If we are not committed to a modern version of fatalism in which whatever exists in a given society must be functional and justifiable, then we can allow that there was an eighteenth-century politics of dower rights in which better or worse choices could have been and were made.

In favor of the liberal view, which would claim that the better choices were made, it can be said that equity courts served women by allowing some of the logic of old dower rules to apply to jointures comprised of important new forms of property like consols or bank stock that would earlier not have afforded dower. Further, by removing dower as a clog on alienability in trust estates and in many mortgage and purchase situations, they may claim to have contributed to a more economic use of land and so to a general increase in wealth women could share. Also, as we shall see in subsequent chapters, whereas in older dower law women forfeited their entitlement to dower by elopement and adultery, equity, in dealing with jointure and other newer separate estates, refused to make the complete analogy to dower by requiring forfeiture for the wife's sexual misconduct. Equity, in these cases, thus permitted married women to reap the benefits of contracts independently of their status.

Moreover, it is one of the finer ironies of this tale that the very consciousness of the dower/curtesy anomaly we have been discussing was not only a sign of the actual inequality between men and women, but also a sign that that inequality was diminishing. The earlier dower and curtesy rules look more equal to later eyes, but S. F. C. Milsom's discussion of inheritance by women in the twelfth and early thirteenth centuries leads to the insight that dower and curtesy were not originally symmetrical rights at all. Early curtesy is not the husband's entitlement to his wife's land by a special favor of the law, as later commentators tended to say; instead, curtesy is a continuation of the husband's possession of land already his as the lord's man and tenant, even if the land had earlier come to him as his wife's inheritance. He needs no action to secure such possession and consequently has no writ. A woman, by contrast, could never have been the lord's man or rendered homage to the lord. Even if she was an heiress, her position was not so much that of an owner as that of a transmitter of the inheritance from her father to her son; hence the inheritance might be forfeit if she did not marry. Milsom's medieval women are not recognized as persons or actors in the feudal system, which is a system of the relations between lords and men. Arrangements concerning them do not belong to this world, already a public world, but rather are internal domestic arrangements within families, already arrangements within a private sphere. Dower was not a right against the lord but a right against the heir and is conceptualized not as the widow's land but as the son's land, to which it is his duty to grant her use rights. Consequently, to compare curtesy and dower as symmetrical rights, as was habitually done in the early modern period, even if it is observed that the doweress's rights are lesser, is already to suppose a greater equality between men and women than existed in the thirteenth century.

Nevertheless, it must be acknowledged that it was not so much a pure liberal desire to make women more autonomous that inspired eighteenth-century doctrines concerning married women's property as a concern that women be effectively protected, prevented from becoming public charges, and a desire that the wife's father's property should pass to his grandson without being wasted by his son-in-law. The power shift that occurs looks less like a shift from men to women than one from the husband's father to the wife's father, as is consonant with the rising prices of daughters' portions in this period. Although curtesy was more difficult to bar than dower, carefully drawn wills and settlements could succeed in defeating the husband's entitlement and securing the inheritance immediately upon the wife's death to her father's grandchildren. Moreover, while some women were able to take advantage of their newly acquired control over property, we shall see that the creation of married women's separate property was generally pronounced a failure by its own creators, who at the end of the century lamented that women with such estates were constantly being induced to part with them by their husbands. They were thus driven to invent the restraint on anticipation to reduce women's autonomy. Indeed, the history of married women's property in this period challenges one of the fundamental principles of liberal ideology, namely, that the ownership of property serves as a basis for political freedom and individual autonomy.

In support of a neo-Marxist view, it should by now be sufficiently clear that the courts in these dower cases were not acting to secure traditional common law rights and that, though they frequently claimed to be driven by the necessities of legal reasoning, they were in fact innovating in what were perceived to be the interests of male property owners and purchasers. Part of the problem, ironically, was that they did recognize some institutional constraints. To the repeated argument that equity was forced to acquiesce in the practices of conveyancers and the expectations they created even when they established wrong rules one obvious reply is to suggest a prospective rule, one that does not penalize good-faith reliance on past mistakes but which allows the right rule to prevail in the future. Parliament actually employed such a rule in the Dower Act, which was to affect only marriages entered into after 1834, and an eighteenth-century parliament did the same thing in the 1724 act abolishing the custom of London. But eighteenth-century judges did not think they could make prospective rules. Confronted by the claims of the expectations and reliance of purchasers, they simply ignored the possible expectations and reliance of women, which was the easier as no women appeared to say what their expectations might have been. Nor did the judges, acting as judges, suppose they might alleviate some of the problems of dower by molding the common law dower rules to follow customary free bench rules, giving the wife rights only in the property of which her husband died seised instead of in all the property of which he had ever been seised during the coverture. As I noted in Chapter 2, that this would have been a fairly obvious response to contemporary complaints about dower as a clog on alienability is shown by a Connecticut statute of 1673 which makes just this change in common law dower. English judges, many of whom had been or were members of Parliament, could have promoted similar legislative changes at home had they wished to do so, but they preferred to support the more complex conveyancing evasions of dower which I have described.

If it is true that forced shares are generally tolerated so long as the women's shares do not represent significant accumulations of property, as suggested before, then we should not be surprised to see the increased individual accumulations of early capitalism leading to the subversion of both dower and forced shares of personality according to local customs, like London's, as in fact we do. In *Drury* it was said that one reason uses had arisen in the first place was that "it was thought unreasonable that where a person of very large estate married a young woman of little or no fortune, she should be at all events entitled to one third of it."[54]

Yet the defeat of forced shares of larger accumulations does not necessarily mean that the subsequent provisions for widows will represent less than what a forced share of a smaller whole would have been. It may be true that a breakdown of traditional community structures in early capitalism left adrift numbers of widows for whom their husbands would earlier have been forced to provide, perhaps even more than the number whose sexual conduct had made them such outlaws in traditional society that they lost their entitlement to protection; but such a result is not intrinsic to the rule changes, and it would be very difficult to establish that it occurred. Also, a crude neo-Marxist notion that an early, happy, rural world in which women were fully recognized as producers of public importance was replaced by an unhappy capitalist world where women are relegated to a private sphere as nonproductive ornaments must be qualified—at least in considering legal history—by realizing that there was already a kind of public/private split in the feudal world, as Milsom has shown, and that early common law rules gave women much lesser entitlement to the products of their labor than men had. Moreover, for traditional status security one must pay the price of role limitations and loss of security for violating status rules. Finally, new capitalist forms of wealth at least potentially put women at less of a disadvantage both as producers and holders than traditional agricultural work.[55]

In support of a feminist analysis of this history of dower, at the very least one has to say that the substitution of jointure and other forms of married women's property for dower was substantially motivated by concerns over the transmission of property from man to man and the retention of property by men rather than by a desire to permit women to enjoy property as men did. This will become especially evident in the discussion of pin money and other forms of separate property in Chapter 5. The more dazzling the artifices of conveyancers and the subtleties of equity judges in dealing with abstractions like equities of redemption or contingent remainders, the more obvious the alienation of women from the whole contemporary system of property law. Equity judges were conscious of having a responsibility to protect women, indeed, of having a responsibility to enforce a husband's moral duty to provide for and to protect his wife, even when the technicalities of common law rules seemed to offer ways for him to evade that duty. Yet evasions were repeatedly supported by equity judges murmuring *aequitas sequitur legem* and *communis error facit jus.*

*A Critique of Arguments Asserting the Paramount Importance
of Security of Title and Promoting Alienability*

Claims that conveyancing evasions of women's dower rights had
to be accepted because of a paramount public interest in security
of title to real property are vulnerable to neo-Marxist and feminist
critiques, despite the fact that the desirability of security of title
was probably the public interest which judges in married women's
property cases most frequently asserted and the one which they
felt most comfortable asserting. At first glance, the desirability of
security of title may appear so obvious and uncontroversial that
it seems virtually tautological to stipulate it as an important public
purpose of a property law system. Is not the achievement of security of title the obvious goal of any system of property law?
Would not everyone have to agree with a pamphleteering barrister
who declared in 1829, "To the inquiry, what is the first requisite
to a *perfect* system of real property law, there can be no doubt that
the answer is *certainty to title*"?[56] Nevertheless, the belief that
judges ought to act so as to promote security of title is ideological,
and like any ideological principle is, in Marx's phrase, an "empty
generality torn away from the facts." It can be and was used selectively in ways that promoted some interests and not others, in
particular, in ways that promoted the interests of propertied men
but not the interests of their wives. As we have seen, in dower
cases like *Chaplin* and *Radnor* public interest in security of title
was asserted to be so important as to prevail over what the judges
characterized as technical correctness.

But the judges and Parliament certainly did not always act as
though promoting security of title were a paramount interest.
Indeed, judicial permissiveness toward complex conveyancing tactics, including the multiplication of contingent future interests, the
manipulation of terms of years, and the multiplication of equitable
interests separate and distinct from legal interests, actually contributed to making titles insecure. Even contemporary admirers
of the rule system admitted that titles were, in fact, not secure.
For example, Blackstone explains why by the 1760s private acts
of Parliament had become increasingly common means of assuring
titles to land: "For it may sometimes happen, that by the ingenuity
of some, and the blunders of other practitioners, an estate is most

grievously entangled by a multitude of contingent remainders, resulting trusts, springing uses, executory devises, and the like artificial contrivances . . . so that it is out of the power of either the courts of law or equity to relieve the owner."[57]

Furthermore, English property owners in this period did not believe security of title was important enough for them to accept one of the best means of achieving it: registration of titles to land. Their hostility to registration was apparently based partly on a desire to evade taxation and partly on owner's fondness for manipulating others, especially dependent family members, with uncertainties about what future interests in the land they had granted or would grant. William Pierepoint opposed early schemes for an estate register in part by arguing:

> These registers will cause differences and discontents in families, between husbands and their wives, parents and their children, and children amongst themselves. Whilst a father keeps his deeds of settlements of his estate private to himself, his wife and children, each hoping for better than is done for them (perhaps than the estate can bear), yet they live in love and quiet; but, if they should know (which by these registers they would know) what the settlements are, wives would be unquiet, children would be undutiful; the eldest brother would think his youngest brothers and sisters had too much; and they, that they had too little.[58]

Then, as landowners increasingly raised cash by mortgaging land, they also resisted registration on the ground that it would allow potential lenders to discover the extent of their current indebtedness. The desirability of registration was repeatedly urged and repeatedly resisted.

The few legislative reforms that were effected were rapidly subverted, essentially by conveyancers with the cooperation of the judges, the same judges who in our dower cases insisted on the paramount importance of security of title. Thus, as Blackstone cheerfully relates, the intent of the Statute of Enrollments (1535) to prevent clandestine conveyances of freeholds was evaded by the conveyancers' invention of lease and release and the judges' acceptance of its validity.[59] The establishment between 1703 and 1708 of two local registers, one in Middlesex and one in Yorkshire, turned out to have less effect than was hoped for partly because registration was not made compulsory in the sense that instruments had to be registered to have legal effect.[60]

But the local registers also had less effect because of early modern judicial rulings permitting mortgage tacking.[61] Tacking allowed one holder of an equitable mortgage to gain preference over another holder of an equitable mortgage (on the same land) by acquiring a legal mortgage which had priority to both. Thus if A mortgaged his property to X by a legal mortgage and then to Y and Z by successive equitable mortgages, Z's mortgage could be given priority over Y's if Z bought X's mortgage, provided Z had no notice of Y's mortgage when he advanced his money. Among the legal estates used for this purpose were satisfied terms; thus, Z could jump ahead of Y by buying a satisfied term, so long as Z had had no notice of Y's interest. According to one eminent and irritated lawyer in the early nineteenth century, conveyancing practice and equity opinions had "annihilated the whole purport of Registry Acts in this country, by rendering it unnecessary, and according to the opinions of some practitioners, unadvisable [lest prior mortgages be discovered and give Z notice that would prevent him from later tacking], to search for incumbrances [on titles to land]."[62] Thus, I claim, judicial assertions that particular decisions in these dower cases are forced by a paramount public interest in security of title to real property cannot be accepted at face value.

Similarly, claims that the decisions in dower are motivated by a public interest in maintaining the alienability of real property are also vulnerable to neo-Marxist and feminist critiques. Clearly, since dower was only a life estate, it hardly threatened to create a perpetuity, but as a forced share it did interfere with the husband's ability to sell or to mortgage his land since the wife could (in theory at least) refuse to give him clear title. If the wife was willing to agree to the conveyance, as wives apparently usually were, then, after examination by a magistrate designed to ensure that consent was freely given, she could join in a conveyance by fine, a secure conveyance which, it was complained, was expensive.

Yet while the judges invoked the importance of the public interest in freedom of alienation and sided with purchasers and mortgagees against doweresses, they did not invoke the public interest in freedom of alienation in two other areas of great importance: their acceptance in the very late eighteenth century of restraints on anticipation of married women's property and their acceptance of the conveyancing tactics which promoted strict settlement. Restraints on anticipation will be discussed in Chapter 5, which addresses pin money and the wife's separate estate. But we have seen, earlier in this chapter, that the conveyancing innovation of a clause to trustees to preserve contingent remainders, a clause which made strict settlement possible, and other such devices which permitted strict settlement were technically dubious at their inception. These devices depended quite heavily on the judges' giving them favorable interpretations—which the judges did. No one, I think, could deny that strict settlement entailing property in tail male and making present occupiers tenants for life without power to alienate were worse clogs on alienability than dower, and yet the judges collaborated with the conveyancers to permit strict settlement. Moreover, as George Haskins has pointed out in an important article on the *Duke of Norfolk's Case* (1681), the case that is usually spoken of as having established the common law Rule against Perpetuities, the rule was originally spoken of as the Rule of Perpetuities (rather than against) and, in fact, instead of prohibiting the settlement of future interests which had previously been allowed, actually permitted settlements which had previously been treated as void for creating perpetuities.[63]

Nor was a public interest in freedom of alienation invoked in a set of eighteenth-century gambling statutes. Quite the contrary, these statutes were explicitly aimed at making it impossible for "young and unwary" heirs apparent and heirs to lose their property through fashionable fecklessness.[64] Gambling has always correctly been understood to be a characteristic social practice of the aristocracy and landed gentry of this period, and stories abound of spectacular sums lost "at play."[65] Most recently, J. C. D. Clark, in an eccentric but lively book extraordinarily sympathetic to the elite classes, describes gambling as actually a significant part of the "aristocratic ethic."[66] Since lords and gentlemen were apt to run through the limited amounts of cash at their disposal rather quickly, they were often tempted to mortgage their interests in land. Contemporaries worried that too many estates would fall into the hands of money lenders, supposedly persons unfit to manage estates or to enjoy the political power that the ownership of land conferred. Strict settlements that succeeded in giving the tenant only a life estate at least prevented a gambling heir from alienating more than his own life interest, leaving the inheritance for his son. But Parliament did not consider such strict settlements an adequate defense.

For our purposes, the most significant feature of the new gambling statutes was the provision in 9 Anne, c. 14, that any effort to mortgage an estate to pay a gaming loss was void as to the winner or lender.[67] A lender who took a mortgage or other conveyance "where the whole or any Part of the Consideration shall be for Money . . . won by Gaming . . . or for the reimbursing or repaying any Money knowingly advanced for . . . gaming" took nothing but a piece of paper worthless at law. Attempts to make such conveyances, void as to the mortgagee, benefited instead the heir apparent of the would-be mortgagor, who took the estate as though the would-be mortgagor "had been naturally dead." That this statute failed to have all the effects desired and had to be supplemented by others in 1739 and 1745 (statutes which in turn also failed to have all the effects desired) shows the resourcefulness at avoidance of gamblers and money lenders alike, but is not relevant to my point.

My point is simply that contemporary legal intellectuals were quite comfortable with anti-alienation provisions when they thought such provisions helped to maintain the social and political order they preferred; they not only lived with anti-alienation provisions already in place, they felt free to add new ones. From a modern economic point of view, the rationality of allowing the landed property of a gentleman who risks it at cards or roulette—very probably doing so in a state of alcoholic intoxication—to fall into the hands of a sober citizen who has prudently accumulated cash and has it to lend appears obvious. Surely the sober citizen is more likely to put the land to its highest and best economic use. But, despite judicial and legislative rhetoric about the undesirability of clogs on alienation, such a prospect would have been truly appalling to the judiciary and the political elite. And they were quite prepared to exercise their powers to prevent its occurring.

It is also worth pointing out that English landowners were already especially insulated from losing their land by means more ordinary than the new gaming statutes. Although general historians do not always realize it, a peculiar feature of English common law was that land was not liable for ordinary personal and contract debts. Thus, landed gentlemen could and did accumulate enormous unpaid bills with tradesmen, as well as gaming debts, and run no risk of having a lien placed on their land, of enduring a court-ordered sale of land to pay such debts, or even of seeing the land go to their creditors at their death. As commercial creditors gained political strength by the very late eighteenth century, they began to introduce bills to make freehold property liable for simple contract debts. These bills were powerfully and successfully resisted by the landed interests and the judiciary, perhaps most notably by Lord Chancellor Eldon. Sir Samuel Romilly struggled in this cause until he finally in 1807 managed to get a limited act making the real estate of deceased traders liable for their debts, but he could not get agreement to extend the provisions to the estates of aristocrats or ordinary country gentlemen.[68] His adversaries insisted that to make land so liable would destroy primogeniture, penalize heirs, and make land unsalable. In House of Lords debates in 1814–15 that led to the rejection of Commons bills to make freehold estates of landowners dying indebted liable for their contract debts, Eldon insisted: "This bill [of 1814], while it went to remove the guards with which the policy of the law had fenced landed property, afforded in fact but little benefit to the creditor; and it was better that he should be left to use his own caution and discretion, than that he should sit down in apathy, under the notion that the legislature would take care of his interests." In resisting the 1815 bill Eldon argued, "all men who gave credit to a landowner well know they had no remedy against his land after his death. The law had always held real property more sacred than personal, and had provided that no transfer of it should be made without certain solemnities."[69] Despite Lord Eldon's position, a Pennsylvania statute of 1700 making land liable for payment of debts makes it evident that, in theory and within the intellectual resources of common law thought, it would have been perfectly possible to promote alienability and fairness to creditors by making land liable for payment of debts at any time during the eighteenth century—if promoting alienability had been a paramount goal.[70]

The selectivity with which both the public interest in security of title to real property and the public interest in promoting alienation were invoked is probably nowhere so nakedly apparent as in the legal rules made for real property in Ireland. The Irish rules show with what freedom legal intellectuals could treat their property rules when they considered that important social or political matters were at stake. As I observed in Chapter 1, during most of our period Irish law was a branch of English law, with all appeals from Irish decisions lying to the English House of Lords.[71] (From 1725 to 1789 all the Irish Lord Chancellors themselves were also English.)[72] Laws for Ireland were either made in the English Parliament or in the (Protestant) Irish Parliament. Laws of Irish origin were subject to the approval of the English Privy Council (including the English Lord Chancellor), which was charged with determining whether laws of colonial origin were repugnant to the fundamental law of England. By a few crucial changes in the law of real property in Ireland—changes in which any general public policy in favor of security of title was spectacularly ignored—the Protestant Irish Parliament and the English Privy Council virtually destroyed the Irish Roman Catholic gentry.[73]

Basically, by a bill of 1704 Roman Catholic landowners who possessed fee simples at common law had their fee simples turned into estates which could not descend according to the rules of primogeniture; instead, at the death of such an owner, his estate was to descend according to the rules of gavelkind, that is, to be divided equally share and share alike among all his sons.[74] However, should an eldest son of a Roman Catholic father be willing to conform to the Protestant Church of Ireland, then he could take the entire estate by primogeniture; should he conform while his father was still alive, then his father from that moment was to have merely a life estate, one he could not alienate. Moreover, Roman Catholics could not acquire land from Protestants by inheritance or marriage. Nor could a Roman Catholic purchase any interest in land greater than a term of thirty-one years. These terms were mere chattel interests, less than life estates, and did not entitle their holders to vote. (Laws affecting the real property interests of English Roman Catholics were, of course, also in force; they affected a small minority of the English population, whereas the Irish laws affected the overwhelming majority of people resident in Ireland.) Ratified by the English Privy Council and the king, the Irish Penal Laws so rudely cutting off interests in Irish real property held by Roman Catholics and so massively destructive of the security of the titles they held were adjudged not repugnant to the laws of England. Lawyers and politicians who quite clearly understood the important relationship between real property rules and social and political power calculated the Irish penal code to ensure, indeed, to create, the dominance of a Protestant landed elite in Ireland—and they did so very effectively. Edmund Burke, son of an Irish attorney and a graduate of Trinity College, Dublin, before he went to England to read for the bar, memorably remarked of the penal code: "It was a complete system, full of coherence and consistency, well digested and well composed in all its parts. It was a machine of wise and elaborate contrivance, and as well fitted for the oppression, impoverishment, and degradation of a people, and the debasement in them of human nature itself, as ever proceeded from the perverted ingenuity of man."[75] For good measure, other provisions of the penal code barred Roman Catholics from becoming solicitors or barristers; one statute even provided that any Irish barrister marrying a Roman Catholic was to be "deemed" a Roman Catholic and subject to all the penalties of Roman Catholics.[76] Under the circumstances of the penal code, the Protestant Parliament might well have judged that to permit Roman Catholics access to knowledge of what were supposed to be the principles of English law would only have served to irritate them further.

Thus, a critical analysis would point out, assertions of public interest in security of title and public interest in promoting freedom of alienability—said to motivate decisions like that in *Radnor* and judicial willingness to see doweress's rights defeated by the interests of purchasers and mortgagors—were very selectively applied. Indeed, had such strict settlements not been permitted, a tenant in tail would have been more able to raise cash by selling land or committing waste, and would not have been so much driven to rely on mortgaging—and thus not so eager to see his wife's dower rights defeated.

Whether the defeat of dower rights represented a loss to married women, however, depends in part on the value of the alternative kinds of married women's property that were in effect substituted for dower in the early modern period: jointure, pin money, and other forms of separate estate. We will look at these newer forms of married women's property in subsequent chapters.

4

Equitable Jointure

Development of the Theory of Equitable Jointure

The classic definition of jointure, repeated and commented upon many times in the eighteenth century, was that of Sir Edward Coke's *Institutes* (1628): "a competent livelihood of freehold for the wife of lands or tenements, &. to take effect presently in possession or profit after the decease of her husband for the life of the wife at the least."[1] Jointures were frequently made on eighteenth-century brides in prenuptial marriage settlements; with different legal consequences, jointures could also be made on wives after marriage. At the upper end of the scale, jointures of £1,500 a year or so are seen in the aristocracy, with Henrietta, Duchess of Newcastle, reported to have enjoyed a relatively lavish £3,000 a year.[2] The widow of the third Duke of Leeds also had a jointure of £3,000; since she lived for sixty-three years after her husband died, she was entitled to £190,000 during the course of her widowhood.[3] More commonly, among the gentry and wealthy citizens provisions ranged in the mid-hundreds of pounds. Judith Bromley, marrying into a family of London goldsmiths, was to have a jointure of the odd sum of £501.10s.[4] Among the less well-off, jointures of £100 or even £15 can be found.[5]

Modern social historians give the impression that widows in the classes that made marriage settlements were rather well-off. G. E. Mingay in his excellent *English Landed Society in the Eighteenth Century* has written of "the generous provision of widows' jointures" and maintained that jointures and other separate property

guaranteed to wives under marriage settlements "gave the wives
of landowners a degree of independence and financial security
which afforded them considerable defence against masculine domination."[6] At another point he observes that given the relationship
that existed between the amount of a woman's portion and the
amount of her jointure, if one allows for the husband's benefit
from the portion during the marriage, the wife became "virtually . . . self-supporting throughout her lifetime, although of
course the heir to the property could hardly be expected to regard
outstanding jointures in this light."[7] Some social historians have
believed that there was a relation between increasing amounts of
women's marriage portions and increasing amounts of jointures.
H. J. Habbakuk, in his now classic and much debated article "Marriage Settlements in the Eighteenth Century," has suggested that
"the increasing flexibility of the jointure in relation to the husband's income is another consequence of the increasing subordination of marriage to the accumulation of wealth. A man who was
particularly anxious to make an advantageous marriage was apt to
persuade himself that he could, without impairing the provision
for other members of his family, offer much more than one third
of his estate," as Habbakuk says was conventional in the seventeenth century.[8] Indeed, concern has been expressed that the
charges imposed by widow's jointures on some estates may have
been such a drain that the economic viability of the heirs' estates
was threatened. Mingay, for example, finds a tendency to make
amounts of portions and jointures "rather larger than the long-
term position of the estates warranted," and notes the great proportion of land burdened by debt.[9] Settlors' concern was expressed
in clauses restricting heirs' power to jointure to limits set in pounds
or in relation to portion amounts, say, a power to jointure out of
given land no more than £100 for every £1,000 of the bride's
portion.

No one, however, as far as I am aware, has made a really sys-
tematic study of eighteenth-century jointure. As we shall see,
agreements in marriage settlements to jointure did not necessarily
mean that the bride, should she become a widow, enjoyed the
jointure so settled upon her—a fact which social historians who
base their remarks on settlements would do well to remember.
Both twentieth-century historians and eighteenth-century commentators also tend to avoid careful comparison between the ear-

lier systems of provision for widows and the eighteenth-century jointure system. Eighteenth-century legal writers, though, usually made some explicit comparison between the widow's older common law right to dower in one-third of the husband's real property and their own modern jointures. As they generally took their basic definition from Coke, they also tended to follow him in maintaining the superiority for women of jointure to dower. Coke had opined that jointure was "more sure and safe for the wife" than any form of dower, giving as his reasons that the widow could enter upon the land without being "driven to her action," and that her husband's treason could bar her of dower but not of her jointure.[10] Blackstone, typically, agreed that the more modern form was better, indeed, "the most eligible species of any" of the provisions for widows. He elaborated on the procedural issue by observing "no small trouble, and a very tedious method of proceeding, is necessary to compel a legal assignment of dower."[11]

Eighteenth-century legal writers also gave attention to the process by which jointure replaced dower. They explained that in the sixteenth century much land was held to uses to avoid feudal taxes. Since, as we have seen, husbands had to be legally, not equitably, seised of land for dower to attach, the wives of these landowners were not entitled to dower in such land held to uses. Some had jointures instead. At marriage a parcel of land might be kept out of the trust and settled on the husband and wife for their "joint" lives or on the wife for her life. Then, when in 1535 the Statute of Uses declared the beneficiaries of uses to be the legal owners of their lands—and hence subject to a variety of feudal incidents which they had hitherto avoided by the uses—some wives who had been given jointures before the statute would suddenly have become entitled to both jointure and dower.[12] In order, therefore, to avoid a Renaissance version of double-dipping, the statute also provided that wives who had jointures were barred of their dower. If a jointure were to be an absolute bar to a woman's common law right to dower, the jointure had to be settled on her prenuptially, and, supposedly, had to conform to certain requirements set forth in the statute.

As eighteenth-century legal writers were vividly aware, an important reason for early modern enthusiasm for marriage settlements was that without such a prenuptial settlement of jointure on the wife, she might have been entitled to dower. A husband who settled a prenuptial jointure on his wife not only prevented her from claiming dower in land he had at the moment of the marriage; he also prevented her from claiming dower in any land which he might acquire by gift, inheritance, or purchase during the marriage. Moreover, by settling a jointure on his wife before marriage, a husband could give her—not only an estate worth more than her dower would have been, as Habbakuk notes—but one worth much less. Although the Statute of Uses attempted to create some comparability between estates in dower and jointure, neither the statute nor subsequent interpretations of it prohibited jointures of much less value than dower from barring dower. Given a ninety-acre estate, a widow's common law dower of thirty acres might be barred by a jointure of three acres or even one acre. Furthermore, as the Statute of Distribution (1670) was interpreted in the eighteenth century, a widow's right to a third of her husband's personal property, if he died intestate, was also barred by her jointure, again, no matter what the amount of the jointure.[13]

What, we may then ask, was to prevent husbands from settling very small jointures on wives and barring them of dower? The obvious answer usually given is that the marriage settlement was a contract that had at least two parties to it, usually more, not only the bride and groom but also both fathers and often other relatives and trustees. The bride's side had some bargaining power arising, first, from the assets she could bring into the marriage and, second, from potential claims to dower she might acquire. Obviously, the husband's side could not have the bride's portion or her personal property unless she agreed to the marriage. The possibility that some dower rights might accrue to the bride existed, but, as we have seen in Chapters 2 and 3, because there were by the eighteenth century so many other ways beside jointure to bar dower (for example, by conveying the land to trustees), the bride's relatives usually could not realistically threaten that she would become entitled to dower in a third of all the husband's real property unless they got the jointure they wanted. Claims that jointures must have been fair because fairness was guaranteed by a process of contractual bargaining require more scrutiny than they have hitherto received, and I will scrutinize them carefully in this chapter.

The exchange of dower for jointure has generally been said to be a more than fair bargain, good for women and good for society.

Eighteenth- and early nineteenth-century commentators congrat-
ulated the legal system for its adaptability and progressiveness in
replacing an old-fashioned, now supposedly dysfunctional dower-
in-land system of entitlement for widows with a modern system
of entitlement to money more appropriate to commercial society.
That there is some merit to this view is evident from a moment's
reflection on how useless entitlement to a third of her husband's
real property would be to many a modern urban wife. Nevertheless, it is also true, I believe, that equity judges and the House of
Lords, acting in its judicial capacity, stripped women of legal rights
in significant ways, and that there is also a more negative side to
the history of this transformation. Just as the legal rights of women
to dower were eroded by equity rulings, the legal requirements
demanded by the Statute of Uses for a jointure adequate to bar
dower were also eroded by the development of a theory of equitable jointure, as we shall see. A widow's entitlement to a life
estate in land was transformed by equity into an entitlement to a
jointure that could be a smaller estate in less secure personal
property for less than the term of her life.

According to the Statute of Uses, to bar dower a jointure had
to satisfy the following seven prerequisites, all presumably intended to guarantee some equivalency between dower and jointure and to ensure that jointure would be a secure provision:

1. It must be an estate of freehold land.
2. It must take effect "presently" after the death of the husband.
3. It must be a life estate or greater.
4. It must be her legal estate, not given to someone else in trust for
   her.
5. It must be given in satisfaction of her whole dower, and not of part
   of her dower.
6. It must be expressed to be in satisfaction of her whole dower.
7. It must be given before marriage; if given after marriage, she may
   elect to take either dower or jointure.

After the statute, however, a doctrine of equitable jointure was
developed by means of which these legal requirements were significantly eroded, only two of the seven (2, 5) being enforced at
equity in the eighteenth century. Indeed, it could be argued that
all the requirements were abandoned.

Three of these developments are of particular interest and significance: the acceptance of an estate determinable on the widow's

remarriage as the equivalent of a life estate, the acceptance of jointures of land in base tenures or chattel interests or personal property as the equivalent of jointure of freehold land, and the acceptance of testamentary devises as the equivalent of postnuptial jointures. I will also analyze in this chapter the issue of whether the consent of the woman is required to create a jointure barring dower, a related issue which does not arise so directly from the Statue of Uses. This question goes to the core of the ideological justification of jointure as fair because based on a bargain entered into freely.

Consider first a simple but important example at law before the further developments of equity in the early modern period. Although dower was an estate for the widow's life and the statute seemed to require that jointures adequate to bar dower be of a life estate or greater, it was decided that a jointure conditional upon the widow's performance of some obligation or a jointure *durante viduitate sua,* that is, one determinable on her remarriage, was a good equitable jointure. A majority of actual eighteenth-century jointures do not seem to contain *durante viduitate sua* clauses, but the clauses do turn up with some frequency.[14] Whatever their actual frequency, what concerns me here is the legal ideology that could find an estate during widowhood an equitable substitute for a life estate. If dower were assigned with condition, the condition would be void, yet here the courts declined to make the analogy. In an anonymous King's Bench case of 1560 the issue was debated by the judges, one finding such an estate less than a life estate, another considering that it was a life estate determinable on a condition and pointing out that a widow was not compelled to remarry.[15] Then Coke himself in *Vernon's Case* (1572) held that an estate *durante viduitate sua* was "an estate for her life, and it cannot determine without her own act, and therefore it is a jointure within the said Act [the Statute of Uses]."[16] Such an estate was considerably less valuable than a life estate without condition, reducing the wife's share of the husband's estate and her return on her portion drastically if she remarried soon after the death of her husband. A jointure *durante viduitate sua* could also interfere materially with a woman's prospects for remarriage.[17] Although the evidence is spotty, remarriage rates of widows do seem to have declined from the sixteenth century to the late seventeenth century and still more from 1660 to 1833.[18] I doubt seriously that a quasi-symmetrical doctrine which found a husband's estate in curtesy determinable on his remarriage to be an equitable substitute for curtesy would have been tolerated.

A more complex change of even greater significance was the transformation of an entitlement to an estate in freehold land to an entitlement to support with no requirement that that support be secured by land. Dower was an estate in freehold land, and jointure by the Statute of Uses was also conceptualized as an estate in freehold land. Nevertheless, although by 1761 Lord Hardwicke still admitted that at the time of the statute "the chief kind of property then regarded was freehold estate in land, and so the statute applied to that only," in his own time, he added:

> How many species of property have gown up since by new improvements, commerce, and from the funds. Equity has therefore held, that where such provision has been made before marriage, out of any of these, she shall be bound [that is, barred of dower] by it. Consider how many jointures there are now made on women out of the funds, and not one of them within the statute of 27 *H*. 8. So multitudes of jointures out of trust estates, not one of them within the statute; yet equity has always supported them. So also of copyhold lands.[19]

By 1820 R. S. Donnison Roper in his treatise on baron and feme could write that the legal requirement that the estate in jointure be an estate in freehold land was entirely unnecessary in equitable jointures on adults, commenting, "in truth, inconveniences which attend a limitation of lands in jointure are so numerous, that it has been the general practice for a long time past to limit or grant a rent-charge to the intended wife during her life, to begin at her husband's death, with powers of distress and entry, secured also by a term of years."[20]

As the Earl of Hardwicke's observation indicated, many jointures had less relation to land than a rent charge did, being made in such forms as annuities, stock, or consols. An excellent midcentury conveyancing book, which prides itself on dealing with "the new Supplies of Stocks, Bonds and Annuities of the public Companies, Exchequer-Annuities, Fortunes in *Ireland* and *Holland,* and Plantations in *America*" as well as with land, prints some very modern marriage articles dated 1721 in which, in exchange for a portion of £2,000 in East India bonds, a ship's captain undertakes to insure and to improve half of the portion on a trading voyage, then covenants either to leave the wife his entire estate or to settle the reunited whole portion to be laid out in lands "or in the Purchase of Stock in the Bank of *England, East-India* Company, *South-Sea* Company, or other Public Stock or Fund."[21]

In *Davila v. Davila* (1716) a husband had covenanted that his wife should be paid a lump sum of £1,500 within a month after his death "in full of dower, thirds, custom of *London,* or otherwise out of his real or personal estate." When he died intestate, the widow claimed her share under the Statute of Distribution, but Lord Chancellor Cowper found the lump sum barred her of her share.[22] In *Vizard v. Longden,* an important but unfortunately poorly reported case, a husband had entered into a prenuptial agreement to settle £14 a year on his wife for her provision and maintenance should he predecease her; this agreement was expressed in a condition of a bond. After the husband did predecease his wife, apparently the husband's brother (his heir) brought a claim to be relieved against the widow's claim of dower because of the settlement made on her in the bond. The widow replied that the sum was not secured by any particular lands and asked to have the annuity made good out of the real estate, the personal estate being insufficient, and also to have her dower. Sir Joseph Jekyll, as Master of the Rolls, found for the widow, not considering this bond a jointure adequate to bar dower. But his decree was reversed by Lord Chancellor King, who ruled the widow was only entitled to the £14 annuity and that the annuity was a bar of dower out of the residue of the husband's lands.[23]

It is remarkable that this right to real or personal property indiscriminately was substituted for a right to real property with such an apparent minimum of legal Sturm und Drang, given the general belief in the superiority of real property and its greater security. Some malaise, indeed, was expressed over the apparently lesser security provided. For example, characterizing the grant in question in his case as a "covenant to pay an annuity," counsel in *Drury* argued, "There was no real security for the performance of the covenant; so that the husband might, before his death, have disposed of all his real and personal estate, and left the defendant destitute of all provision."[24] Moreover, the security which comes from the immovability of land is diminished by the substitution of personal property, which can be alienated by inter vivos conveyance and can also literally be stolen by a thief or taken away by a deserting husband. In so far as there was an answer given to this objection, it seems to have been that at the death of the husband, the absence of sufficient personal property to support the jointure would have constituted "an eviction in equity, and consequently would have given [the widow] her right to dower, like the case of an eviction at law."[25] This might have been a remedy in some cases, though imposing an additional burden on the widow to litigate and subject to the risk that the husband might not have sufficient land or might have land to which dower had been prevented from attaching. Equity developed no such doctrine allowing similar substitutions for the widower's right to his deceased wife's real estate by curtesy, and, in general, such substitutions for rights to real estate were not made in the Restoration and eighteenth century.

The treatment of copyhold land is revealing in this connection. Copyhold land (treated in Chapter 2) was clearly distinguished from freehold land and in principle supposed by eighteenth-century lawyers to be an inferior, "base" tenure.[26] There was no dower of copyhold land, but instead a widow's free bench, somewhat variable according to the local custom, though usually amounting to a life estate in half or even all the land the husband held at his death.[27] It was early said that a jointure of copyhold land was not a good legal jointure. There were still a variety of land tenures in the eighteenth century, and land held in particular tenures was supposed to be treated according to the set of rules belonging to that tenure. For instance, land held by gavelkind passed to all the sons together, not to the oldest son as ordinarily.[28] In *Walker v. Walker* (1747) a widow entered upon land that was her husband's copyhold, claiming free bench. She was sued at equity by her husband's heir at law on the ground of a prenuptial marriage settlement giving her part of her husband's real estate as a jointure, which the heir claimed ought to operate as a bar of her free bench as well as of her dower. It was clear that at law the widow would prevail.

Nevertheless, when the heir sued in equity Lord Chancellor

Hardwicke decided that free bench was here sufficiently "analogous to dower" that by a "nice construction" he could find for the heir. The marriage settlement had said that the wife was to be barred of all claim from the husband's estate "of freehold or inheritance," and copyholds were sufficiently estates of inheritance "by the custom of the realm." "A contrary construction," he thought, "would introduce a dangerous precedent in families; for there are few estates that have not some copyhold mixed; of which perhaps the owner knows not; and it would be mischievous to let the widow claim it."[29] This is an interesting argument if the justification for barring a woman's dower is taken to be her consent to accept a substitute estate in the marriage settlement rather than the husband's mere desire to bar. Lord Hardwicke presumably did not imagine brides were more accurately apprised of the tenures by which grooms held their lands than grooms were, so his argument implies that, if the groom's general intention is interpreted as a desire to bar all such entitlement, brides can waive free bench without knowing that they are doing so.

Election

The requirement of the Statute of Uses that jointures barring dower had to be life estates or greater and the requirement that they had to be estates of freehold land were thus abandoned. The requirement that such jointures be expressed to be in satisfaction of the wife's whole dower had a more complex history and became entangled with the final requirement that only prenuptial jointures could bar absolutely while postnuptial jointures left the wife with a right to election. According to the Statute of Uses, if a jointure were made on a woman not before but after her marriage, then, should she survive her husband, she had a right to elect either dower or the postnuptial jointure. The statute did not contemplate jointuring by testamentary devise, for the obvious reason that until the Statute of Wills (1540), five years later, landowners did not have the legal power to dispose of freeholds by will. At first it was held that a devise of land by the husband to the wife was not a jointure barring dower but a "benevolence" to be enjoyed in addition to dower. But in *Bushe's Case* (1560), after a husband devised a third of all his lands to his wife in recompense for her dower and the wife entered into a third of the fee-simple lands only, it was decided that she was barred of her dower.[30]

Yet when the new rule that a testamentary devise could bar dower was combined with the developing ideas of equitable jointure in the eighteenth century considerable confusion arose and some questionable results were reached. According to a straightforward reading of the Statute of Uses, it would appear that should our original husband (in the hypothetical example at the beginning of Chapter 2) with his thirty acres of hop fields make no explicit provision for his wife but a testamentary devise of "one acre to my beloved wife," then his widow would take both her dower in ten acres and the devise of one acre. The heir at law could not claim that the bequest of one acre was a "jointure" forcing the widow's election between dower and jointure because the bequest had not been expressed to be in satisfaction of dower. Nevertheless, numerous wills in the eighteenth century, including wills obviously drawn up by legal professionals, seemed to show no awareness on the testator's part that there was any such thing as a common law right to dower. Nor did eighteenth-century testators always have the details of their marriage settlements firmly in mind. Thus, a variety of cases arose in which wives, having been given testamentary devises not expressed to be in satisfaction of their whole dower or not expressed to be in satisfaction of an earlier covenant to jointure or not even denominated "jointures," were then challenged by heirs at law or remaindermen when they tried to take both dower and devise or both jointure and devise. Suppose a woman had been entitled to a specific jointure under her marriage settlement, but the property promised to be settled to support her jointure had never been settled as promised, a fairly frequent occurrence. Should some other property bequeathed to her in her husband's will be counted as in satisfaction of her original prenuptial jointure and so as absolutely barring her right to dower? Testamentary devises not expressed to be jointures could nevertheless be construed either as postnuptial jointures in and of themselves or as in satisfaction of a prenuptial jointure. Table 1 is a rather abstract representation of the principal possible combinations of circumstances (in the first three columns) and their theoretical outcomes for the widow (in the fourth column).

Table 1. Jointure and election

Prenuptial agreement	Agreement during marriage	Testamentary devise	Result for widow
Prenuptial jointure	—	—	Must take jointure
Prenuptial jointure	Jointure not settled	Devise found satisfaction	Must take devise
—	Postnuptial jointure	—	Elect dower or jointure
—	Postnuptial jointure not settled	Devise found satisfaction	Elect dower or devise
—	—	Devise found jointure	Elect dower or devise
—	—	Devise not found to be jointure	Take dower and devise

Had the original statutory requirements that jointures barring dower be of freehold land and so on been maintained, then the rules concerning election here displayed would have been relatively simple to administer and probably fair enough. But, as we have seen, by the early eighteenth century at equity jointures of personal property as well as of real property could bar dower. Did that mean that a testamentary devise of personal property could force a widow to elect between the bequest of personal property and dower? Was it possible that a testamentary bequest of personal property could be found to be a satisfaction of a prenuptial jointure of land, the land having never been settled? The general trend at equity away from requiring freehold property as the only form of jointure barring dower and toward counting virtually any kind of property as adequate to bar increasingly made bequests of any sort and any size look more "jointure-like" and so more like possible bars. Yet it would have been grotesque to have allowed a bequest of only one shilling or of a single family portrait to be treated as an equitable jointure barring dower.

Increasingly the courts strayed from the formalistic requirement that a jointure be expressed to be in bar of dower (or a testamentary devise be expressed to be in satisfaction of jointure) and wandered into the realm of speculation about the testator's intention. As dower became a more archaic and less frequently enjoyed right, it became more plausible to suppose that a testator must have intended to bar dower—even if he neglected to say so. Perhaps the most controversial and ideologically revealing set of cases in this area arose when testators silent about dower or jointure made bequests to their wives out of real property but left the bulk of their property to another beneficiary, either devising it outright or creating a trust of which the other was a principal beneficiary.

In *Lawrence v. Lawrence* Dulcibella Lawrence had been given a bequest of lands and houses to the value of £130 a year to enjoy during her widowhood.[31] She had had no marriage settlement and so claimed both dower and the bequest. Trustees for the first remainderman, a godson of the husband, protested that the bequest was for her jointure and that, consequently, she was not entitled to both dower and the bequest. In 1698 Common Pleas gave her her dower, but in 1699 Lord Chancellor Somers issued a perpetual injunction against her enjoying dower. When Somers was succeeded in office by Lord Keeper Wright, Dulcibella was granted a rehearing. In 1702 Wright, having "fully considered of the matter," "conceived there was nothing in the testator's will that did intend that the defendant should be barred of her dower," and reversed Somers's decree. When the first remainderman died, the next remainderman made another attempt to oust Dulcibella from the dower land. By this time it was 1715 and Cowper was Lord Chancellor. Not very boldly, he declared, "as to the point of dower, that it being a point of right, and so doubtful in its nature, as that the Court had been of different opinions therein, and the last determination . . . was so long ago . . . [he] did not think fit to make any variation from what was then determined as to that point." This second remainderman, however, appealed to the House of Lords, who heard argument on the election question and affirmed Lord Keeper Wright's determination. *Lawrence* thus became a strong case for widows in subsequent litigation. (The determination was all the stronger on the point of law because Dulcibella herself had been a servant who married a member of the landed gentry, had no children by him, yet ended by enjoying during a long widowhood lands worth nearly £400 a year out of an estate said to be worth about £550 a year—as the remaindermen bitterly complained.)

Some midcentury cases, however, forced widows to questionable elections between dower and testamentary devises even
though those devises were not expressed to be in satisfaction of
dower. Judges asserted a theory of "incompatibility" between
dower and certain sets of testamentary devises. For example, in
Arnold v. Kempstead (1764) a husband devised two leasehold houses
to his wife for her life and also an annuity of £10 "during her life,
so long as she continued a widow"; he also devised all his freehold
estates to his nephew for life, subject to the £10 annuity. When
the widow entered into possession of the leasehold houses and
also brought a writ for her dower of the freehold, Lord Chancellor
Northington ruled that, despite the absence of any marriage settlement and despite the husband's not having expressly devised
the leaseholds or the annuity in lieu of dower, because the freehold
estates were subject to the annuity it was the husband's "manifest
intention . . . to give the annuity in satisfaction of dower."[32] Were
she to take the devise, it would be a postnuptial jointure which
she elected and so defeat her claim to dower. Were she to insist
on dower, that would be an election "in contradiction to the will,"
violative of what Northington understood as the gift to another
of a life estate in all (not the two-thirds left after dower) of the
freehold—and no one can take under a will without abiding by
all the provisions of that will. So the widow was forced to elect
either dower or the bequest.

Similarly, Lord Chancellor Camden in *Villareal v. Gallway*
(1769) decided that a husband's devise of all his real and personal
property to trustees to the use of his daughter subject to an annuity
of £200 to his wife would force the widow to elect dower or the
bequest.[33] His reasoning resembled Northington's: "The widow,
by the claim of dower, disappoints the will in the most essential
part of the testator's plan; by reducing the interest of the devisee,
and loading the estate with an additional burthen."[34] Less positive
by temperament than Northington, Lord Camden also took note
of the fact that he had inherited conflicting authority on the question before him, with *Lawrence* and the later case of *Pitt v. Snowden*
decided by Lord Hardwicke on the widow's side and *Arnold* on
the other. "I wish these cases could have been reconciled," he
lamented, "feeling in myself a modest unwillingness to sit in judgment upon two men greatly superior to myself in learning as well
as capacity: but . . . I undertake [decision] with more ease of mind,

knowing that there is a jurisdiction superior to us all, which is able to confirm or reverse my opinion by a final decision."

Assuming that Camden meant by "a jurisdiction superior to us all" the House of Lords, rather than the deity, his wish for higher authority on the vexed question of when election should be forced was soon enough answered in *Broughton v. Errington* (1773), when a decree by Lord Chancellor Bathurst that a wife was to have both jointure and bequest was affirmed by the House of Lords.[35] *Broughton* involved a larger estate than *Arnold* or *Villareal* and probably not coincidentally one in which there had been a marriage settlement. But the lands settled in jointure on the wife had never actually been settled, so after her husband's death, although other lands had been devised to her, she put in a bill for specific performance of the marriage articles giving her the jointure worth £1,000 a year. The case was ably argued on appeal in the House of Lords, with Wedderburn (later Attorney General, and still later Lord Chancellor Loughborough), leading the team for the husband's brother, and Thurlow (later Lord Chancellor), leading the team for the widow. Wedderburn contended that the testamentary devise ought to be presumed to be in satisfaction of the jointure despite the fact that the will made no reference to jointure. The usual presumption that a bequest was intended as a bounty, he claimed, should be overweighed "by a still stronger presumption" that, since there had been marriage articles, the devise was intended to be in satisfaction of jointure; such a general presumption "that where two provisions are made for a wife . . . the testator intended the one to be a satisfaction for the other" was "grounded on the known custom of this realm, to give the bulk of the family estate to the eldest son or heir at law. . . ." Thurlow, however, won with the contention that "every devise or bequest in a will, *prima facie,* imports a bounty," so that for equity to consider a testamentary devise a satisfaction of dower or jointure, it must be shown either that the testator expressly intended to satisfy or that by "the clear and necessary implication from the will" satisfaction was necessarily implied. The principle that there could be no "collateral satisfaction for dower," he further argued, applied also to jointure, and here "a bequest of a personal estate cannot be averred to be, or be considered as a satisfaction for a jointure in lands, or a rent charge upon a real estate." (Her husband had not completed the purchase of some lands devised to her; hence, Thurlow con-

tended, that devise was merely of so much money as he had agreed
to give for the purchase.) Bathurst's decree allowing the widow
to take both the annuity and the devise was affirmed by the lords.

In the 1780s and 1790s judges generally felt that the midcentury
cases had gone too far in their willingness to find implied intentions
to bar and in their discoveries of incompatibilities between dower
or jointure and testamentary devises. Kenyon, Loughborough,
Thurlow, and Arden as judges demanded more than the mere
circumstance that a rent charge or annuity devised to the widow
was to issue from land devised to another in order to force election
and more evidence that testamentary devises were in satisfaction
of jointure.[36] Thurlow in *Foster v. Cook* (1791) had a case in which
the wife's testamentary devise was payable by trustees out of a
fund composed of all the husband's real and personal property,
with another the principal beneficiary of the trust. With characteristic bluntness, Lord Chancellor Thurlow found the obvious
retort to the argument that for a wife to claim dower and a bequest
under such a will would defeat the testator's intentions toward the
principal beneficiary. Dower, after all, had attached to the husband's land during the coverture, before his death; it was a kind
of prior lien on the land, certainly prior to any testamentary disposition of the residue remaining of the husband's estate at his
death. Mocking the claims of counsel against the widow in *Foster,*
Thurlow said sarcastically: "But, here, it is to be gathered from
circumstances, that she is not to have [dower]; and because he has
given all *his* property to the trustees, I am to gather from his
having given all he has, that he has given that which he *had not.*"[37]

More temperately, Sir Richard Arden as Master of the Rolls
shed considerable light on the subject of testamentary devises and
election in a careful opinion in *French v. Davies* (1793), yet another
case in which it was contended that a testamentary devise to a
widow should force her to elect the devise or dower. Critically
reviewing the competing authorities and finding them difficult to
reconcile, he nevertheless rejected the argument that the testator
could not have intended that the widow should diminish the value
of the estate to be sold by insisting on her dower. "If I am to
admit the extent of that argument," he observed, the [absurd]
consequence would follow, if it was the case, not of a wife, but
of any incumbrancer, to whom an annuity was given."[38] It is one
of the ironies of these election cases and a symptom of how weak

the common law right to dower had become that many of the testators involved—and their lawyers who, from the language of the wills cited in the cases, obviously drew up their wills—simply forgot about dower. In *French,* Arden observed that he was privately convinced that the testator, if he had "recollected" his wife's right to dower, would have made her renunciation of it a condition of her enjoying the bequest.

Although some of the most dubious judicial presumptions of intent to bar were thus cut back at the end of the eighteenth century, several aspects of election remained treacherous for women. In cases where testamentary devises were ruled to be satisfactions of prenuptial jointures which had never been settled as promised, the woman lost her right to the particular jointure for which she had supposedly bargained and had to take the testamentary devise. Even if the wife considered her prenuptial jointure in quality and quantity an adequate satisfaction for jointure, it did not necessarily follow that she would have been equally prepared to accept the different devise the court pronounced a satisfaction. More serious, although in theory a right of election might seem fair enough, and although it might abstractly be supposed that widows would always elect the more valuable of the two choices offered them, in practice election could adversely affect the interests of widows. If a widow was unaware of the existence of her right to election and took *any* benefits under the will, for instance, receiving an installment on an annuity or continuing to live in the house in which she had lived with her husband, she might find herself judged to have given evidence that she had elected to take under the will.[39]

Furthermore, in order to elect the widow had to be prepared to cast herself in the role of a wife rejecting her husband's will. Social, psychological, and moral inhibitions could prevent her from doing this. The will could be and often was read not merely as a legal document but as a solemn expression of the man's desire and command. Even a woman so intelligent and spirited as Lady Mary Wortley Montagu, and one so little in love with her late husband, having no marriage settlement but a bequest in her husband's will barring dower if she elected to take under the will, was exquisitely distressed at a mere rumor that she might elect dower rather than acquiesce in her husband's will. Her husband, Edward Montagu, had left her £1,200 a year from an estate estimated to be worth £800,000 in money and £17,000 a year from land. "I dare be poor, I dare not be dishonest," she wrote to her son-in-law, repudiating any thought of electing dower.[40] (This same husband had shortly before their marriage published an essay denouncing the modern fashion of settlements, stating, among other points, that they were unnecessary because "the law of our country has given an ample and generous provision for the wife, even the third of her husband's estate.")[41] Many eighteenth-century gentlemen made their wills only when they were approaching death, and it is easy to understand the psychological and moral force a dying husband's will could have for his wife, whatever her common law rights or even her marriage settlement might have been. Horace Walpole in a letter gives a vivid account of one deathbed scene in which a wife entitled to thirds under a settlement was, despite an unhappy relationship with her husband, persuaded to relinquish much of her entitlement to her children for a deathbed postnuptial jointure: "On Friday perceiving her alarmed by his danger, he had the amazing presence of mind and fortitude to seize that only moment of tenderness, and prevailed on her to accept a jointure. He instantly dispatched your brother Ned to London for his lawyer, and by five o'clock on Saturday, after repeated struggles of passion on her side, the whole was finished—Dear Gal! he could not speak, but he lifted up his hands in thanks!"[42] After scenes like these, widows were likely to elect the husband's devise.

The testamentary devise cases may be seen as way stations on the road to the Dower Act of 1833. Judicial interest in the issue of whether the husband testator had intended to bar and presumptions that he must have intended to bar threatened to obliterate concern with whether the wife had intended to make such a bargain and with the social value of a forced share system. Indeed, the very point of wills is to allow individualistic deviations from communal forced share systems. The judges themselves all (or almost all) made wills, as is evident from David Duman's having been able to find the wills of 93 percent of the judges in his study of the bench during the years 1727–1825.[43] It increasingly came to be believed that the husband rather than society was the right judge of proper provision for his wife—not only during marriage, as had always more or less been the case—but after the marriage had been ended by his death as well. Obviously, estates much smaller than dower or a distributive share of personality could be devised.

Doctrinal debate over forced election, tipped back in the direction of allowing both dower and devise by judges like Kenyon and Arden at the very end of the eighteenth century, was silenced by legislative determination (in the Dower Act) that dower could be barred by a declaration in the husband's will (s. 7), that it could be subjected to whatever restrictions the husband chose to declare in his will (s. 8), and that the husband's devise of *any* land out of which the widow would otherwise be entitled to dower (or any estate or interest in such land) to the widow would bar her of dower in *all* the husband's land in which she would otherwise have been entitled to dower (s. 9). Thus, Parliament went back to the logic of the midcentury cases like *Arnold* and presumed incompatibility between dower and devises of real property. The burden shifted over to the wife to negotiate prenuptially a certain provision for herself, a jointure or, under the Dower Act, a covenant that the husband would not bar dower. If the wife were passive and did not arrange such provision, her husband could bar her in his will of any share in either his real or his personal property.

Questionable "Virtues" of Jointure

Particularly given the development of these eighteenth-century doctrines of equitable jointure, the judicial willingness to find testamentary devises satisfactions of jointure, and the complexities of election, it is not as obvious as Coke claimed that jointure was intrinsically "more secure and safe for the wife" than dower. Nor is it as obvious as Blackstone claimed that the procedures for demanding dower were so much more "troublesome" and "tedious" than those for demanding jointure. After all, Blackstone frequently enough decided to characterize complex and archaic procedures not as "troublesome" but as guarantors of liberty and property. In the ideal course of events, the heir cooperatively sets out the widow's dower, and she has nothing to do but occupy the land. Only should the heir fail to cooperate, does she have to invoke her writ—and other kinds of writ procedures Blackstone often enough characterized in highly favorable language. Also, he omitted to take notice of a provision of the Statute of Merton (1235) providing a widow kept out of her dower land with damages to the value of the dower from the time of the death of the husband to the time she recovered seisin, a statutory provision we know was enforced in the eighteenth century.[44] On the whole, the argument that jointure was better than dower for widows because dower procedures were cumbersome seems feeble. And, of course, contemporaries were capable enough of altering real property procedures they no longer liked, either by conveyancing devices or by statute.

Moreover, despite theoretical claims that jointure was obviously better for women than dower because dower had to be claimed by a cumbersome legal process and jointure made the surviving wife's entry "more secure and straightforward,"[45] even when the wife thought she had had a prenuptial jointure, her confidence might turn out to be unfounded. As I have noted, property covenanted in a marriage settlement to support a jointure was not always so settled, and specific performance of the covenant could not always be obtained. The complexity of the land law and the variable skills of legal professionals in this period also created a state of affairs in which, as social and economic historians have remarked, marriage settlements and wills were "notoriously subject to legal disputes."[46] Indeed, problems with jointures were sufficiently familiar to contemporaries that Samuel Butler could make a joke about them in his Restoration comic epic, *Hudibras.* When Hudibras, the deceitful Presbyterian comic villain, is forced to confess his true intentions toward the widow he has been courting, he admits he would have:

> . . . laid her Dowry out in Law,
> To null her Joynture with a Flaw,
> Which I before-hand had agreed
> T'have put, of purpose, in the Deed. . . .[47]

Less comically, the letters of Charlotte Smith reveal how insecure a provision a settled jointure could be. Charlotte, the daughter of a landed gentleman, had been married at fifteen with a settlement. Some years after her marriage, while she was trying to support herself and her children by writing novels, she lamented:

It is now above seventeen months since I have heard from [Mr. Smith] and the few people who know [where he is] . . . have received instructions not to let me know . . . I believe he has another family by a Cook who lived with him, and has hid himself in Scotland by another name; so that if I were disposed to commence any process against him to compell him to allow me my own income for his childrens support I know not where to find him. But I have no such design. My marriage articles in which there are two flaws that deprive me of any jointure in case of his death, make no provision for a separation. I was not quite fifteen when my father married me to Mr. Smith and too childish to know the dismal fate that was preparing for me.[48]

Social historians must remember that marriage settlements indicating a woman was entitled to a jointure of a certain sum do not necessarily indicate that, once widowed, she actually had it to spend. Even when women did obtain jointures, they sometimes yielded all, or, more often, part of them back to the heir or other family members. Combinations of familial affection and social pressure on occasion prompted such relinquishments. Thus in 1676, the year of her son's marriage, Dame Elizabeth Whitley agreed to accept an annuity of £170 for herself and a guarantee that her daughter's portion would be paid in exchange for surrendering her jointure lands worth £200 a year to the son.[49] A good sense of the social pressures that could be brought to bear on a jointress whom other family members thought had "too much" is given in a private letter of Sir Horace Mann discussing Margaret Rolle, Countess of Orford: "It would be extremely natural for so rich a mother to give up at least her jointure, which must distress her son so much to pay, instead of insisting upon the arrears, and the deficiency being made good to her for the future, as she seems determined. Those even who were only solicitous for her welfare ought to have given her that advice upon her second marriage."[50]

Certainly, many eighteenth-century widows did receive and enjoy their jointures. But clearly, also, eighteenth-century jointures gave widows much smaller fractions of the total estate of husband and wife than the thirds established as forced shares by dower and by the Statute of Distribution (which applied to personal property in intestates' estates only). To the argument that dower had to be replaced by jointure because personal property was replacing landed property as the principal form of wealth, the obvious response is that dower could simply have been supplemented by a statutory forced share of one-third of the husband's personal property. Instead of requiring statutory thirds of personal property for the widow, the scheme which the ecclesiastical courts had earlier used when they had the administration of wills of personal property and a scheme revived in the Inheritance (Family Provision) Act of 1938, the English legal system in the seventeenth and early eighteenth centuries moved toward complete freedom of testation.[51] The conclusion that jointure replaced dower in part because contemporaries resisted forced thirds as too much for women is irresistible. Supposedly, women traded their thirds, which had become insecure, for smaller shares, which were more secure. Dower, as we have seen, had become insecure because of the judicial rule of no dower of a trust and because of a variety of conveyancing techniques. The question we must consider next is whether women can reasonably be said to have exchanged larger shares for smaller, more secure shares in a fair process of contractual bargaining.

The Fairness of Contractual Bargaining

Claims that jointures must have been fair because fairness was guaranteed by a process of contractual bargaining require more scrutiny than they have hitherto received. Although some women upon entering marriage were as capable of bargaining on their own behalf as some men, certainly many women were ill-equipped to bargain on their own behalf through a combination of ignorance and social, religious, and moral sanctions against their asserting their own material interests. Even today, most women seem to think it would derogate from the attitude of love, respect, and trust they ought to have and want to have toward a husband-to-be to insist on a prenuptial agreement. But many who would concede that most eighteenth-century first-time brides were not very capable of bargaining on their own behalf, would nevertheless insist that the fathers of brides were at least equal matches for grooms and the fathers of grooms in the bargaining process. Thus, in a disagreement I have had with Professor Lloyd Bonfield on this subject, he has stated that his "assumptions regarding human behavior require [him] to believe that as fathers [males] tried to exact the most favorable terms for their daughters either because they loved them or the chase: they drew a sense of accomplishment by striking a hard bargain."[52] Certainly, I would concede, many fathers desired to exact favorable terms for their daughters "either because they loved them or the chase." My assumptions about human behavior and my knowledge of eighteenth-century social history, however, do not force me to conclude that these were the only motives of fathers. Some fathers were incompetent or indifferent. Moreover, in the negotiations over marriage settlements between 1660 and 1833 the interests of brides and the interests of their fathers were not always, or perhaps even ordinarily, identical.

Fathers, in fact, could have needs or desires at odds with the interests of their daughters. Fathers and other male relatives supposedly negotiating on the bride's behalf sometimes wished to advance their own visions of dynastic or familial interests in ways that could be very weakly connected to any individual interests the daughter might have. In extreme cases, such as that of Sir Edward Coke's efforts to advance himself and his family by forcibly marrying his daughter to the insane John Villiers, Viscount Purbeck (noted in my introduction), contemporaries might disapprove or think things had gone a bit too far, but they were not therefore prepared to interfere with paternal prerogatives. When the novelist Samuel Richardson in *Clarissa* treats the efforts of the Mr. Harlowes, father and son, to marry Clarissa in what they judge to be their best interests, Richardson obviously believes that he cannot assume contemporary readers will be sympathetic to Clarissa's efforts to resist their marriage bargains in what she considers her own interests. Nor did judges necessarily see anything wrong with fathers' arranging daughters' marriages to advance personal or familial economic or dynastic interests. Lord Hardwicke had a case in which a girl of fifteen had been married to her first cousin, the heir male of her mother's family. She had had a portion of £5,000 and contingent future interests amounting, apparently, to £58,000; her husband's land had been charged with mortgages of £15,000. Her second husband, whom she married at nineteen, after having been widowed, attempted to overturn the first marriage settlement on the ground that, having been a minor at the time of settlement, she ought to have a right at twenty-one to repudiate it. Lord Hardwicke rejected this attempt and commented:

... the second objection, that the parents of *Dorothy* did not make
so beneficial a bargain for her as they might have done; admitting
this was so, I apprehend that it would not be a sufficient reason to
set aside the marriage agreement; the law has intrusted parents with
the marriage of their children; there are many considerations that
may induce a parent to agree to a marriage besides a strict equality
of fortune, as the inclination of the parties, their rank and quality ... the convenience too and propriety of such a match as to
preserve the whole estate in the family, which are matters proper
for parents to judge of.[53]

A particularly important conflict of interest between fathers (or,
if fathers had died, brothers or other heirs) and brides in the
eighteenth century, I believe, had to do with the payment of
portions. It was in the bride's interest that a portion settled on
her in her parents' marriage settlement be paid in cash immediately
upon her marriage. Such prompt payment was likely to secure her
the most favorable jointure. Grooms were frequently in need of
ready cash and prepared to exchange future interests for it; even
should the groom not absolutely need ready cash, if the portion
came to him immediately on marriage it was secure and he could
also immediately begin to enjoy income from it. But fathers were
not infrequently reluctant or actually unable to pay on marriage
the portions that had been settled on their daughters. Like
grooms, fathers had cash flow problems too. Peter Roebuck in
his study of Yorkshire baronets between 1640 and 1760 observed that payments of the principal sums of portions due could
normally be delayed, as long as those to whom they were due
received interest on them. "It seems clear," he added, "that as
the period progressed the payment of a growing number of
portions was via loans or by instalments, and that the receipt
of many was temporarily postponed or deferred indefinitely."[54]
A. P. W. Malcomson similarly notes in his study of marriage practices in the Irish aristocracy "the landed class's lack of liquidity"
and consequent interest in negotiating over "whether all, part or
none of the portion should be paid into the hands of the bridegroom's father."[55] A bride's father who needed or wished to persuade a groom to agree to a deferred (and possibly uncertain)
payment of a portion might well accept a smaller jointure on his
daughter's behalf.

Jointures on Infants

A final exceptionally difficult and revealing doctrinal problem in the jointure cases arose over the issue of whether the consent of the woman was necessary to create a jointure barring dower, and, if so, whether that consent could only be given by an adult woman. On the one hand, as contract ideology began to operate as a legitimizing force in the field of married women's property, it was extremely appealing to justify the barring of a common law right on the ground that the individual who possessed the right had consented to waive it and to exchange it for another one, the right to jointure, even if the jointure might not be of equal value. Lord Alvanley in 1794 distinguished one case of a minor from that of an adult, observing, "I do not say, that if she had been adult, she might not have bound herself. She might have taken a provision out of the personal estate [instead of a more secure provision of land], or she might have taken a chance [an estate not to commence immediately upon the death of her husband but dependent upon another life, for example], in satisfaction for her dower, acting with her eyes open, but an infant is not bound by a precarious interest."[56] Roper in his treatise on baron and feme similarly defended equitable jointures inferior to legal jointures as binding on an adult woman who consents "because she, being able to settle and dispose of all her rights, is competent to extinguish her title to dower upon any terms to which she may think proper to agree."[57] On the other hand, historically, jointure did not originate out of a full-blown eighteenth-century contract ideology, so there was some difficulty formulating a coherent doctrine including the earlier cases. Furthermore, practically, men were not prepared to postpone marrying girls until the girls reached the age of twenty-one.

Some early cases seemed not to require the woman's consent. In *Cannel v. Buckle* (1724) an infant female gave her husband-to-be a bond that she would convey her lands to him on marriage, and Lord Chancellor Macclesfield permitted the husband's heir to bring a bill to compel her to convey the lands. He added, "suppose a feme infant seised in fee, on a marriage with the consent of her guardians, should covenant in consideration of a settlement to convey her inheritance to her husband, if this were done in consideration of a competent settlement, equity would execute the agreement."[58] In *Jordan v. Savage* (1732) a husband had covenanted in a settlement to settle some copyhold land on his wife "in Lieu of her customary estate." Despite the facts that the wife was not a party to the marriage settlement, that the wife was an infant, and that copyhold was not legally a jointure adequate to bar dower, Lord Chancellor King ruled that the settlement barred her of her free bench.[59] Lord Chancellor Hardwicke in *Price v. Seys* (1740) thought it "extremely plain, that if a Man marries an Infant, and before the Marriage makes a Jointure upon her, such Jointure will bar her of her Dower." Should the jointure be inadequate to her portion, "much more if there was any Collusion between her Friends and the Husband in the making of the Jointure," she might have an equitable remedy against the husband.[60] Similarly, in *Harvey v. Ashley* (1748) he decided that a female infant was bound by a settlement made by her parents and guardians: "Consider the trust put in parents and guardians; suppose a female infant is married to a gentleman of great estate, the dower is one third, and yet she has a jointure made to her of only one tenth the value; and notwithstanding this, as the law has intrusted parents and guardians with the judgment of the provision for infants, she shall not set it aside upon the inequality between the dower and the jointure."[61] Two basic ideas supporting these cases were, first, that some prenuptial provision had been made for the wife and, second, that the courts were extremely reluctant to revise marriage settlements, even if they were very unequal, since they could not "set the wife *in statu quo,* or unmarry the parties" and since children might have been born who were entitled to rights under the settlement.[62]

But there was an obvious difficulty in justifying a rule which apparently permitted husbands to substitute tiny jointures for substantial dowers without the wife's consent. As one lawyer pointed out, "a man of a great real estate might procure an infant of the tenderest years to marry him, and by settling a small part of his real estate on her by way of jointure, bar her of dower, while he at the same time acquired an absolute property in all her personal estate."[63] Lord Macclesfield's hypothetical in *Cannel* had conveniently provided the female infant with the consent of her guardians, and Lord Hardwicke elsewhere was tempted by the idea that the consent of the parents or guardians might bind the infant.[64] This, however, would have been quite peculiar. Even so staunch a conservative and so enthusiastic an advocate of protection for women as Lord Thurlow had to admit that it was difficult to see how guardians' consent could be said to bind an infant: "I cannot conceive that the parent's or guardian's consent can make any essential difference in the contract."[65] Lord Macclesfield's hypothetical also suggested that perhaps only "competent" settlements were to be binding without consent. Yet this raised what Lord Northington forcefully pointed out was the extreme difficulty of the court's attempting to rule on competence. He asked on what grounds a court was supposed to decide that a husband's provision was disproportionate to his wife's entitlement: "What measure is the court to make of this disproportion? The husband's estate? The wife's fortune? Her family? Her person? Her endowments? I am lost in the impossibility of equity's interposing, and frightened with a jurisdiction that I should attempt to introduce."[66]

Other cases suggested that female infants could not be bound by a settlement. In 1715 Dennis and Ellin Daly, who had been married when they were both sixteen, appealed to the House of Lords against a marriage settlement in which they claimed Ellin's mother had made a better provision for herself than she was entitled to by law from the estate Ellin had inherited. It was held that their settlement was void as against them, "they being then minors, and no parties."[67] In *Cray v. Willis* (1734) Sir Joseph Jekyll, Master of the Rolls, decided that a female infant having a jointure made on her before marriage, might after she came of age elect either jointure or dower, thus treating jointures made on infants like jointures made on feme coverts, who, as we have just seen, also had a right to election, based, some argued, on their inability to consent during coverture.[68] Lord Chancellor Hardwicke himself in *Glover v. Bates* (1739) had found that a wife who had been an infant at the time of her marriage settlement had a right of election. The widow in *Glover* obtained her share of personal property under the Statute of Distribution despite a settlement barring her "right and claim of dower, or any claim or right by common law, custom of the city, *or any other usage, law, or custom notwithstanding.*"[69]

The position that an infant could not be bound by a settlement was also supported by the practice of obtaining private acts in Parliament to permit such settlements. In 1756, for example, such a private act was obtained for Esther Hanmer to enable her to settle her estates pursuant to her marriage articles with Asheton

Curzon.[70] Typically, as in "An act to enable Sir Watkin Williams Wynn, baronet, a minor, to make a settlement on his intended marriage with the Lady Henrietta Somerset" (1768–69), these acts state the desirability of the marriage contemplated and stipulate something like, "But by reason of the Minority of the said Sir Watkin Williams Wynn . . . such Settlement cannot be effectually made and carried into execution without the Aid and Authority of Parliament."[71] Had marriage settlements been clearly binding on infants, it is difficult to see why such private acts would have been purchased and passed. But that more acts were obtained for male infants than for female infants may suggest that settlements were more likely to be assumed to be binding on female infants. Also, the total number of such acts is of an order of magnitude much smaller than the total number of infants who married with settlements, which may suggest not only that many could not afford private bills but also a more general assumption that settlements on infants would bind.[72]

These conflicts were most fully aired in *Drury v. Drury* (1760–61), decided by Lord Northington, overruled in the House of Lords in *The Earl of Buckinghamshire v. Drury* (1761). The jointure involved, made on a female infant, was an annuity not charged on particular lands and supposed to bar both her dower and her distributive share in her husband's personal property. Lord Northington ruled that such a jointure made on an infant left her with the power of election.[73] Significantly, he seems to have considered that the motives behind the opposite rule were to permit jointures less than dower, the dower third having been defined by law "as a reasonable provision." Repudiating the masculine selfishness and sordidness behind resistance to a third, he observed with apparent sarcasm: "The law has been indeed much arraigned as being too liberal in its provisions to the wife; and it was asked [presumably by those in opposition to his rule], what man of £15,000 *per annum* would marry, if the wife was to take a third, when the heir was to be cramped to £10,000 *per annum* and stinted in luxury, expense, and diversion for the sake of his mother?"[74]

As we have seen in Chapter 3, in cases involving dower and other similar rights frequently involved in marriage settlements, the practice and opinion of conveyancers was usually accorded weight, both on the ground that conveyancers were learned in the law and on the ground that the security of property generally depended upon the trustworthiness of their practice and upon the confidence reposed in them. In *Drury* plaintiff's counsel, arguing for a rule giving validity to infant consent, insisted that convey-ancers never regarded whether jointure was made on an infant or an adult and warned that this "opinion has so far prevailed, that half the settlements in the kingdom would be overturned by a contrary decision."[75] Lord Northington took note of the fact that opposing counsel gave opposing representations of conveyancing practice, and, again, indulged in sarcasm, here concerning "the want of curiosity and oscitancy" of the plaintiff's supposed con-veyancers, "who, it is said, when they hear the word jointure are satisfied, and never inquire whether the woman is a minor or not when she is married; that is, in other words, whether the dower was barred or not; a point which, unless we have much misspent our time, was certainly worth inquiring about."[76]

After this judgment for the defendant widow in *Drury,* however, one of the plaintiff daughters married the Earl of Buckingham-shire, who appealed. Of seven judges giving their opinions to the lords, three (Gould, Parker, and Pratt) supported Lord Chancellor Northington and four (Wilmot, Adams, Bathurst, and Smythe) did not. The Earl of Hardwicke, formerly Lord Chancellor, speaking not as a sitting judge but as a member of the House of Lords, presented a long argument for reversal, which was decreed. His argument depended upon defining jointure as a "provision" for the wife rather than as a payment under contract. It seems to have been assumed that were infant females to have a right of election, the threat of their electing more valuable dower in preference to less valuable jointure would constitute a problem. The Earl of Hardwicke featured in his parade of horribles that would result from Lord Northington's rule: "No person of a great estate will be able to marry an infant, unless she finds surety to bar herself at twenty-one by a fine. Beauty, virtue, and merit, cannot always find such surety."[77] Lord Mansfield, also speaking not as a sitting judge but as a member of the House, agreed: "Were infants not bound by such agreements as this, no lady could marry without her father or some near friends becoming security that she would, when of full age, join in fine to bar herself of dower, which, if she should afterwards refuse to do, the husband must have his remedy for a collateral satisfaction against the heir of her father, or such next friend, which would make wild work."[78] Concern was also expressed about nonfamily purchasers of land, who would be distressed to find dower claimed in land they had purchased.[79]

Drury was thus a close case, and one in which Northington apparently continued to believe he had been wrongly overruled. As Sir Robert Henley, he had been given the seals as Lord Keeper in 1757 because Pitt demanded that preferment for Northington in exchange for Pitt's agreeing to Newcastle's demand that Hardwicke have a cabinet seat. But he was neither elevated to the peerage nor made Lord Chancellor at this time. According to his grandson and biographer, he thus suffered "the mortification of having to preside for nearly three years in the House of Lords as a commoner, while the office of directing that assembly when sitting in its judicial capacity devolved exclusively upon Lord Hardwicke and Lord Mansfield. . . . [both of whom] regarded his elevation with no favorable aspect."[80] He was created Baron Henley so that he could preside as Lord High Steward at Lord Ferrar's trial, but he did not get the seals as Lord Chancellor until January 16, 1761, after the accession of George III. According to an anecdote of Horace Twiss, Henley as Keeper was more than once frustrated by not being able to enter into lords debates to defend his opinions when there were appeals from his judgments, especially when Hardwicke or Mansfield argued for reversal.

> He was frequently much out of temper with the proceedings in which his opinions were reversed, when he thought it impossible to maintain that they were wrong. In the famous case of Drury and Drury, the Bar of the time when his judgment was given, and all subsequent times, held his judgment to be perfectly right, and that it was impossible for sound lawyers to impeach it. The law Lords however prevailed upon the House to reverse it. The Keeper was very angry: and tradition tells us, that in going up Saint Martin's Lane, in his way home, his coach stopped, and in some anger he said to the coachman, "Why don't you drive on?" The coachman replied, "My Lord I can't, yet—if I do I shall kill an old woman." "Drive on," said the Keeper, "if you do kill her, she has nothing to do but appeal to the House of Lords."[81]

The reversal in *Buckinghamshire v. Drury,* while perhaps pragmatically satisfying to gentlemen, was theoretically and ideologically embarrassing. Having decided that jointures on female infants were binding, equity in the later eighteenth century was neither prepared to go on to decide that marriage settlements were binding on male infants nor to articulate a clear rule that female infants could be bound and male infants could not.[82] An attempt, therefore, was made to narrow the holding in *Buckinghamshire* by distinguishing between jointures which would bar female infants and jointures which would not, requiring that the former conform to certain legal requirements of the Statute of Uses. In *Caruthers v. Caruthers* (1794) a jointure had been made on an infant of land in possession of the husband's mother, in trust for the use of the husband's mother for her life, remainder to the husband for his life, remainder to the wife for her life for her jointure.[83] The wife was widowed while the husband's mother still survived, so her life estate could not commence until the husband's mother died. This was an obvious case of a jointure not barring dower under the Statute of Uses because the wife's estate failed to commence "presently" at the death of her husband. However, the heir's counsel argued, citing *Buckinghamshire,* that the jointure should bar the widow of her dower, free bench, and statutory share of the personal estate. Sir Richard Arden, Master of the Rolls, rejected the idea that *Buckinghamshire* decided that guardians have a power to bind the infant and found that *Buckinghamshire* only decided that jointures "equally certain with the dower" were bars. Thus, since the jointure in question was obviously not a certain provision, he allowed the widow to elect her dower and free bench, which she did. Lord Chancellor Eldon similarly engaged in criticism of *Buckinghamshire,* and in *Milner v. Lord Harewood* (1811) determined that a female infant was not bound by an agreement to settle her freehold estate on marriage without an option to refuse at twenty-one.[84]

Turn-of-the-century treatise writers also showed signs of finding *Buckinghamshire* problematic. Fonblanque in an important equity treatise of 1793–94 found that in the wake of *Buckinghamshire* "how far the real estate of an infant can be bound by any agreement entered into during infancy, appears to be still subject to some doubt." Commenting on *Harvey v. Ashley,* he believed that Lord Hardwicke had "considered the leaving of issue, as well as the adequacy of the settlement, material to its binding the rights of the infant." He also noted that in *Williams v. Williams* (1782) Lord Thurlow had said that "to bind an infant, the settlement must be fair and reasonable."[85] Edmund Gibson Atherley in an 1813 treatise on baron and feme found the rule to be that a female infant may be barred of dower by a prenuptial settlement, but that provision must be "certain," not "precarious." He raised the issue of competence in the form of whether such a jointure must be adequate in amount, but found no possibility of measuring adequacy short of a provision for the wife so small as to constitute fraud. No cases, in Atherley's judgment, had yet expressly held that male infants could bar themselves of curtesy or of their rights to the wife's personal property, but given the decisions concerning female infants, he could see no reason why male infants should not be treated similarly, nor any reason why male infants could not settle their real property.[86] Roper in 1820 observed that the question of the female infant was "for a considerable period involved in uncertainty" until decided by *Buckinghamshire,* but he found the issue of the competence of the jointure still problematic:

> From *dicta* in some cases, it had been inferred that jointures in equity upon infants, although not within the statute, would be binding if such provisions were *competent.* But what shall or shall not be so considered, is so vague and uncertain as, it would seem, to afford no sufficient data to induce a Court of Equity to interpose and compel a person to abandon a legal ascertained right, in consideration of a provision . . . which may happen in the result to prove far below the value of the legal title in lieu of which it was substituted.[87]

To a limited extent, the problems created by *Buckinghamshire* were resolved by the development of a doctrine of two types of equitable jointure: jointure on adult women, which could be uncertain and precarious because adult women were presumed competent to dispose of their rights by contract, and jointure on infants, which had to conform to minimal requirements of certainty. But the development of tests for the competency of infant jointures did not progress very far. We have seen in Chapter 2 that any conveyance to trustees for herself by a woman in contemplation of her marriage was adjudged to be a fraud against the husband's marital rights unless he consented to the conveyance. There the judges confidently presumed that the husband was entitled to enjoy *all* his wife's property during the marriage unless he explicitly waived that right. When it came to determining how small a jointure had to be to constitute fraud against an infant bride, however, the judges had no such confidence in what her entitlement was. They certainly were not prepared to determine that any jointure which gave the infant bride a provision smaller than thirds constituted a fraud against her marital rights. Everyone knew that a social and economic purpose of jointures and devises was to prevent women from enjoying as much as thirds and that adult brides regularly agreed to jointures smaller than thirds. The idea of thirds had been so far abandoned in practice that it was not available in theory to the judges to use as a test of fraud— and no other test occurred to them.

It is hard to reconcile, on the one hand, insistence on the marriage settlement as a contract and on the adult woman's contractual capacity to justify substitution of a possibly precarious entitlement to jointure for a common law right to dower, and, on the other hand, denial that the marriage settlement was a contract to justify regarding "provisions" for jointure on infants as binding. Moreover, in other areas of doctrine the marriage settlements were said to be contracts. For example, although dower was forfeit by elopement and adultery, jointure was said to be by contract and not forfeit for adultery unless there was an explicit clause providing for such forfeiture in the marriage settlement.[88] Some further resolution, although hardly one which spoke to the basic contradiction, was attempted in the Victorian Infants Marriage Bill (1855), which permitted men of twenty and girls between the ages of seventeen and twenty, or their guardians, to petition Chancery for approval of their settlements, with a proviso that the act did not extend to any powers which it was expressly declared should not be exercised by infants.[89]

Conclusions

I would argue that three deep problems were not confronted in the litigation and theory of jointure in the eighteenth century. First, the ways of measuring the "value" of an estate had shifted between 1535 and 1800. The Statute of Uses, in requiring freehold and a life estate, had been making value requirements in terms intelligible in the early sixteenth century. But, in the eighteenth century, as an estate's annual revenues in money came to seem a more relevant measure of the value of the estate, with questions of free or servile tenure fading in the light of cash income of so many pounds a year, there was no apparent procedural way to substitute these new measures. Indeed, one might suggest that it was in the interest of husbands to describe the equity of the system by reference to requirements couched in the language of the old categories, to mask the absence of requirements in the more modern language of cash income. Thus, the courts continued to structure decisions about jointure around traditional categories of freehold, copyhold, leasehold, and so on, at the same time suffering some embarrassment at the fact that a dower right worth £1,000 a year could be barred by a jointure of £100.

A second deep problem not confronted in the contemporary theory of jointure was that, as we have observed in comparing the origins of dower and curtesy, historically provisions for women were not symmetrical with the property rights of men. It was probably reasonable to argue that the Statute of Uses had intended no distinction between adult and infant women. But the eighteenth-century rhetoric of individual "rights" and property and contract rights made it seem that the same rules ought to apply symmetrically to men and women—unless, of course, the women were married, which justified some difference. The Marriage Act of 1753, breaking with the earlier asymmetry of the ecclesiastical ages for marriage, had treated men and women alike, declaring any marriage involving any person under twenty-one void, unless contracted with the approval of parents or guardians, or in case of incompetent or unreasonable parents or guardians, the approval of Chancery.[90] Perhaps this also made it more likely that the age of twenty-one would be thought of in connection with marriage as the age of consent. Thus, it was difficult to promulgate a rule that female infants were bound while male infants were not.

Third, and most crucial of the problems that were not fully confronted, the nearly fatal weakening of the dower system in the eighteenth century made the legitimization of jointure on the grounds of contract or election increasingly spurious. There were, as we have seen, three kinds of jointure, each with a different rationale for its fairness. The fairness of prenuptial jointure on an adult as an absolute bar to dower was supposed to be guaranteed by contractual bargaining that occurred before the woman was subject to coverture. The fairness of prenuptial jointure on an infant was supposed to be guaranteed by a court-imposed "strict-scrutiny" which held such jointures to a higher level of "certainty" by requiring them to conform to statutorily imposed requirements like that of commencing presently on the death of the husband (though, as I have just said, these requirements no longer reflected what contemporaries thought were the most relevant measures of fairness.) In the case of postnuptial jointures or satisfaction by testamentary devise, treated as a special kind of postnuptial jointure, fairness was supposed to be ensured by the widow's right to elect dower or jointure.

If jointure is contracted for in the presence of a meaningful dower right or if jointure is elected instead of a meaningful dower right, then jointure may seem eminently fair. In eighteenth-century litigation, objections to unfairness were repeatedly met by appeals to the fairness of contract or election. But dower was a less and less meaningful alternative because it could be so easily barred and was, in fact, so often barred.

A brief but clear glimpse of this iron fist in the velvet glove of contract and election is afforded by Justice Wilmot's argument in *Buckinghamshire*. Taking what might be the most historically correct position, that any jointure at all made on an infant bars her of her dower (though, of course, the result of this was very different before and after the legal requirements of the Statute were eroded by equity), requiring not even that she or her guardian be a party to the settlement, he meets the objection that such a rule may cheat women by giving them very small jointures with the observation that every day estates are put in trust or purchased after marriage in ways that prevent dower "and, at the same time, preserve to the Husband an absolute dominion over the Estate"; "and therefore, all the Objection of prejudice to Infants, as the Law now stands, vanishes in a moment: for what detriment can it be to Infants to preclude them from Dower, by a small Estate, when they may be equally precluded from it without giving them any Estate at all?"[91]

What has vanished, in practice, although not in theory, is the communally enforced right to a third. Its persistence in theory actually serves to legitimate jointure, the bargain so private that the courts decline to inquire into the issue of whether or not an individual jointure or testamentary devise is a fair bargain or a competent maintenance. When Chancery's practice of approving (and sometimes even negotiating) marriage settlements for its own wards is recalled, judicial disclaimers of institutional competence to determine fair amounts of jointures appear to have strategic and ideological value. The woman's real protection is not the refusal of jointure for dower but the refusal of the offer of marriage with the individual man. As Justice Wilmot says, "This is a kind of Condition annexed by the Husband to the disposal of himself. If she takes him, she ought in justice to abide the terms on which she accepted him; She ought not to retain the benefit of the Contract, and then reject the Condition upon which the Husband entered into it."[92] But the extent of variation on the offers made by individual men is controlled only by the market. There is no publicly enforced forced share system to support women's claims. The absence of dower in practice transforms jointure from a simple substitution for dower or even a benefit secured under contract in exchange for valuable consideration, transforms it almost magically, into the husband's private, individual gift.

5

Pin Money and
Other Separate Property

Although there were major changes in the law of dower and jointure between 1660 and 1833, the basic concepts of dower and jointure were already familiar in the Renaissance. Both dower and jointure were intended to support the wife after the marriage had been terminated by the death of the husband. But what about provision or income for the wife during coverture, during what twentieth-century lawyers like to call "on-going marriage"? Normally, the law has taken relatively little notice of on-going marriage, in earlier times ceding the regulation of the household to the husband and in modern times deferring to the idea of a private domestic sphere with which it would be inappropriate for public law to meddle. At common law the husband did have a duty to maintain his wife, that is, to see that she received the necessities of food, clothing, shelter—and probably, if required, medicines and medical attention. Should a husband fail to provide such necessaries, a wife could—if she could find cooperative vendors— purchase the necessaries herself and charge them to her husband. Creditors were to recover against the husband and juries to decide whether the purchased items were or were not sufficiently necessary to bring them under this rule and make the husband liable. Necessaries for women of various classes were presumed to differ according to the class of the husband. Compared to the elaborate doctrines of dower and jointure, this doctrine of the husband's duty to support his wife had been developed in only a rudimentary way.

In the early modern period, however, marriage settlements introduced new areas of doctrine concerning married women's property during on-going marriage. As we have seen, jointures were normally settled on brides in marriage settlements. Less frequently, but still quite often, the settlements also provided for separate income for the wife during the marriage itself. This income was popularly called pin money. In the fifth act of Vanbrugh's comedy *The Relapse* (1696), Miss Hoyden, the simpleminded daughter of an almost equally simple-minded country gentleman, eagerly anticipates her approaching marriage to Lord Foppington and all the concomitant delights of fashionable London life. Attempting to rebut some of her old nurse's doubts about the marital happiness to be expected with fashionable lords, who have been known to give their money "to their sluts and their trulls" instead of to their wives, Miss Hoyden declares that Lord Foppington, at least, is "as free as an open house at Christmas": "For this very morning he told me I should have two hundred a year to buy pins. Now, nurse, if he gives me two hundred a year to buy pins, what do you think he will give me to buy fine petticoats?" The nurse enlightens her: "Ah, my dearest, he deceives thee faully, and he's no better than a rogue for his pains. These Londoners have got a gibberidge with 'em, would confound a gipsy. That which they call pin-money is to buy their wives every thing in the varsal world, down to their very shoeties: nay, I have heard folks say that some ladies, if they will have gallants, as they call 'um, are forced to find them out of their pin-money too."[1] As the nurse suggests, pin money was paid by husbands to wives, so much per year, and was supposed to be spent on clothes, amusements, charities, and such other out-of-pocket expenses as a wife incurred—not, of course, including the maintenance of a lover. In 1696 even a girl more worldly-wise than Miss Hoyden might have found "pin money" a puzzling term, since it seems to have been a relatively new social phenomenon in the late Restoration and early eighteenth century.[2]

Although the term was used more loosely, for my purposes, it will be convenient to define pin money as payments under a contract by a husband to a wife during coverture of a set annual sum. Often the contract was the marriage settlement, but some-

times husbands entered into other pre- and postnuptial agreements to pay pin money. Richard Brinsley Sheridan in *The School for Scandal* (1777) realistically enough makes Sir Peter Teazle's failure to settle any pin money or separate estate on Lady Teazle a bone of contention between them; then, in the famous screen scene of the fourth act, he has Sir Peter appear with the drafts of two deeds, one giving Lady Teazle property after his death, the other giving her "eight hundred a year independent" while he lives.[3]

Pin money was thus one species of married women's separate property, that is, one species of property that women could be said to own despite the coverture which under common law made the wife's property belong to her husband. In the eighteenth-century lawyer's mind, the paradigmatic form of married women's separate property was the wife's separate estate put in trust for her at the time of the prenuptial marriage settlement, an estate which the wife was to possess "for her sole and separate use," not subject to the control of her husband and not available to her husband's creditors. One aim in creating the married women's separate estate was to increase the security of the wife and the minor children should her husband prove feckless or unlucky. Another was to secure some of the wife's father's property for his grandchildren without risking its being swallowed up in the husband's estate; thus, the wife's separate estate was likely to be settled on her for life with remainders to the children of her body. Most lawyers preferred to have the property which was to be the wife's separate estate conveyed to trustees "for her use," apparently both because they supposed male trustees would manage it better and because the contract could then be thought of as between the husband and the trustees with the wife as a sort of third-party beneficiary, thus softening the common law objection to contracts between husbands and wives. But by 1725 in *Bennet v. Davis* the courts had permitted a wife to possess separate property without trustees.[4] In the early nineteenth century an attempt was made to distinguish pin money clearly from the married woman's separate estate; unfortunately, though a clear distinction would make my exposition here easier, no such distinction was made in the eighteenth century.

The eighteenth-century idea of pin money, while in some ways simple enough, was, in other ways, almost hopelessly tortuous and contradictory. On the one hand, pin money reflected a tendency to construe marriage as contractual and imported into the matrimonial relationship elements of the eighteenth-century ideology of contract. On the other hand, neither the legal establishment nor society generally was prepared to see all the traditional status incidents of marriage become the subjects of purely private negotiation, to allow those rights and duties of the matrimonial relationship thought to be fundamental to social order to be bargained over as individual whim might dictate. The husband's obligation to support his wife and to provide her with necessaries was a crucial status incident of marriage. Insofar as pin money was supposed to contribute to the wife's maintenance, it was by no means clear that a contract for the performance of what was, prior to the contract, a common law duty could have any validity. Moreover, time was required to work through the consequences of construing either marriage or marriage settlements as contractual, and what seemed to be logical corollaries of this construction sometimes proved disturbing. As we have seen in the doctrine of jointures, when jointures were seen as sufficiently contractual to make jointures made on minors voidable, then the idea of jointure as contractual was rebutted with assertions that jointure was simply a provision for the wife.

Throughout the eighteenth century the legal system had two general problems with women and property which I will venture to state here with brutal simplicity. New forms of women's property had supposedly been created in part to provide greater security for women and children, forms of property secured by contract, and consequently to assure that one man's women and children did not become public charges to other men. But the first general problem was that these new forms of property, under contract logic, did not seem to provide the social control over women that had been part of the customary and other earlier systems of maintaining women and children. For example, under some customary tenures a widow's free bench was forfeited by her unchastity, and under the Statute of Westminster the Second (1285) dower was forfeited by elopement and adultery, but a widow's jointure in the eighteenth century was secured by contract and so not subject to forfeit for sexual misconduct. The second general problem was that, although according to liberal political theory a wife who had separate property legally secured to her ought to have gained power and although male contemporaries certainly complained enough that married women with separate property were entirely too powerful and too independent, it frequently happened that, despite separate property being secured to them, women were unwilling or unable even to hang on to it, being, as contemporaries said, "kissed or kicked," "bullied or coaxed" out of it by husbands who had physical or emotional power that rendered their wives' legal powers nugatory.

The history of the legal thought concerning pin money from about 1690 to 1834 shows how judges responded to these two perceived problems by developing a set of special rules to maximize the probabilities that married women's separate property would provide secure maintenance for the women and children upon whom it was settled and to minimize the possibilities that women could take property intended for maintenance and use it as capital. In order to do this, it was necessary to develop different rules for women's property and for men's property, and to have idiosyncratic protective rules that restricted the powers attendant upon ownership when the owners were married women. Some of the earliest late seventeenth- and very early eighteenth-century cases involving pin money express doubt that a husband's agreement to pay his wife can have legal consequence.[5] In the eighteenth century, however, the validity of these contracts was recognized, and the consequences of treating pin money as a contract debt were developed—up to a point. From the Restoration through the early nineteenth century, as we shall see, the history of pin money reflects a variety of contradictions. First, pin money was construed as a contract debt, but judges developed an idiosyncratic rule of no arrears beyond a year, based on the assumption that if the husband and wife cohabited, the husband had maintained the wife. Second, the actual purposes of paying pin money could not be fully acknowledged either in official discourse or in legal theory, and this contributed substantially to the incoherence of the legal theory. Third, pin money came to the wife as cash payments which were her separate property, but if she bought certain things other than clothes with that money, she might discover that the traditional law of baron and feme had gone into effect and that the things she had bought either were subject to rules different from those normally governing married women's separate property or had become her husband's property. Fourth, marriage settlements frequently gave the wife a fund "for such uses and purposes as she shall direct or appoint," which might seem to imply that the wife could do anything she wished with the fund, but when experience showed that some wives elected to mortgage or alienate the capital, to "sink the fund," as contemporaries said, ways were found to prohibit such alienation.

Conveyancing Practice

Although I shall be concerned principally with the development of the legal theory of pin money from about 1690 to 1834, it will make the subsequent discussion of cases easier to follow and may be of use to historians and biographers who encounter such documents among family papers first to consider briefly the forms in which agreements to pay pin money were usually made. It was usual to settle some property as the capital fund which was to support the annual payments. The property so settled might be land or it might be in another form, long leases or stock or consols, for instance. In the forms of conveyances most approved by lawyers, the capital fund was conveyed to trustees who became responsible for managing the fund and paying the wife, customarily in quarterly installments. A marriage settlement or other instrument (for example, a bond) might make it clear either that an annual sum was denominated "pin money" or that an annual sum was to be spent for such items as the wife's clothes. Other agreements, it is important to realize, made provisions for similar payments without denominating them "pin money" or specifying the purposes for which expenditures from the fund were to be made.

Gilbert Horsman's *Precedents in Conveyancing* prints a sample marriage settlement, dated 1729, providing for a jointure and also for pin money. In this particular settlement the bride has brought a portion of £6,000 and is to have a jointure from lands the yearly value of which is £500 "or thereabouts"; the pin money payments are to be £120 a year in the first three years of the marriage and £250 a year thereafter (glosses mine):

And this Indenture further witnesseth, that in Consideration of the said intended Marriage and Marriage Portion, and of the great Love and Affection which he the said *Aaron Assley* hath and beareth unto the said *Frances Eave* his intended Wife, and, the sum of 10s. . . . to him in Hand paid by the said *Charles Castor* and *Daniel Darby,* at and before the Ensealing and Delivery of these Presents, the Receipt whereof is hereby acknowledged, he the said *Aaron Assley,* hath granted, bargained, sold and demised, and by these Presents doth grant, bargain, sell and demise unto the said *Charles Castor* and *Daniel Darby,* their Executors, Administrators and Assigns, all and every the said Messuages, Farms, Lands, Tenements, Tithes, Hereditaments and Premisses herein before granted, settled, limited and appointed, unto and upon the said *Frances Eave* for her Life, for her Jointure as aforesaid, with their and every of their Appurtenances, and the Reversion and Reversions, Remainder and Remainders, yearly and other Rents, Issues and Profits thereof, and of every Part and Parcel thereof; To have and to hold the said Messuages, Farms, Lands, Tenements, Tithes, Hereditaments . . . unto the said *Charles Castor* and *Daniel Darby,* their Executors, Administrators and Assigns, from the Day next before the Day of the Date of these Presents, for and during the full Time and Term, and unto the full End and Term of ninety-nine Years from thence next ensuing, and fully to be compleat and ended, if they the said *Aaron Assley* and *Frances* his intended Wife shall both of them so long jointly live, upon the Trusts, and to and for the Intents and Purposes, and under and subject to the Provision and Agreements herein after mentioned, expressed and declared of and concerning the

the groom, *A.A.,* sells specific land, described earlier in the settlement, to the trustees, *C.C.* and *D.D.,* for the nominal sum of 10s.

the trustees to hold the land to the use of the wife (i.e., in trust for the wife, to be a capital fund from which will issue her jointure payments after her husband's death)

raises a 99-year trust term on the same land for the same trustees to pay pin money to the wife during the coverture, i.e., these payments to be made only during the joint lives of the husband and wife same Term, (that is to say) . . . upon Trust, and to the Intent and Purpose, that they the said *Charles Castor* and *Daniel Darby,* and the Survivor of them, his Executors, Administrators and Assigns, shall and do yearly and every Year, by and out of the Rents, Issues and Profits of the said Messauges, Farms, Lands, Tenements, Tithes, Hereditaments and Premises so demised . . . pay, or cause to be paid by four equal quarterly Payments, on the four most usual Feasts or Days of Payment in the Year (that is to say) the Feasts of the Birth of our Lord *Christ,* the Annunciation of the blessed Virgin *Mary,* the Nativity of Saint *John* Baptist, and Saint *Michael* the Archangel, by even and equal Portions, free of all Taxes and Deductions whatsoever, the several yearly Sums of Money, . . . the

trustees to pay out of rents and profits from this land, annually, in quarterly installments, payable on days stipulated

yearly Sum of 120 l . . . until the Feast-day of Saint *Michael* the Archangel which shall be in the Year of our Lord 1732, (if they the said *Aaron Assley* and *Frances* his intended Wife shall both of them so long jointly live) and then and from thenceforth, and from and after the said Feast-day of Saint *Michael* the Archangel 1732 the yearly Sum of 250 l . . . , for and during the Joint Lives of them the said *Aaron Assley* and *Frances* his intended Wife; both the said yearly Sums to be paid unto the proper Hands of her the said *Frances Eave,* or to such Person or Persons, and for such Uses and Purposes as she, without the said *Aaron Assley,* by any Note or Writing under her Hand, shall from Time to Time, notwithstanding her Coverture, direct or appoint; the same to be for her own sole and separate Use and Benefit, exclusive of the said *Aaron Assley,* and not to be liable or subject to his Controul, Debts or Incumbrances, but to be disposed of by her for her Cloaths, and such other Uses and

£120 a year until St. Michael's Day in 1733, and £250 a year thereafter

pin money not subject to the husband's control or liable for his debts

Purposes as she shall think fit; and her Receipt, or the Receipts of the Person or Persons to whom she shall appoint the said Monies to be paid as aforesaid, under her or their respective Hand or Hands, shall from Time to Time, notwithstanding her Coverture, be sufficient Discharges to the Person or Persons who shall so pay the same, for so much of the said several yearly Sums for which such Receipts shall be given.[6]

only the wife's receipts or the receipts of her assignee to be a discharge of the trustees' obligation to pay the pin money

The somewhat casual status of the term "pin money" is indicated, for example, by Horsman's describing one precedent as containing a "term for pin money" in the table of contents, then printing a text which speaks only of raising a term for ninety-nine years for the wife, describing this in the marginal gloss as a sum "for her separate use."[7] Most settlements and similar documents providing payments under a contract by a husband to a wife of a set annual sum—as I have defined pin money here—probably did not use the term "pin money" or even a descriptive phrase like "for her Cloaths" in the body of the document, and many probably did not use the term or descriptive phrase in a title on the document either. Such practices caused difficulty for the courts at the beginning of the nineteenth century, when an attempt was made to develop different rules for "pin money" and for "the wife's separate estate." Moreover, not every agreement was so well drawn as Horsman's sample precedents. Since all these agreements were private contracts, in practice they could be drawn in an infinite variety of ways, with or without trustees, and with the payments dependent upon more or less well-secured capital funds, or, indeed, not secured by any fund.

Rules by Analogy to Men's Property versus Idiosyncratic Rules

Once these agreements were drawn, it remained to be seen what legal effect the courts would give them. Since married women's separate property was a new species of property, basic questions arose of whether or to what extent it should be treated by analogy to men's property or, alternatively, whether idiosyncratic rules were required for it alone. These questions, of course, occurred in the context of a system of property law where there were special rules for many categories of property. On the one hand, cases could be decided by simple analogy, the property constituting a married woman's separate estate being treated as though she acquired it by contract and as though it were the property of a man or a feme sole. For example, in *Milles v. Wikes* (1694) it was said that a woman who "by Management or good House-wifry" saved money out of her pin money or separate maintenance allowance might "dispose of such Money so saved by her or of any Jewels bought with it" by "Writing in Nature of a Will" if she died before her husband or, if her husband predeceased her, might retain such savings against her husband's creditors or heirs.[8] On the other hand, cases could be decided by emphasizing the peculiar status of married women's separate property as a "creature of equity" and stressing its ostensible special purposes, including the maintenance of wives and children and the preservation of some property for children no matter what the financial fate of the husband. This peculiar status and these special purposes were invoked to justify the development of special rules.

Questions naturally arose as to what would happen should a wife entitled to payments under a marriage settlement leave her husband and live in adultery with another man. Should she be treated like any other contract debtor who was entitled to his money no matter what her personal morality? (Agreements to pay pin money almost never stipulated for good behavior.) Or should either the analogy to dower—forfeit for elopement and adultery— or social policy arguments be invoked to deny her payment? At first the analogy to dower and social policy prevailed, but by the 1730s these arguments tended to be displaced by contract logic. Thus, in an early case, trustees were not permitted to recover pin money for a wife who eloped and lived in adultery: "for *Pin-Money was never designed to make Women independant of their Husbands,* and *support them in Vice.* But if *she left him by ill Usage,* or other reasonable Grounds, or the *Husband acquiesced in her Departure,* Equity won't interpose."[9] In 1734, however, Lord Chancellor Talbot in *Sidney v. Sidney* decreed specific performance of marriage articles providing for jointure and pin money, despite the husband's contention that his wife had eloped with an adulterer and that he, as presumptive heir to a peerage, particularly dreaded the introduction of a bastard as his heir.[10]

Among the earlier pin money cases decided by the invocation of contract logic and by analogy to men's property was *Moore v. Moore* (1737).[11] The marriage settlement of 1707 between Sir Richard Francis Moore and his wife put certain land in trust for a term of ninety-nine years to secure £100 out of the rents payable to Lady Moore for her separate use. In 1728, "some differences and disputes arising between the husband and wife," Lady Moore went to live in France and subsequently sued Sir Richard for several years' arrears of the payments of her allowance. Sir Richard's counsel argued that the wife's behavior should forfeit her entitlement and, moreover, "that this allowance was only to promote harmony between the plaintiff and the defendant, and to enable her to do acts of bounty in her family, therefore, when the reason for it ceases, the allowance ought to cease likewise." Lord Chancellor Hardwicke rejected both the husband's social policy arguments and his offer to take his wife back instead of paying her, finding for the wife on the explicit language of the contract, which gave her property and the allowance and was silent about forfeiture for elopement. Similarly, in *Blount v. Winter* (1781), specific performance of marriage articles was decreed on a contract logic despite the husband's proof that his wife was living apart from him in adultery.[12]

Idiosyncratic rules for married women's separate property, on the contrary, were derived in part from analysis of the purposes the property was intended to serve and are, consequently, revelatory of those purposes. The most important idiosyncratic rule developed in the pin money cases is that arrears of pin money were not to be paid beyond one year. Normally, of course, contract creditors could sue for their debts under a contract over the full term of the contract. In *Powell v. Hankey and Cox* (1722), a case of a widow suing her husband's executors for the arrears of her pin money, Lord Chancellor Macclesfield determined to construe the wife's not having demanded the pin money "for several years together" as her consent that her husband "should receive it."[13] He invoked three ideas to justify this construction. First, he said that since married women's separate property is "against common right," "all reasonable intendments and presumptions were to be admitted against the wife." Second, he invoked a social policy argument that sudden demands for many years' arrears of pin money might ruin husbands, or, if the husband were dead, cause substantial injury to his heirs. Third, he assumed that the wife, living with her husband, had in any case shared in the enjoyment of her presumed gift of the pin money to him. Rejecting the wife's contention that she had feared to press for payment during her husband's life "by reason of the husband's passionate temper," the Lord Chancellor replied that she might have applied to her trustees, "whom she must be supposed to have had a confidence in, as persons who would have protected her against any resentment of her husband, had there been occasion." Despite the conventionality of clauses like the one in the Horsman settlement I quoted earlier, which stated that only the wife's receipts or the receipts of her assigns were to be discharges of the trustees' obligation to pay pin money, the rule in *Powell* implying the wife's consent that the husband should receive her money was regularly applied in subsequent cases in the obvious absence of any such receipts. Under special circumstances, this presumption of the wife's consent to make her husband a gift of the arrears of her pin money could be rebutted, as, for example, in *Ridout v. Lewis* (1738), in which a widow succeeded in collecting the arrears of her pin money from her husband's executors because he had made partial payments, explicitly referred to as such, and had accompanied these partial payments with promises to pay the rest later.[14]

This rule of no arrears beyond one year meant that a wife whose husband did not pay her by the usual quarterly dates would normally have had to sue him at least each year for the debt or lose her entitlement; if she sued him and he lacked the will or the resources to pay her, she would also have to have been prepared to see him imprisoned for failure to pay. It is hard to imagine that a gentlewoman who had had her husband imprisoned for failure to pay her pin money would have been warmly received in polite society. Joseph Addison, for one, satirizes the idea of a wife's presuming to insist on her entitlement to payment. He has a presumably fictitious correspondent in the *Spectator,* Josiah Fribble, complain that his pin money payments have furthered his wife's adultery and the birth of children to her not his own. When he asks her to permit him to use the pin money to make provision for these children, "This Proposal makes her noble Blood swell in her Veins, insomuch that finding me a little tardy in her last Quarter's Payment, she threatens me every Day to arrest me; and proceeds so far as to tell me, that if I do not do her Justice, I shall die in a Jayl."[15]

There has been a long and not entirely unreasonable prejudice against interspousal suits in either contract or tort. Relations within the family are said to be too intimate to be made the subject of contract. In contract, there is the idea that "within the closely-knit family demands for a contractual spelling out of obligations will seem to imply an inappropriate distrust."[16] Moreover, relations, rights, and obligations within the family—the wife's obligation to provide her husband with service and consortium, for instance—are to a considerable extent already determined by law in ways which contract is not permitted to alter. Judges have also disliked invading the supposedly private sphere of the family and are likely to despair of successful fact finding there. Furthermore, if spouses are going to continue living together after the suit, success for one and defeat for the other has been thought likely to poison the matrimonial relationship. Indeed, when only very recently interspousal tort suits have been allowed, the old rule has been abandoned partly on the ground that many tort claims are now actually against insurance companies, so that one spouse who injures another by his act or negligence could ordinarily be presumed to be relieved and happy to see insurance pay for the injury.[17] In contract, anxieties similar to those in tort made judges worry that they might have to listen to litigation about private trivia, to decide, for instance, a question of whether a husband was entitled to make a deduction from his wife's allowance if she spent an afternoon "visiting her mother, instead of making jellies."[18] This general prejudice against interspousal suits certainly affected the results in pin money, the courts finding it more bearable to inquire into recent events within a family than to try to uncover more remote and more tangled family history.

Contradictory Purposes of Pin Money

The establishment of the rule in *Powell* raised a fundamental problem concerning the nature of pin money: was pin money for the ordinary maintenance of the wife or was it for expenses other than ordinary maintenance? To justify the rule of no arrears beyond a year as a special case of laches grounded on hostility to interspousal suits and on fear of the disruptiveness of claims for large lump sums when smaller periodic payments had been intended is at least intelligible, though the interval of one year is startlingly short. However, to justify the rule by assuming that as long as the wife has lived with her husband she has shared in the enjoyment of her presumed gift is trickier because this strand of the argument comes perilously close to assuming that pin money is for the wife's maintenance and that if she has lived with her husband she has been maintained. In *Thomas v. Bennet* (1725), shortly after *Powell,* where the executors of a wife demanded ten years' arrears of her pin money and there was no proof that she had demanded it herself, the court ruled that if the husband and the wife cohabited and the husband maintained the wife, then arrears of pin money were not recoverable.[19] In *Moore,* after both *Powell* and *Thomas,* where the spouses were living apart and the husband not maintaining the wife, the court did not invoke its no-arrears rule.

When we ask the question of whether pin money was for maintenance, then, I believe, we confront the problem that the actual social purposes of paying pin money were not and could not be fully acknowledged either in official discourse or in legal theory. The actual social purposes of paying pin money are probably fairly described by saying that—beyond the general purposes of creating the wife's separate estate, which I mentioned earlier—pin money was normally paid for partial maintenance (clothes and tips to servants, but not food or house rent), for some extras above maintenance (though upper-class women were entitled to some frills as maintenance), and for "insurance" for the wife should the husband prove so stingy as to be unwilling to support her at an appropriate level, should the husband lose his assets, or should the marriage prove so unhappy that the couple separated.

Let us consider the partial maintenance function. That partial maintenance was one intention is suggested not only by explicit provisions for clothes in some settlements and by the general understanding that clothes were to be bought with pin money, but also by the fact that the annual sums specified for pin money, usually enough to outfit the woman appropriately, were commonly although not invariably less than the annual sums specified for jointure for the same woman, the woman often having to provide housing and food as well as clothes out of her jointure money.

The Horsman settlement giving £120 to £250 for pin money and £500 for jointure is a good example. Lord Chancellor Brougham, after consulting his own experience and that of other peers, reported: "It is . . . clear that no nobleman or person of however high and honourable degree, being in ever so wealthy circumstances, would ever dream of making an allowance to his wife for pin-money, if he were at the same time to be paying all her bills year after year, her milliner's bills and others, over and above her pin-money."[20]

With respect to the insurance function of pin money, in theory the wife should not have needed such insurance unless her husband lost his assets, in which case her separate property would then be shielded from his creditors. At common law, as already noted, her remedy against a stingy or cruel husband was simply to charge her purchases of the necessaries appropriate to her rank, leaving merchants to recover from her husband, who had a duty to provide his wife with necessaries. But there seems to have been some appreciable practical gap between a wife's common law right to such necessaries and a wife's ability to obtain credit for them. Moreover, the wife lost her right to the husband's support if she left him without what the courts considered sufficient legal justification. There was, therefore, an impulse to offer secure support to the wife by the method of pin money. Addison reported that women had defended pin money to him as "a necessary Provision they make for themselves, in case their Husband proves a Churl or a Miser; so they consider this Allowance as a kind of Alimony, which they may lay their Claim to, without actually separating from their Husbands."[21] Such motives, I suspect, were even more likely to inspire fathers of brides than young brides themselves. Lord Hardwicke observed, "possibly this agreement before marriage might be designed to provide for the wife, if such dissention should happen between the parties, as would be a just inducement for them to separate, though their quarrels should be of such a nature as are not proper to be laid before a court."[22]

Although contemporaries paid pin money with these intentions of partial maintenance and insurance in mind, to justify either of these intentions in terms of legal theory posed significant difficulties. If pin money is to be understood as intended for maintenance and if the husband's maintenance of the wife is to bar claims for arrears, then it would seem that the husband has contracted to perform what was in any case his legal obligation to maintain his wife, an obligation which existed independent of any marriage settlement, and thus, that agreements to pay pin money were invalid in the first place. In other words, the husband could be seen as attempting to make one of the status incidents of marriage the subject of contract, which has traditionally been impermissible. Given the support/service reciprocity which is supposed to constitute the marriage relationship (the husband's obligation to support the wife and the wife's obligation to provide him with service), a husband's attempt to make his obligation to support or maintain his wife the subject of contract should be like a wife's attempt to make her obligation to provide her husband with service the subject of contract—which has been repeatedly disallowed.[23] To say that partial rather than full maintenance was intended would not improve the situation because contracts for partial maintenance are still contracts for maintenance.

As for insurance, to admit openly that that was a function of pin money not only seemed to denigrate the effectiveness of the wife's common law right to necessaries, but, what was worse, looked like approving a contract for future separation. As we shall see in Chapter 6, as separate maintenance contracts grew more common, there was increasing temptation to plan ahead and to provide in prenuptial agreements for possible future separations, but eighteenth-century judges disliked doing anything to facilitate separations, and these agreements for future separations were eventually found to be void as against public policy.[24] Even in *Moore,* where Lord Hardwicke at one point referred to the wife's allowance secured by the marriage settlement as a "separate maintenance," he also insisted, "These separate maintenances are not to incourage a wife to leave her husband, whatever his behaviour may be; for, was this the construction, it would destroy the very end of the marriage contract, and be a public detriment."[25] Only if the agreement to pay pin money was understood as an agreement to pay for expenses "above and beyond the call of duty" or for extra "frills and furbelows" would it seem to have constituted a valid agreement. But the social reality was, as the sums contracted for suggest and as Lord Brougham's statement indicates, that men did not bind themselves to pay merely for extras. During the eighteenth century these contradictions about the purposes of pin money were not squarely faced or resolved, and this theoretical problem remained, as we shall see, to erupt in a spectacular early nineteenth-century case involving the executors of the Duke and Duchess of Norfolk.

Categories of Women's Property

In addition to the anomalies of the no-arrears rule and the difficulties of reconciling the social purposes of paying pin money with any legal justification of those purposes, another kind of problem arose over what might be described as the "categories" of women's property. To what extent were various kinds of chattel or real property bought with pin money or with the savings from or interest on pin money to be considered as falling into the category of pin money and thus as "owned" by the wife? In the simple world of a medieval village, a husband might maintain his wife by letting her lie in his bed under his roof, eat the produce of his land, and clothe herself with wool from his sheep or cloth made from his flax. But an eighteenth-century wife's pin money came in the form of cash, and cash could be spent to acquire property in any form. Clearly a wife could buy a dress with her pin money, but was she equally entitled to buy bank stock or to save her pin money and buy a cottage? (After all, it might not take a frugal woman who was getting £300 a year very long to save enough to buy a cottage.) If she did buy bank stock or a cottage, what rules should be applied to her property? Was the new property as much hers as the pin money had been or was pin money more or less like the later "household allowance" in the sense that any savings from it and any property bought with it *"prima facie* remained the husband's property"?[26]

It is probably true that at the deepest level the development of the legal theory of pin money in the eighteenth century was confused by a conflict between, on the one hand, the older sense of the naturalness of having particular rules pertaining to the ownership of particular kinds of things (for example, forests or a wife's clothes) and, on the other hand, the development of a more modern, general, abstract category of "property" and stress on alienability or the right to exchange one kind of property for another as the fundamental sign of ownership. Older rules tend to provide for the appropriate present enjoyment of a particular kind of thing according to its "nature" rather than to allow for the exercise of individual will to determine the future use of the thing or to exchange it for another kind of thing. Thus, in the fourteenth century a tenant of a forest could cut branches to repair his house but he could not turn the forest into a meadow for grazing without incurring penalties for waste; in the fourteenth century, also, the "owner" of land could not make a will determining how that land should descend.[27]

In the realm of married women's property, there is the old category, paraphernalia, describing a particular kind of thing, namely, the wife's clothes and personal ornaments (such as jewels). Such things are appropriately usable by a woman and not by a man and are "owned" by the wife in a particular sense. Pollock and Maitland observe that "very ancient Germanic law knows special rules for the transmission of female attire; it passes from female to female."[28] At common law, while the wife's paraphernalia may be alienated by the husband during coverture (as her other chattels may), the husband cannot bequeath them to another, and, if he predeceases her, unlike her other chattels, which go to his representatives, her paraphernalia goes to her, subject to rights of his creditors. Although in the thirteenth century some wives made wills disposing of their own clothes and ornaments, it later came to be common law that a wife could only devise her paraphernalia with the consent of her husband; if she predeceased her husband without having secured his consent to a testamentary devise, her paraphernalia were his. Thus, questions arose as to whether paraphernalia-like objects bought with pin money should be treated according to paraphernalia rules.

Some settlements gave the wife explicit testamentary power over her separate property, and some cases suggest that a wife was to be considered as the absolute owner of the savings or other proceeds of her pin money. In *Milles v. Wikes* (1694), we recall, it was decided that the wife could devise the savings from her pin money if she predeceased her husband or alienate them if she survived. Similarly, in *Gore v. Knight* (1705), equity ruled that if a wife had reserved the power of disposing of her separate estate, "all that she dies possessed of is to be taken to be her separate Estate, or the produce of it, unless the contrary can be made appear, and as she has a Power over the Principal, so she may dispose of the Produce or Interest."[29] Also, in *Wilson v. Pack* (1710), it was decided that "where the Wife has a *separate* Allowance *made before marriage,* and *buys Jewels with the Money* arising thereout, *they will not be Assets liable to the Husband's Debts.*"[30] Results like these weaken the contention that pin money was for current maintenance.

However, in *Peacock v. Monk* (1750–51) Mrs. Lestock, an admiral's wife, having a prenuptial agreement providing for pin money and giving her the right to devise her own real estate, used some of her money to buy a house. She devised this real estate to a person of her choice and died. After her death and her husband's death a dispute arose over whether this house should go to her heir or to her devisee. The court decided that while the prenuptial agreement permitted her to devise property specified in that agreement, the husband's "bare agreement" concerning real estate she acquired after the marriage could not deprive the heir of his rights: "For though in respect of the husband, money to be laid out in land will be considered as part of her separate estate, yet it is going a great way to say, that it shall be considered as personal [that is, as personal property] as between her heir and executor; for she having made it realty, this court would say, it was in that manner [that is, it was real property, not personal property]; and she has purchased it so as to go to the heir."[31] In other words, by turning what was personal property into real estate, Mrs. Lestock had lost her right to devise it. A similar case, discussed in *Peacock,* in which a married woman with real estate to her separate use was found not to have the power to devise it, was said to have provoked "a good deal of discourse"; "it seeming extraordinary that she should not have this [the power to devise] in equity as incident to her ownership" and that she "should not be in equity considered as the absolute owner of it."

These results might seem extraordinary if one thinks in terms of a certain modern idea of "absolute ownership," but the more traditionally minded might find it equally extraordinary that in *Milles* the wife could treat jewels—paraphernalia—bought with her pin money as though she were the absolute owner of them. Logic would seem to decree that to make *Milles* and *Peacock* symmetrical, the court in *Milles* should have said of the wife, "she having made her pin money paraphernalia, the court would say that it was paraphernalia, not her separate estate, and she has purchased it so as to go to her husband's creditors." Indeed, in *Lady Tyrrell's Case* (1674), where Lady Tyrrell said she had bought jewels with her pin money and attempted to retain them as her paraphernalia, Lord Keeper Finch ruled that they must go to her husband's creditors:

> As to the point of buying them with her own money, that should make no difference, so long as the husband and wife do cohabit; for if the wife out of her good housewifery do save any thing out of it; this will be the husband's estate, and he shall reap the benefit of his wife's frugality; and he said, the reason of it is, because when the husband agrees to allow his wife a certain sum yearly, the end of this agreement is, that she may be provided with clothes and other necessaries, and what soever is saved out of this redounds to the husband.[32]

One can only speculate as to why symmetrical results were not reached in *Milles* and *Peacock;* it is unlikely that equity felt significantly more concern for heirs than for creditors, but it is quite possible that equity was inclined to be more conservative with respect to real property than with respect to chattel property.

The rule of no arrears beyond a year from *Powell* and a result like that in *Peacock,* which resists the conversion of pin money into real property, helps to maximize the probabilities that such property would provide maintenance for the woman upon whom it was settled and to minimize the possibilities that women could take property intended for maintenance and use it as capital. An additional key issue was whether a wife could alienate the capital fund, or a substantial part of the capital fund, from which her yearly payments were to come. In the usual language of the settlements the wife was to have her money, in the words of the Horseman settlement quoted earlier, "for such Uses and Purposes as she . . . shall from Time to Time, notwithstanding her Coverture, direct or appoint . . . for her own sole and separate Use and Benefit, exclusive of [her husband], and not to be liable or subject to his Controul, Debts or Incumbrances." But suppose the use the wife wished to appoint was to pledge her entire interest in the fund as security for a large loan to herself for some present expenditure? Or suppose, though the separate estate was established as not subject to her husband's control or debts, she wished to make him a gift of it? It was natural enough that some wives would wish to use their assets to advance their husbands in their careers or businesses, like the wife in *Tate v. Austin* (1714), who raised

£400 out of her separate estate to equip her husband as an officer in the army.[33]

But for a wife to "sink the fund" from which her maintenance was to come defeated her father's attempt to provide her and her children with a kind of insurance against her husband's fecklessness or ill luck and, moreover, tempted greedy or unscrupulous husbands to coerce wives to make such gifts. As one contemporary song recommended to a man with a troublesome wife possessed of a "separate Fortune" which she refused to pay him, she might be locked up alone in a room:

> There a while let her dance,
> Without cordial or Nantz,
>   Til sober and penitent grown,
> She submits to your Will,
> Consent, Sign, and Seal,
>   And make all her Fortune you're own.[34]

Eighteenth-century novelists depict similar scenes of domestic coercion. In Fielding's *Tom Jones,* for example, Mr. Fitzpatrick has mortgaged his estate to the hilt and spent all the ready money that came to him with his wife. He first tries behaving more fondly toward her to induce her to sign over the remaining estate, which is her separate property. But she refuses, and according to her version of the story: "I told him, and I told him truly, that had I been possessed of the *Indies* at our first Marriage, he might have commanded it all: For it had been a constant Maxim with me, that where a Woman disposes of her Heart, she should always deposite her Fortune; but as he had been so kind, long ago, to restore the former into my Possession, I was resolved, likewise, to retain what little remained of the latter." After much quarreling, he finally confines her to her room, depriving her of writing and reading materials, allowing her to see no one but the servant who brings her food, and declares she will never be let out until she agrees to make over her separate property to him.[35] A wife, as we have seen, could only convey away her dower by a fine and with a separate examination, but she could convey both jointure and her separate estate more easily and without separate examination.

A number of eighteenth-century cases contain rather sweeping dicta that a married woman is to be considered as a feme sole with respect to her separate estate, thus implying that she is free to "sink the fund." For example, in *Grigby v. Cox* (1750) a wife sold part of her separate estate, then complained that she had executed the deeds "by compulsion of her husband, and for fear of losing her life if she refused," and that her trustees should have been consulted. Lord Chancellor Hardwicke ruled in favor of the purchaser and said, "the rule of the court is, that where any thing is settled to the wife's separate use, she is considered as a feme sole; may appoint in what manner she pleases; and unless the joining of her trustees with her is made necessary [which would have been uncommon], there is no occasion for that."[36] In *Fettiplace v. Gorges* (1789), Sophia Charlotte Fettiplace during her life had been entitled to £200 pin money a year, had after marriage acquired £1,000 in bank annuities as separate property bequeathed to her by an aunt, and with savings and gifts had had £1,900 in consols purchased for her separate estate with a female relative as trustee. Sophia Charlotte bequeathed all her personal estate to her niece, who was sued by Mr. Fettiplace on the ground that he had never assented to his wife's having such separate property and that, therefore, it belonged to him. Lord Chancellor Thurlow found for the niece, declaring, "All the cases shew that the personal property, where it can be enjoyed separately, must be so with all its incidents, and the *jus disponendi* is one of them."[37] In *Pybus v. Smith* (1791), Thomas Vernon, a trader, eloped to Scotland with a ward of Chancery, married her, then agreed to a postnuptial settlement giving her separate property. Shortly after the marriage, he persuaded her to pledge this property as security for his debts, then went bankrupt three years later. Despite some apparent temptation to find that the words "from Time to Time" in the settlement prohibited an appointment of the capital fund, Lord Chancellor Thurlow felt compelled to rule in favor of the husband's creditors, on the principle that "a *feme covert* had been considered by the Court, with respect to her separate property, as a *feme sole.*"[38]

But by the end of the eighteenth century, allowing married women such powers of alienation with respect to their separate estates was found to be intolerable. Some earlier cases offered support to this effort, for example, *Caverley v. Dudley and Bisco* (1747), in which Lord Hardwicke decided Lady Dudley's purchase of an annuity from her separate estate was "too large an anticipation," and gave her leave to redeem what was supposed to have been an irredeemable annuity.[39] Great frustration was expressed over *Pybus v. Smith,* and very late eighteenth-century cases contain lamentations that wives have the power to defeat provisions intended for their protection. For instance, in *Whistler v. Newman* (1798), Lord Loughborough was confronted with a wife who had had £1,300 in bank annuities settled on her, had then sold them after marriage to provide her husband with capital for his trade, and then, when her husband died insolvent, was left a widow with six children to support. Mrs. Whistler, he observed, "was prevailed upon in the common manner, in which things bad in themselves are done, partly by being coaxed, partly by being bullied."[40] Out of frustration over the difficulty of providing married women with inalienable security for their maintenance, Lord Thurlow invented the "restraint on anticipation" by inserting into a settlement words positively restricting alienation of the capital fund.[41]

By 1839 in *Tullet v. Armstrong* restraints on anticipation were well established, and Lord Chancellor Cottenham was able to decide that, though admittedly "inconsistent with the ordinary rules of property," these restraints might come and go with coverture, allowing a father to give his daughter a separate estate before her marriage, with the assurance that once married the daughter would be unable to alienate the fund, but that if she happened to be single or widowed, she could deal with the property as though a feme sole. Lord Cottenham in the course of this decision gave a rather candid history of the problem, making the social policy considerations clear:

> When this Court first established the separate estate, it violated the laws of property as between husband and wife; but it was thought beneficial, and it prevailed. It being once settled that a wife might enjoy separate estate as a *feme sole,* the laws of property attached to this new estate; and it was found, as part of such law, that the power of alienation belonged to the wife, and was destructive of the security intended for it. Equity again interfered, and by another violation of the laws of property supported the validity of the prohibition against alienation. . . . Why then should not equity in this case also interfere; and if it cannot protect the wife consistently with the ordinary rules of property, extend its own rules with respect to the separate estate, so as to secure to her the enjoyment of that estate which has been so invented for her benefit?[42]

Howard v. Digby

In my earlier discussion of the rule of no arrears of pin money, I noted that under special circumstances the wife's presumed relinquishment of her entitlement to the arrears could be rebutted. One such special circumstance seemed to be the insanity of the wife; an insane person cannot waive his right to payment under a contract. The most elaborate pin money case ever was produced when the executors of the Duchess of Norfolk, who had been certified a lunatic, sued the executors of the Duke of Norfolk for arrears of her pin money. This case provoked a serious reconsideration of the legal theory of pin money.

Since Charles Howard, later Duke of Norfolk, and Frances Fitzroy Scudamore had married in 1771 with suitably elaborate and lavish settlements, and since she had been a certified lunatic for decades, the arrears of her pin money arguably amounted to £33,000. Vice-Chancellor Shadwell decreed payment of that sum. Considerable confusion arose over whether pin money was supposed to be for a wife's maintenance or whether it was supposed to be for expenses, perhaps "fanciful and luxurious," over and above the maintenance appropriate to the wife's station. The Duke in this case had provided the Duchess with clothes, carriages, and even for many years a separate establishment. As we have seen, there were some earlier cases where the husband's having maintained his wife was apparently added to her failure to demand payment to reach a result of no arrears due. But Vice-Chancellor Shadwell in *Howard v. Digby* (1831) refused even to let the Duke's executors set his account of expenses incurred on her behalf off against the arrears, on the principle that the Duke was liable to maintain the Duchess "notwithstanding the income which was provided for her separate use."[43] Shadwell considered that pin money "never could be intended to be applied to the necessary maintenance of the duchess" but could only be for extras, and that, consequently, the justification of the no-arrears rule in *Powell* could only be the wife's implied consent to her husband's receipt of the money. Since a lunatic could not have so consented, the no-arrears rule could not apply to the Duchess.

Shadwell's decision in *Digby,* however, was overturned on appeal to the lords in 1834. Lord Chancellor Brougham gave an opinion for reversal and reported that he had been driven not only to a careful examination of the earlier cases but also to introspection and to interviewing various peers on the question of what they considered the purposes of pin money to be. This unusual bit of empirical research by the Whig chancellor contributed to his insistence that pin money was to go toward maintenance. He reported, as I noted earlier, that no man, however wealthy, would pay pin money if he were also expected to pay bills for dresses and hats, and he decided that "the general opinion of all those who give pin-money" is a very material fact.[44] Not surprisingly, Lord Brougham did not think to interview a sample of those who received pin money. Indeed, since it would seem more ordinary to speak of "paying" someone to whom you are indebted under a contract than to speak of "giving him money," his phrase "give pin money" suggests how far he was from thinking of wives with pin money allowances as contract creditors.

Lord Chancellor Brougham's opinion depended upon making a distinction between pin money and the married woman's separate estate, a distinction which he was honest enough to admit "is very obscure" and does not seem to have been made with any regularity earlier. Commenting on his researches in the books, he noted, "you cannot trace the line which divides [pin money] from the separate property of the wife, with any distinctness."[45] This is quite true and supports the Duchess's executors' claim that there were not two separate sets of rules for pin money and for married women's separate property in the earlier cases. Moreover, though the Lord Chancellor in *Howard* encountered a settlement which actually used the term "pin money," as I observed in my earlier discussion of conveyancing practice, many settlements conveying what even Lord Brougham would have wished to consider pin money did not use the term. (Lord Brougham, among other aims, wished to use his distinction between pin money and separate property to say that while there is a rule of no arrears of pin money, there is no such rule for separate property, and that, further, though the wife's personal representatives after her death have no claim to arrears of her pin money, obviously the personal representatives of a wife with a separate estate have a claim to that.)

Pin money, as opposed to the wife's separate property, Lord Brougham determined, was to pay "the ordinary expenses" of the wife. It was a modern "refinement" to relieve the wife of "the somewhat humiliating necessity" of asking her husband's consent every time she wishes to "go to the milliner's shop." "The money," however, "is meant to dress the wife so as to keep up the dignity of the husband, not for the mere accumulation of the fund; and as it is meant that the money should be expended for the husband's honour, to support his and her rank in society, if the *femme* [*sic*] did not choose to pay away the money to the *baron's* honour, she would in vain come to the Court of Chancery and pray, 'order payment of £9000 into my banker's, for 10 years; for I only spent £1000, when it was meant that I should spend £10,000.' "[46] Lord Brougham even fancifully hypothesizes, absent any cases for authority, that if a nobleman's wife "chose to dress herself like a mechanic's housewife, or a farmer's dame," spending only £25 of her £1,000 a year for dress, she would appeal in vain to Chancery for the savings. Later he insists: "The purpose [of pin money] is not the purpose of the wife alone; it is for the establishment, it is for the joint concern, it is for the maintenance of the common dignity; it is for the support of that family whose brightest ornament very probably is the wife; whose support and strength is the husband, but whose ornament is the wife."[47] Thus, without having reference to the waiver of consent argument, the Lord Chancellor was able to justify denying arrears on the ground that pin money is for present expenditure, and, the Duchess being dead, there can be no call for ornamenting her and no point in paying money intended for such a purpose to her personal representative.

Moreover, rejecting Shadwell's claim that pin money was for expenditure over and above maintenance, Brougham argued that since pin money was for the normal expenses of maintaining a wife and the Duke was liable for tradesmen's bills for maintenance, it would be inequitable to make him liable also to the Duchess's personal representatives for the same expenses. A lunatic could not release a debt, but he could receive payment of a debt and thereby make himself or his executors liable in discharge for what he had received, so the Duchess's enjoyment of the maintenance provided by the Duke could be considered in discharge of his pin money debt to her. On Lord Brougham's theory of pin money as intended for maintenance, he was struck by the apparent unfairness of a husband's being doubly liable for the same expenses, once under common law if sued for his wife's debts for necessaries by tradesmen who had supplied her and again under contract for payments to his wife to cover these same expenses. Although in separate maintenance cases, as we shall see, there was for a time a rule that a husband who paid his wife a separate maintenance allowance was not liable to tradesmen for his wife's bills, no similar rule was developed in pin money. On Lord Brougham's logic, it might have made sense to delineate which maintenance expenses pin money was to cover (for example, milliner's bills but not house rent) and then let husbands who paid pin money avoid direct liability for tradesmen's bills for those expenses. But Lord Brougham took it that a husband, as long as he and his wife lived together, had another, presumably better, protection from double liability: "He has an opportunity of controlling her, so that she shall not go and game, for example, with her pin-money, and leave him to pay her milliners' bills."[48]

Conclusions

The self-conscious airing of some of the contradictions in the theory of pin money in *Howard* was probably provoked by a number of factors beyond the obvious importance of the Norfolk estate. Of some significance, I believe, was a phenomenon noted in my introduction: the progressive improvement in law reporting and in the availability of fuller reports over the course of the eighteenth century. This seems to have promoted more awareness of competing cases. Also probably of significance was another phenomenon noted in the introduction: a changed and rationalized style of treatise writing and the growing number of treatises. New treatises appeared on baron and feme and on contract. Whereas R. S. Donnison Roper in 1800 in *A Treatise on the Revocation and Republication of Wills and Testaments: Together with Tracts upon the Law Concerning Baron and Feme* has no separate discussion of pin money and describes a no-arrears rule pertaining to "the produce" of the wife's "separate estate," his 1820 *Treatise on the Law of Property Arising from the Relation between Husband and Wife* devotes a chapter to "Gifts and Allowances by Husband to Wife" and establishes three different categories for pin money, household allowances, and paraphernalia.[49] Roper there attempts to reconcile the cases and to articulate an integrated set of rules. Similarly, although Edmond Gibson Atherley does not use the term "pin money" in his *Practical Treatise on the Law of Marriage and Other*

Family Settlements (1813), he does have two relevant chapters, one "Of Settling Property to a Married Woman's Separate Use" and one "Of Settling Real or Personal Estate so as to Enable a Feme Covert to Dispose of It." Brougham's retreat from contract logic to the logic of protection and publicly controlled maintenance in *Howard* is also congruent with a similar retreat (to be discussed in Chapter 6) in separate maintenance contract cases, where contract logic is given some play in the mid-eighteenth century, then cut back in the very late eighteenth century and early nineteenth century.

Lawrence Stone in *The Family, Sex, and Marriage in England, 1500–1800* has argued that "the hardest evidence for a decline in the near-absolute authority of the husband over the wife among the propertied classes is an admittedly limited series of changes in the power of the former to control the latter's estate and income," adding that "the introduction of the practice of inserting into the marriage contract a clause about pin money now guaranteed the wife an independent fixed income at her exclusive disposal."[50] It is true that under certain circumstances wives with pin money did attain some increased autonomy in spending and even that some women could use pin money to support themselves if they separated from unsatisfactory husbands. Yet there was not much self-congratulation over the institution of pin money in the eighteenth century.

Indeed, that the law and modern fashion allowed pin money was a subject of satire and a fact almost universally lamented by gentlemen moralists. Agreements requiring the husband to pay pin money, it was said, gave the husband and wife separate interests (the wife could sue the husband on the contract), allowed the wife to make independent judgments about expenditure, and, what was perhaps worst, made the husband's payments to the wife seem to depend on her right rather than on his generosity, thus, it was said, not inspiring appropriate wifely gratitude. Addison, writing as a "professed Advocate for the Fair Sex" in the *Spectator*, lamented the introduction of pin money and explained: "Separate Purses, between Man and Wife, are, in my Opinion, as unnatural as separate Beds. A Marriage cannot be happy, where the Pleasures, Inclinations and Interests of both Parties are not the same. There is no greater Incitement to Love in the Mind of Man, than the Sense of a Person's depending upon him for her Ease and

Happiness; as a Woman uses all her Endeavours to please the Person whom she looks upon as her Honour, her Comfort, and her Support."[51] Similarly, Samuel Richardson, who might also reasonably have described himself as a professed advocate for the fair sex, in an essay written for Johnson's *Rambler* complained that in the mid-eighteenth century, "settlements are expected, that often, to a mercantile man especially, sink a fortune into uselessness; and pin-money is stipulated for, which makes a wife independent, and destroys love, by putting it out of a man's power to lay any obligation upon her, that might engage gratitude, and kindle affection."[52]

Propaganda against pin money reached a nearly melodramatic climax in Mrs. Catherine Gore's novel, *Pin Money* (1831). Her basically good heroine spends her allowance on progressively disastrous things, beginning with a white marble fountain for their garden, progressing through a subscription to the opera, which exposes her to the attentions of a peer who thinks nothing of trying to seduce married women, and finally ending by incurring, before she is aware of it, a debt of £280 at the écarté table. Distressing experience leads her to understand the moral: "Had I found it necessary to have recourse to [my husband] for the detailed payment of my debts,—had full and entire confidence been established between us in the defrayment of my personal expenses,—never, never should I have been plunged into the excesses which embitter [my] destiny. . . . when by referring [to my husband] for the immediate payment of my bills, I expose myself to reprehension for any prodigal or frivolous action, I shall be insured from all danger of further extravagance."[53]

The contemporary complaint that modern women demanded pin money payments as matters of right instead of trusting to their husbands and being grateful for the allowances they received is actually quite a peculiar complaint. Although usually presented as a longing for the good old days before marriage settlements, the complaint reflects a male demand for an even greater privatization of the family than is represented by negotiated and legally enforceable marriage settlements. The complaint manages to ignore the husband's common law duty to maintain his wife and to provide her with necessaries appropriate to their rank, an obligation which meant that the wife had a corresponding right to that support. It is unlikely that women's "demands" had much to do with the existence or the forms of marriage settlements. The reasons for these settlements were not to bestow new rights on wives or to increase the autonomy of wives. On the contrary, as we have seen, marriage settlements providing jointure were needed by husbands and husbands' families in order to deny wives their common law rights to dower. Eighteenth-century theories of equitable jointure permitted jointures of considerably less value than the corresponding estates in dower to bar dower. The husband's family's desire for a marriage settlement with jointure and other features advantageous to their side gave the wife's family some bargaining power when they wished to preserve some property free of the husband's control as the wife's separate estate. Contemporary complaint about settlements which make "a wife independent" displaces responsibility onto women's "demands" and masks the dynastic motives and the interests of husbands' families in these settlements. The complaint itself seeks to substitute for the publicly enforceable wife's right to support a private exchange of the husband's "gift" for the wife's gratitude.

There is evidence that such propaganda had an effect and that even among those upper-class women who were allowed and who allowed themselves to participate in discussions of their marriage settlements some were reluctant to ask for or even to accept pin money. Lady Mary Pierrepont (after her marriage, Lady Mary Wortley Montagu), who was capable of reminding Edward Montagu that she could have £300 a year pin money from another suitor and of asking Edward for a jointure, also wrote to Edward: "I say nothing of pin money etc. I don't understand the meaning of any divided interest from a Man I willingly give my selfe to."[54] The less famous Mrs. Peach, widow of a former governor of Calcutta, who brought a fortune of £20,000 to her second marriage, persisted in refusing to have any pin money settled on her despite the best efforts of the groom's father, Lord Lyndhurst, to persuade her. According to Lord Lyndhurst, "she persevered in her resolution, thinking that my son's love and her happiness would depend on her putting this trust in him."[55] In the event, in the first year of the marriage, son Thomas deserted his wife to run off to Paris with a barmaid. Furthermore, as the cases already discussed suggest, even when wives did have pin money settled on them, the extralegal powers of husbands, including various sorts of psychological and physical intimidation, could keep wives from enjoying those allowances.

Moreover, the development of the legal doctrines concerning pin money between the Restoration and the early nineteenth century shows that the law, having created a potentially threatening source of women's power in the married women's separate estate, soon appreciated that threat and responded by creating idiosyncratic rules for pin money and other forms of married women's separate property which minimized the possibility that such property could become a source of women's power or the material basis for equality between men and women. These legal rules helped ensure that women's property was for the maintenance of the woman and the family, and, as Lord Brougham said, "expended for the husband's honour."

Although the development of these idiosyncratic rules occurred within conveyancing practice, equity judgments, and rulings of the House of Lords without the influence of new statutes, it was a cultural and political choice, not an inevitable development decreed by abstract legal logic. Indeed, legal logic alone could also have justified a more liberal reliance on the argument by analogy to men's property (as it did in *Moore*). It could even have justified the leap made in *Slanning v. Style* (1734), a creative case in which, despite the absence of any written contract providing for pin money payments, the court decided to construe a husband's statements that his wife should have the proceeds from the sale of eggs and such on their farm as an implied contract for pin money.[56] Judges might have ignored the political pressures of patriarchy and elected to build on the logic of *Slanning* instead of on that of *Powell*. But they did not, and the alternative historical development of idiosyncratic rules for pin money and other forms of married women's separate property was one reason why married women's property did not then lead to married women's power.

6

Separate Maintenance Contracts

Description and Ideological Significance

In Oliver Goldsmith's *Citizen of the World* (1762) Lien Chi Altangi, Goldsmith's fictional Chinese philosopher, and his friend, the Man in Black, one day walk down a London street and come upon a man and his wife engaged in a heated argument, right in the middle of the street. Even before Altangi and the Man in Black get there, the argument between Dr. Cacafogo, an apothecary, and Mrs. Cacafogo has already drawn a mob of onlookers, "not to prevent, but to enjoy the quarrel." Dr. Cacafogo, it seems, has discovered his wife *in flagrante* with her lover. As one would expect a follower of Confucius to do, Altangi expresses humane concern over the fate of a woman guilty of such an offense. Ignorant of the English methods of discipline, he inquires of his friend, "Will they burn her as in India, or behead her as in Persia; will they load her with stripes as in Turkey, or keep her in perpetual imprisonment, as with us in China?" To his amazement, he learns from his English informant that though Dr. Cacafogo must expect to be laughed at as a cuckold, Mrs. Cacafogo will simply be "packed off to live among her relations," supported by separate maintenance payments which her husband will supply. "Is it not enough," exclaims Altangi, "that she is permitted to live separate from the object she detests, but must he give her money to keep her in spirits too?" The two friends conclude the chapter by contrasting the supposed customs of the Russians, said "to behave most wisely in such circumstances," among whom a father ceremoniously cudgels his daughter three times before relinquishing both the daughter and the cudgel to the bridegroom.[1]

Goldsmith's story conveys a rather common eighteenth-century worry: that the balance of power in domestic relations was shifting from husbands to wives in ways that were both unfair and socially disruptive. Goldsmith's choosing to set this domestic quarrel in the street is also of interest, since another concern contemporaries often expressed was that the sordid details of domestic life were now all too often aired in the gossip columns of newspapers or magazines or in public courts. Like many of his contemporaries, however, Goldsmith seems not to have known quite what to make of the apparent changes in relations between husbands and wives, as is evident from the ironies of his narrative. The story is told in such a way that Goldsmith both satirizes the apparent privileges of wives in the modern state of matrimony and distances himself from what by 1762 seemed the barbarities of punishing errant wives by cudgeling, beheading, or burning.

Marriage itself can be said to be a contract, a relationship formed by mutual promises, leading—it is hoped—to mutual benefits. In England during the eighteenth century, as Goldsmith suggests, should these benefits not materialize, the relationship could be altered by means of a separate maintenance contract, that is, a private agreement between husband and wife that they should live apart. These contracts had no necessary connection with either ecclesiastical or parliamentary divorce; they could be and were entered into by couples when neither had grounds for divorce. A paradigmatic eighteenth-century separate maintenance agreement, one likely to be drawn up by a good lawyer, would be between a husband and a wife and trustees for the wife. The husband would agree to allow the wife to live apart from him without molestation and to pay to her or to her trustees or assigns some annual sum, the sums I have seen ranging from £12 to £3,000 a year, depending on the economic and social position of the parties. The trustees for the wife, for their part, would agree to indemnify the husband for the wife's debts. The husband and the wife might also agree not to litigate issues arising from the marriage in either the ecclesiastical or secular courts. The husband, for instance, might renounce any right to sue the wife in the ecclesiastical court for a restitution of conjugal rights, or the wife might agree not to sue the husband there for cruelty or adultery. Some agreement might be made concerning children; most commonly the husband might agree to let young children live with the wife, though at law he was their legal guardian. Sometimes, though apparently not frequently, the agreement might contain a *dum casta* clause, that is, a clause stipulating that the wife's payments were to continue only while she continued chaste.

In *Players' Scepters* I have written about separate maintenance agreements in the Restoration, emphasizing their importance as part of a process of transfer of jurisdiction away from the ecclesiastical courts and also as instances of contract rather than status ideas being invoked in the domestic sphere.[2] Because of the importance of contract ideas in Restoration and eighteenth-century political ideology, the application of those ideas to marriage served an important legitimating function. If the political sovereign's authority over his subjects was justifiable by a contract ideology, so the husband's authority over his wife was similarly justifiable. Indeed, use of contract ideology to legitimize domestic authority was more plausible than its use to legitimize political authority. A citizen might reasonably wonder when exactly he personally had assented to the social contract, but a wife could easily enough remember the words she had spoken on her wedding day. In the eighteenth-century classes with which I am here concerned, those supplied with legal advice, she might also remember those other contracts, the marriage settlements, which families and their lawyers negotiated before the marriage ceremony. Moreover, a wife who could in effect renegotiate her marriage contract into a separate maintenance contract would appear to be in some respects in a position analogous to that of the king's subjects after the Revolution of 1688. Like the king's, the husband's authority appeared less absolute.

A contrast between two leading cases involving wives living apart from their husbands, *Manby v. Scott* (1663) and *Moore v. Moore* (1737), conveniently illustrates the displacement of an older view of the marital relation in which the husband's authority has a religious and hierarchical justification by a newer view more dependent on the rhetoric and logic of contract.[3] In the earlier case, *Manby v. Scott,* Mr. Justice Hyde was arguing that it would be wrong to hold a husband whose wife had left him liable for her debts. He quoted Genesis, "Thy desire shall be to thy husband, for thy will shall be subject to thy husband; and he shall rule over thee," and reasoned:

> If the contract or bargain of the wife be made without the allowance or consent of the husband shall bind him upon pretence of necessary apparel, it will be in the power of the wife (who, by the law of God and of the land, is put under the power of the husband, and is bound to live in subjection unto him) to rule over her husband, and undo him . . . and it shall not be in the power of the husband to prevent it. The wife shall be her own carver, and judge of the fitness of her apparel, of the time when it is necessary for her to have new cloathes, and as often as she pleaseth, without asking the advice or allowance of her husband: and is such power suitable to the judgment of Almighty God inflicted upon Women for being first in the transgression? . . . Will wives depend on the kindness and favours of their husbands, or be observant towards them as they ought to be, if such a power be put into their hands?[4]

In the later case, *Moore v. Moore,* one of the pin money cases noted in the preceding chapter, Cox was arguing for another wife living apart from her husband and succeeded in persuading the court that the husband was nevertheless obliged by the marriage settlement to continue paying pin money. Counsel for the husband in *Moore* suggested that the payments to the absent wife should stop "in order to induce her to return to her duty." Cox for the wife replied, "according to the words and legal operation of the deed, there is a provision at all events for the defendant of £100 a year, and *quoad hoc,* she is to be considered as a feme sole, and as a stranger to the plaintiff." Having contended that the husband "made her not only as a cypher in his family, but took from her even the respect due to her from his servants," he went on to cite not Genesis but Puffendorf "in his book of the Law of Nature and Nations, in the chapter of Marriage, that in case the husband denies his wife the respect due to her sex, and her relation, so as to shew himself not so much a kind partner, as a troublesome vexatious enemy, it should seem very equitable, that she might be relieved by divorce."[5] In *Manby* Hyde saw the husband alone as representing the family in the public sphere, whereas in Cox's view in *Moore* the husband and wife could both appear before the court, in public, as individuals with rights under a contract, rights that the court could be asked to enforce.

To some extent the eighteenth-century separate maintenance cases do indicate that contract ideas subverted traditional patriarchal relations of male dominance and female subordination. The cases also show, however, that toward the end of the eighteenth century the apparently deeper structures of patriarchy reappeared, albeit transformed.

It is important to understand that rules protecting women or rules "advantageous to women" are not necessarily inconsistent with patriarchy. It is not in the interest of patriarchy for women to be so oppressed or bereft of subsistence that they die out altogether, or even so bereft that they fail to make desirable wives and competent mothers. Thus, within patriarchy there are some social rules promoting the protection and support of women, especially rules designed to ensure that women who have been possessed or enjoyed by one man do not subsequently become the public charges of other men. For example, as we have seen in earlier chapters, common law dower was just such a social rule of patriarchy, providing widows with a forced share of their husbands' estates, thus attempting to ensure that they did not become public charges.

The replacement in the early modern period of such common law entitlements as dower by entitlements under individual marriage settlements to new forms of married women's separate property like jointure and pin money is potentially construable as the replacement of a patriarchal regime by a more egalitarian regime in which women can negotiate for individual rights under a contract (the marriage settlement) and, consequently, appear, even as married women, as legal persons with entitlement to separate property. Thus, Lawrence Stone in his discussion of property rights and status in "the companionate marriage," argued that "the hardest evidence for a decline in the near-absolute authority of the husband over the wife among the propertied classes is an admittedly limited series of changes in the power of the former to control the latter's estate and income."[6] Moreover, at least at first glance it does seem reasonable to suppose, as Stone does and as my argument in *Players' Scepters* implies, that the possibility of a wife's securing a formal separation from an impossible husband and by virtue of the separate maintenance contract enjoying separate property in the form of a separate maintenance allowance also constitutes evidence for the weakening of patriarchy. Yet, I now believe, this conclusion is too simple.

Contract ideology was used in the eighteenth century to legitimize the husband's power over his wife and so was part of a process of mystification. This application of contract ideology to the domestic sphere was not merely a cynical attempt to preserve patriarchy in another disguise. On the contrary, the separate maintenance cases show that the uncynical application of contract ideas to domestic relations was felt to lead to consequences so genuinely subversive of patriarchy that after some decades of experimentation men had to realize, as the lady says in "The Love Song of J. Alfred Prufrock," "That is not what I meant at all. / That is not it, at all." My analysis of the cases will show that after an initial period of pursuing and developing a contract logic in dealing with separate maintenance contracts, in the later eighteenth century the courts attacked the relevance of this logic in domestic cases and repudiated some of the earlier decisions.

Because these separate maintenance agreements were private agreements between two (or more) parties—contracts—the parties could in practice agree to do anything they liked. But it did not follow that the courts were willing to enforce any agreement merely on the ground that it had in fact been made. The legal ideology of marriage is in part defined by the issue of which provisions of separate maintenance contracts the courts will enforce and which they will decline to enforce, so my analysis of the cases will focus on this issue.

A short and simple parenthesis on contract enforcement may make this point clearer to the reader who is not a legal historian or a lawyer. In the heyday of contract ideology in the nineteenth century, the progress of law was described in Sir Henry Maine's classic *Ancient Law* (1861) as a progress from status to contract. Individual freedom was freedom to exercise individual will without state coercion, freedom to make whatever contracts one chose. The role of the state was not to limit or to fix the nature of what the individual willed, but merely to enforce performance of private agreements already made. Convinced contract ideologues today still argue for the moral superiority of private contract over state regulation. But it has never been the case, and is not now the case, that society is prepared to enforce whatever agreements individuals decide to make without exercising very considerable control over the content of those agreements. In the modern world, including the eighteenth-century world, much of that control is exercised by means of private law rules. Some contracts which individuals want to make, or, indeed, which they actually do make, will be found at law void or invalid. Contracts to provide illicit sexual services are a traditional example of invalid contracts. Whether or not contracts between "surrogate mothers" and would-be adoptive parents ought to be invalid is a related question now being debated. On the other hand, sometimes when individuals have made no agreement at all, the law may find that they have entered into a contract "implied in law." For example, an unconscious person found on the street and treated by doctors at a hospital may be found to have entered into a contract implied in law to pay for their services.

Marriage itself, though often called a contract, and in some ways treated as contractual, has not been contractual in the sense that the two parties could negotiate whatever provisions were dictated by their individual wills. Historically, married people have not been allowed to make enforceable agreements thought to be violations of the marital relationship, for instance, agreements not to have sexual intercourse or agreements that the husband has no responsibility to support the wife. Moreover, many of the terms of the marriage contract are implied in law; so many, indeed, that marriage may seem more like a status than a contract.

Separate maintenance agreements constituted an attempt to make marriage more genuinely contractual, to make it less a status and more a contract, to subvert the rights and obligations of married persons implied in law. As we have seen in Chapter 5, a major contemporary complaint about eighteenth-century wives was that they had contracted for new privileges and contracted out of their traditional status. Wives' access to pin money and other forms of married women's separate property within on-going marriage were repeatedly said to be bad for them, bad for marriage, and disruptive of society. The possibility of a wife's contracting out of her duty to provide her husband with consortium and nevertheless receiving his economic support under the terms of a separate maintenance contract seemed, if anything, more noxious—especially if, as in Goldsmith's story, the wife had been guilty of sexual or other delinquency. At common law, an adulterous wife who eloped from her husband lost her entitlement to dower and to support, yet many wives guilty of adultery succeeded in negotiating (often with the help of other family members) separate maintenance allowances.

Why, then, were these contracts allowed? One reason, as I have suggested, was that contract ideas newly legitimized in political philosophy in the seventeenth century were applied to relations of domestic authority. There was some conscious awareness that husbands, like kings, might exercise their authority unjustly, and a liberal desire to offer some state protection to the victims of domestic tyranny. Noting the willingness of equity to enforce specific performance of articles of separation, Mr. Justice Buller observed: "The infirmities of human nature have given rise to cruelties and other ill treatment on the part of husbands, and to cases in which this Court has thought it indispensably necessary to interpose."[7] Wives might be inferior to husbands, as even eighteenth-century subjects were still inferior to the king, but they nevertheless had some rights which the legal system was prepared to protect.

New contract ideas within the field of married women's property also offered considerable benefits to men. As we have seen, the development of married women's separate property was in part motivated by the desire of the wife's father to continue to exercise some control over the property he gave the wife to bring into the marriage, especially to ensure that it was not wasted or lost by a feckless or unlucky husband and to ensure that at least some of it remained for the wife's father's grandchildren. Furthermore, our study of the process by which jointure replaced dower also shows that contract ideas could be and were invoked to support women's loss of traditional status rights to property. With respect to agreements for separate maintenance, it is clear that they could allow men to live apart from wives whom they could not have divorced in the church courts—wives who were nags rather than adulteresses, for instance, or wives whom they simply preferred to leave for more appealing mistresses, as Vice-Admiral Nelson separated from his faithful wife Frances at the time his mistress, Lady Hamilton, was pregnant with their daughter.[8]

Also of importance was the fact that separate maintenance agreements allowed husbands to contract out of their obligation to be responsible for their wives' debts. Anxiety over ruin at the hands of a spendthrift wife is a common eighteenth-century theme. Lord Mansfield observed in 1783: "Within the last century a great change has been introduced into the law relating to married persons, by means of trusts; and there is also a system of cases for the protection of the husband against the debts of the wife."[9] To this class of cases, he said, belonged those involving women with separate maintenance allowances known to their creditors, and the allowances of such women were liable for their own debts.

Some study of the particular economic arrangements made by various couples also suggests that underneath the idea that the wife's property belonged to the husband, and underneath the outrage expressed by contemporaries that a man after a separation must support an unsatisfactory or erring wife with *his* money, lay the idea that the property the wife brought into the marriage in another sense continued to "belong" to her and the understanding that whatever allowance the separated wife got was to come from the interest on her property.

Three Separations

It is impossible to say what percent of eighteenth-century couples entered into separate maintenance contracts. Sifting through such sources as appellate cases, letters, and biographies, however, it is easy to find couples with these agreements. It happens that some of the leading cases involve people otherwise well known. *Rex v. Mead* (1758) turned on a contract between Mary Mead Wilkes and her husband, John Wilkes, later famous as a radical politician. *Hatchett v. Baddeley* (1776) turned on a separation between Sophia Baddeley, a singer and actress, and Robert Baddeley, an actor most remembered as Moses in Sheridan's *School for Scandal*. *Corbett v. Poelnitz* (1785) turned on a contract between Anne Stuart Percy Poelnitz, a daughter of Lord Bute, and Hugh Percy, famous before his separation as the British commander who marched out of Boston to cover the British retreat after the battle of Lexington. It would be rash to say that these three couples were typical. It does seem to me, though, that the Wilkes, the Baddeleys, and the Percys give a reasonable idea of the range of circumstances that led to separate maintenance contracts, and that a brief description of how the contracts figured in these three marriages will give some useful social and economic context for more abstract analysis of the legal theory.

John Wilkes, the son of a wealthy distiller, was educated at a Dissenting Academy and at Leyden and apparently intended to be a gentleman.[10] In 1747 at age twenty-two he married Mary Mead, a spinster heiress aged thirty-two. Much later John claimed, unconvincingly, that he married in his "non-age" only to please his father, and asked, "Are such ties, at such a time of life, binding?—and are school boys to be dragged to the altar?" Israel Wilkes settled property on the couple sufficient to provide £330 a year and stipulated that that was John's portion; no more was to come to him on the death of his father. Mrs. Mead settled a Prebend House in Aylesbury and the Manor of Aylesbury on Mary. Mary appears to have been a pious, sober woman with no taste at all for John's libertine pleasures. The couple lived part of the year at Aylesbury in a house that came to them from the Meads. There John spent more money than the Meads thought wise improving his new estate and buying up adjacent properties. In 1752 he persuaded Mary to settle the Aylesbury estate on him by a deed of gift. During winters in London he was part of a very fast crowd. Over the objections of his family, but with the encouragement of Lord Temple, Wilkes tried to become M.P. for Berwick-upon-Tweed, spending £3,000 or £4,000 in losing the election. He spent more money electioneering to become M.P. for Aylesbury, an object he attained in July of 1756 at an estimated cost of £7,000.

In September of 1756 John informally separated from Mary, taking their little daughter, Polly, with him into lodgings at St. James's Place. The following spring Polly got the smallpox. According to John—Mary's version of this episode has not survived—John begged Mary to come to their daughter's bedside and Mary refused. Again according to John, "he bitterly resented the inhuman conduct of his wife, which in his eyes was as infamous as a breach of the marriage vows."[11] Shortly afterward, a formal separate maintenance agreement was negotiated by which Mary gave up much of the property she had brought into the marriage and bargained to be allowed to live with her mother, to see her daughter occasionally, and to get £200 a year as an allowance.

John's various debts had him so hard up for cash that he was borrowing money at high interest rates. In March 1757 John sued Mary and her trustees at equity to have the separation deed giving him her separate property executed. The court decreed, Mary being present in court and consenting, that the deed be executed. Looking to his wife for help, John apparently tried to get her also to surrender her annuity but found she refused even to see him. In 1758 John sued out a writ of habeas corpus against Mary's mother, no doubt hoping that the court would say that the separate maintenance contract was not enforceable, and that, once Mary was back under his influence, he could profit from the money she was in due course to inherit. The court, however, held the separate maintenance agreement "to be a formal renunciation by the husband, of his marital right to seize her, or force her back to live with him."[12] John then launched on his better-known adventures. While he was in France in 1764 he had an agent sell the Aylesbury property for £4,100 and continued to live rather high on the hog, eventually getting his debts up to about £30,000, when assistance from the Supporters of the Bill of Rights helped pay them off. He died insolvent in 1797. Mary had inherited about £100,000 when her mother died in 1769 and had died, solvent, in 1784.

The second couple comes from a humbler sphere. Robert Baddeley, orphaned early and with no known family support, first appeared on the London stage in 1760.[13] His salary was £3 a week in 1764, rising to £9 a week in 1789, with an additional £100 or so a year from benefits. At thirty he eloped with eighteen-year-old Sophia Snow, daughter of a sometime theatrical musician. Sophia made her own stage debut in 1764. In 1765 the couple were apart, Sophia playing at Liverpool, Robert at Manchester. Sophia's long and complex career of adultery seems to have begun at this time. In the 1760s she is said to have had affairs with, among others, the actor Charles Hamilton, and when he died, his physician, Dr. Hayes. David Garrick, in his role as manager and moralist of Drury Lane, insisted that she stop living with Hayes, a demand with which she complied on the condition that Garrick pay her salary to her directly rather than paying it to Robert. In 1770 there was a notorious but noninjurious duel between Robert and Garrick's brother George, who undertook to defend Sophia's honor, a duel in which Sophia appeared on the Hyde Park Ground, kneeling to Garrick and begging him to spare her husband.[14] Shortly after this, a separation was negotiated with the assistance of Arthur Murphy, a lawyer as well as a playwright.

After the separation, Sophia continued her career, occasionally appearing on stage with Robert, though it was said the two did not speak to each other off stage. In 1776 Sophia was sued by John Hatchett, a coachmaker, for labor and materials; Sophia's counsel pleaded that she did not owe the money on the ground that she was a married woman whose husband was still living. All argument proceeded on the premise that there was no formal separate maintenance agreement, a premise which was almost certainly incorrect.[15] *Hatchett v. Baddeley* contributed to the development of a rule that eloped wives living in adultery without separate maintenance are not to have credit in their own right, nor are their husbands to be responsible for their debts. Blackstone, who was among the judges who decided *Hatchett,* took the opportunity to defend the evolving rule as desirable public policy: "And I see no hardship in a man's losing his money, that avows upon the record, that he furnished a coach to the wife of a player, whom he knew to have run away from her husband. If this were universally known to be law, it would be difficult for such women to gain credit, and this would consequently reduce the number of wanderers."[16]

In fact, Sophia personally seems not to have been so discouraged that she did not continue to take other lovers, including Lord Melbourne. She also continued acting, specializing in innocent young women in genteel comedy. In the 1780s, however, her health and fortune declining, she took refuge from her London creditors by acting in Dublin, then Edinburgh, and finally—after playing Jane Shore—retiring, consumptive, from the stage. Supported in her last year by a stipend from fellow actors, she died in 1786. Robert also continued his acting career after the separation. He died in 1794 leaving his house and property to one of the mistresses with whom he had lived.

Our final couple is an aristocratic one. Hugh Percy was the eldest son of Hugh Smithson, who took the name of Percy and became Duke of Northumberland.[17] Hugh began a military career as a teenager and was already a lieutenant colonel and member of Parliament when he married Anne Stuart, a seventeen-year-old daughter of the Earl of Bute. A marriage settlement of a complexity suitable to the rank and fortune of the parties had as one of its provisions a jointure of £1,600 a year for Anne should one or both of Hugh's parents survive him or £2,500 should they both predecease him. In 1766 Hugh went off as a colonel to America while Anne went to live with her sister Augusta, who had married one Drew Corbett, a sublieutenant in the horse-grenadiers. When Hugh returned, there were various matrimonial problems, including a discovery of letters from four different men in Anne's desk drawer. In 1769 Anne and Hugh entered into a separate maintenance agreement providing Anne with £1,600 or £2,500 (depending on the same contingencies as the jointure in the marriage settlement) "so long as she should live in Great Britain." Hugh's military career continued apace, his reputation as a humane commander much increased by his paying out of his own pocket to send home those soldier's wives widowed at the battle of Bunker Hill.

In 1777, according to depositions later produced on Hugh's behalf, Anne began to have an affair with a young gentleman of about twenty-three, William Bird. Aside from the usual servant's testimony to adultery for the ecclesiastical divorce trial, a clergyman deposed that Anne and William Bird at Southampton "showed a degree of familiarity . . . that was exceedingly indiscreet, and was observed by everybody as such." Horace Walpole in May of 1778 gossiped in a letter that Anne was pregnant with her lover's child. In 1778, having demanded his recall from America after a dispute with General Howe, Hugh sued Bird for criminal conversation, won, sued Anne for an ecclesiastical divorce, and won that. In 1779 he got a parliamentary divorce and two months later married Frances Julia Burrell. The private bill granting the divorce recites the marriage settlement and also settles the £1,600 or £2,500 on Anne as a separate maintenance.

Since the essence of a separate maintenance contract is to adjust arrangements to individual circumstances, no single couple can be regarded as typical. Yet the idea that the wife's support is to come from interest on property she brought into the marriage and be somehow proportionate to that property is an important one. The jointure could serve as a convenient bargaining point, though other wives and their families might be less successful negotiators than Anne Stuart and her family. Since the expenses and hazards of litigation such as that engaged in by Hugh were considerable, pledges not to litigate issues arising out of the marriage or not to contest litigation initiated by the other spouse could also have economic value. Other wives, like Mary Mead Wilkes, innocent of any matrimonial fault themselves, but anxious to live apart from unsatisfactory husbands, were willing to settle for allowances that represented much less than the interest on property they had brought into the marriage.

Decreed Separate Maintenance and Party-Created Contracts

Now, with some sense of what separate maintenance contracts were and how they functioned in people's lives, we can examine the development of legal thought concerning them. For the sake of discussion, the cases may be described in three rough stages. In the first stage (1675–1778), equity courts were increasingly hospitable to the idea of separate maintenance and contract logic. In the second stage (1778–1800), there was a struggle over whether the common law courts would accept the principles developed at equity, criticism of contract logic, concern that it had subverted the marital relationship in socially disruptive ways, and an attempt to overturn some earlier cases. In the third stage (after 1800), courts reaffirmed the legitimacy of separate maintenance contracts but developed rules that controlled party autonomy in the contracts, reasserted public control over the marital relationship, and, I argue, revived patriarchal structures temporarily overcome by contract. (The dates here are meant as guidelines only; there is significant overlap between what I am distinguishing, for analytic purposes, as stages.)

An important part of the first stage, in which the courts were hospitable to separate maintenance, were cases where equity decreed separate maintenance on the premise that to do so was to do justice to women whose husbands behaved badly. These cases tended to involve a de facto separation, an unsatisfactory husband, and property which came into the marriage through the wife. For example, in *Williams v. Callow* (1717), the wife of a glover who wasted his stock, drunkenly wandered from ale house to ale house, and fired a pistol at her, brought a bill to have the interest of her £500 portion paid to her as a separate maintenance.[18] The court decreed that she should have the interest of the £500, which came from her family, "until the said husband shall have applied himself to some course of business, or some way of living, suitable to receive his said wife."[19] Sometimes the court went so far as to resettle the wife's property in imitation of a normal family settlement, giving her in effect a life estate to support the separate maintenance payments and decreeing that at her death the property would go over to the husband or to the issue of the marriage. In *Watkyns v. Watkyns* (1740) a wife who had remarried as a rich widow asked the court to provide her with a separate maintenance after her new husband, having promised to secure her jointure by a bond of £1,700, took the bond from her cabinet and went abroad. The Lord Chancellor ordered an accounting of her personal estate before remarriage so that what remained of it could be put in trust to yield her interest until her husband returned to "maintain her as he ought" and so that the £1,700 could be paid to her if her husband predeceased her.[20] There do not seem to be cases in which equity decreed a separate maintenance to a woman from property the husband brought into the marriage or afterward acquired in his own right.

Cecil v. Juxon (1737), an early equity case decreeing separate maintenance, directly anticipated the married women's property acts of the nineteenth century. In this case a wife deserted by her husband later went into the millinery business with goods supplied by her mother. The wife supported herself and her two children with this business until the husband returned after fourteen years, broke into the house, and carried away all her goods. When the wife's mother brought a bill for redelivery of the goods, Sir Joseph Jekyll held that what the wife had acquired in her husband's absence to support herself and her family was "her separate property, and not liable to the disposition of the husband when he should please to come home and plunder her."[21] These decreed separate maintenance cases, though they certainly represented secular interference with the husband's prerogative in the name of justice to the wife, still involved public control—the court's control—of the relationship between the spouses, and they do not seem to have been perceived as so challenging to the patriarchal social order as those cases which entailed enforcement of separate maintenance contracts created by the parties.

To a remarkable extent, cases arising from party-created contracts developed on a logic looking to the explicit language of the actual agreement in each case, rather than to the court's understanding of what was implicit in the marital relationship. In *Angier v. Angier* (1718) equity decreed specific performance of articles of separation requiring the husband to pay his wife £52 a year separate maintenance, rejecting his contention that only the ecclesiastical courts could decree separation and alimony and unmoved by his proofs of her drunkenness and "perverse, morose, and malicious temper."[22] In *Rex v. Mead* (1758), the case in which John Wilkes's efforts to force his wife Mary to live with him despite their separation agreement were rebuffed, and in similar cases, even the law courts held that husbands who entered into separate maintenance contracts had renounced their marital rights to compel their wives to live with them.[23] A wife who had a separate maintenance allowance could be sued as though she were a feme sole, meaning that, by virtue of the contract, she was found to have relinquished her entitlement to her husband's support.[24] At the end of the eighteenth century, it was sometimes claimed that only contracts between husbands and trustees for the wife could be valid, not contracts between the husband and the wife directly, but in this first stage contracts not involving trustees were enforced. For example, in *More v. Freeman* (1725) articles of separation under which a wife agreed to pay her husband £200 a year from her separate estate in consideration of his permitting her to live apart from him were held good despite her trustees' not having been party to the articles.[25]

Party-created contracts in which fathers relinquished their common law right to custody of children to mothers seem also to have been frequent and were enforced. Fathers were most likely to relinquish custody of young children and of girls. In *Guth v. Guth* (1792) a contract between husband and wife providing not only for separation and payments but also for the youngest child to live with the wife was enforced at equity. Having entered into a separate maintenance contract in 1785, Guth said he had become insolvent in 1789, could no longer afford the payments, and offered instead to take back his wife and child and support them in his home. Sir Richard Arden declined to consider the circumstances that prompted the original agreement, decided to enforce the contract, and remarked, "in such cases, where parties have been found unhappy, and it has been expedient to enter into such a deed of separation, surely, it was neither necessary nor fit that the wife should proclaim to the public every circumstance which may have occasioned it."[26]

Disputes over Contract Logic

In the second stage (1778–1800) of the development of the legal theory of separate maintenance contracts this relatively untrammeled play of contract ideas was checked. A series of cases at both law and equity attempted to reassert the "general principle" that a husband and wife being in law one person cannot contract with each other against what were now said to be mistaken exceptions. Much of the criticism centered on what were claimed to be the hopeless confusions and illogicalities of allowing an anomalous middle state between feme covert and feme sole, a situation in which a married woman with a separate maintenance contract would be for some purposes feme covert (not being able to marry, for instance) and for others feme sole (being personally liable for her own debts to tradesmen, for example). Earlier statements that a woman with a separate maintenance was to be considered as a feme sole were now said to have gone much too far.

These separate maintenance contracts being in a sense the creatures of equity, although earlier cases like *Todd v. Stoakes* and *Rex v. Mead* had allowed them to have effects at law, there was now some question of whether they would have effect at law, particularly with respect to creditors of wives with separate maintenance allowances. In *Lean v. Shutz* (1778), a creditor following what had by then become common practice sued, in Common Pleas, a wife with a separate maintenance allowance for goods sold and delivered. When the wife pleaded her coverture, Chief Justice De Grey found for the wife on the narrow ground that the creditor had not joined the husband in his writ. He did, however, also say: "And though a wife may acquire a separate character, by the civil death of her husband, as by exile, profession, or abjuration; yet by a voluntary separation she does not acquire such a character, which may be called a civil widowhood, nor is taken notice of by the law as such."[27]

Shortly after this decision, however, Chief Justice Mansfield of King's Bench decided a series of subsequently controversial cases recognizing separate maintenance contracts at law. Mansfield, it should be noted, was famous as a bold judicial spirit, sometimes criticized for allowing the spirit of equity to contaminate his rulings at law; he "often acted on the principle that 'as the usages of society alter, the law must adapt itself to the various situations of mankind.' "[28] In *Ringstead v. Lady Lanesborough* (1783) Lady Lanesborough, after having entered into a separate maintenance agreement, tried to avoid the claims of a creditor by pleading coverture, as Sarah Shutz had in *Lean*. Mansfield found for the creditor, branded Lady Lanesborough's plea a "most iniquitous defence," and declared: "To hold a woman liable under such circumstances is justice to the creditor and mercy to the woman herself, for it enables her to obtain credit. . . . The agreement of separation bound both the parties in the same manner as if they had been sole, and the Court will not suffer either of them to break through it. Under this agreement the wife possesses a separate property."[29] Mansfield reaffirmed this position in *Barwell v. Anne Brooks* (1784). Although counsel for the wife cited *Lean* and complained that Mrs. Brooks's maintenance was not even stated to have been secured by deed, Mansfield again found for the creditor.[30]

In 1785, in *Corbett v. Poelnitz,* Mansfield rejected what was arguably an even stronger plea of a separated wife against her creditors. Anne Percy (discussed earlier) had after her divorce married Baron Karl Hans Bruno Poelnitz. While she and Baron Poelnitz were still enjoying the separate maintenance allowance from Hugh Percy, they were sued by Anne's brother-in-law Corbett for a debt of £1,800 she owed him. Anne's counsel sought to avoid payment by arguing that even if it were then the rule that a woman with a separate maintenance was liable for her own debts for necessaries and maintenance, surely such an exception to the general principle that "the contract of a married woman was not only voidable, but actually void" could not extend to a transaction like the one here, which they characterized as sinking "the fund from whence the maintenance is to come." Lord Mansfield rejected their argument and considered Anne liable for the debt as a feme sole under the separate maintenance agreement. "In modern days," he declared, "a new mode of proceeding has been introduced, and deeds have been allowed under which a married woman assumes the appearance of a feme sole, and is to all intents and purposes capacitated to act as such."[31]

The key case rejecting party autonomy in this second stage was *Marshall v. Rutton,* first argued in 1798 but not finally decided until May of 1800. In *Marshall* Lord Chief Justice Kenyon, who had succeeded Mansfield in 1788, reasserted what he now claimed to be the "general principle" that husband and wife being in law one person cannot contract with each other. Consequently, he overturned *Ringstead, Barwell,* and *Corbett* and ruled that a woman with a separate maintenance allowance could not contract or be sued as a feme sole. The validity of separate maintenance contracts had also been questioned earlier in the 1790s. Sir Richard Arden in 1797 reported that he had recently heard Kenyon question *Corbett* and for himself also questioned the logic and public policy represented by *Corbett;* he said, too, that he wished it to be understood that *Corbett* "may not be understood as quite acquiesced in."[32] Similarly, Lord Chancellor Loughborough in *Legard v. Johnson* (1797) criticized *Guth* and doubted that equity "upon the general and simple question between husband and wife can entertain a suit upon a contract, in which the wife only claims a separate maintenance against the husband."[33] Shortly before *Marshall* itself was decided, Lord Eldon in *Beard and Arabella His Wife v. Webb and Another* (February 5, 1800) also expressed doubt about the foundations of *Ringstead, Barwell,* and *Corbett* and puzzlement over how it could be maintained that the contracts of a married woman "are good, because she is in a state of separation, her existence in that state originating in a deed or contract executed and entered into before she is separated."[34]

None of these judges, however, so boldly repudiated the earlier cases as Kenyon did in *Marshall.* This case, "on account of the magnitude of the question," was argued once in 1798 before all the then judges except one and argued again in 1800, again before all the then judges except one. Kenyon went back to Littleton to insist that husband and wife were in law one person and "on that account unable to contract with each other." Even were such a contract to be valid, he opined, it would

> without dissolving the bond of marriage . . . place the parties in some respects in the condition of being single, and leave them in others subject to the consequences of being married; and . . . would introduce all the confusion and inconvenience which must necessarily result from so anomalous and mixed a character. In the course of the argument some of these difficulties were pointed out; and it was asked, whether, after such an agreement as this, the Temporal Courts could prohibit, if either party were to sue in the Ecclesiastical Court for the restitution of conjugal rights? Whether the wife, if she com-

mitted a felony in the presence of her husband, would be liable to conviction? Whether they could be witnesses for and against each other? Whether they could sue and take each other in execution?— and many other questions will occur to every one, to which it will be impossible to give a satisfactory answer.[35]

Lord Kenyon's argument here presents his decision not to recognize the contract between the Ruttons as valid as a decision forced by legal logic, when in fact it was not. Given that husband and wife are in nature two persons, whenever the law wishes to say that they are one there have to be "exceptions" allowing the recognition of their separate identities, unrecognized exceptions like providing for the survival of one spouse after the other dies or recognized exceptions—which, of course, were well known to Kenyon—like allowing the testimony of a wife against her husband in cases of forcible marriage. What is "impossible" is maintaining an absolute that husband and wife are one person, not deciding where to draw the line between treating them as one and treating them as two, since a line must be drawn. To pile up problems such as those Kenyon lists and claim that it is beyond the intellectual resources of contemporary legal thought to deal with a middle category between feme covert and feme sole seems virtually disingenuous, especially as the law of husband and wife at this point was almost childishly simple compared to the law of real property. The oxymoronic category of chattels real within which the law of leases and the law of mortgages made rapid development in the eighteenth century is one of many examples of the ability of contemporary legal thought to deal with middle categories. In fact, as we have seen, the courts had by 1800 already gone a considerable way in solving the problems of dealing with this very category of separated women. Another problem like the ones Kenyon poses had recently been decided: should a husband who had entered into a separate maintenance agreement with his wife be allowed to recover criminal conversation damages in case of her subsequent adultery? No, said the court, on the perfectly plausible ground that a husband who "voluntarily relinquished" the consortium of his wife ought not ask for damages for the subsequent loss of it.[36]

Some of the anxieties expressed in this second critical stage had to do not with the legal logic of recognizing separate maintenance contracts but rather with economic worries. Henry Ballow in his early *Treatise of Equity* (1756), which identified contracts as its principal subject, had dealt very briefly with separate maintenance agreements in a section entitled "The Assent Required in Agreements." There he noted that at equity a wife may have separate estates with respect to which she is like a feme sole: "And if she has a separate Maintenance, and lives separate, and this known to Tradesmen, they cannot trust her and recover of the Husband at Law."[37] In 1793 John Fonblanque published an edition of Ballow's treatise with extensive notes of his own. To Ballow's brief recognition of married women with separate maintenance contracts, Fonblanque appended a long note, unusual in the context of eighteenth-century treatise writing in its direct criticism of recent cases. Citing *Lanesborough, Barwell,* and *Corbett,* Fonblanque observes that none of these "though they are supposed to furnish at least a general rule of law" pays any attention to the adequacy of the particular separate maintenance allowance or to whether the husband's resources are sufficient to pay it. Should the payments be inadequate, Fonblanque worries, the wife might become chargeable to her parish, which would be an injustice to the parish.[38] Some might argue that Fonblanque's criticisms here do not apply to the validity of separate maintenance contracts but merely express an equitable concern over fairness. I would point out that court-imposed scrutiny of the adequacy of an allowance restricts party autonomy at least in part for what are explicitly identified as public policy reasons. Furthermore, although equity courts in this period were repeatedly invited to scrutinize the fairness of jointure agreements, they refused to do so. Resistance to party autonomy in separate maintenance agreements, therefore, cannot be simply explained as an inevitable application of equity principles.

Another economic worry expressed more elaborately in the cases was that separate maintenance contracts negotiated between husband and wife could constitute fraud against creditors. Concern about creditors, however, prominent in the midcentury cases when the commercial law generally was undergoing rapid development, could cut two ways. On the one hand, if the courts were to refuse to recognize these agreements, there was the problem of separated women running up bills, then pleading coverture when they were sued for their debts. Mansfield clearly was sensitive to the interests of commercial creditors in *Ringstead* and *Barwell.* On the other hand, suppose the husband and wife, anticipating the husband's bankruptcy, were to conspire to enter into a separate maintenance agreement securing some of his property to her in order to keep it from his legitimate creditors? In several cases creditor plaintiffs tried to overcome separate maintenance agreements as fraudulent under 13 Eliz., c. 5, arguing that even if the agreements might be of some force as between husband and wife, they could not affect third party creditors or purchasers for valuable consideration. In *Fitzer v. Fitzer,* a suit between a wife with a separate maintenance contract and her husband's creditor and assignee in bankruptcy, the husband became indebted to the creditor after the separate maintenance deed had been executed.[39] Lord Hardwicke could not find any sufficient consideration in this particular separate maintenance deed, which did not involve trustees indemnifying the husband against his wife's debts, and finessed the issue by decreeing that upon the wife's paying the creditor the remainder of his debt, the creditor should release his right to the annuity.

It is difficult to say what caused this second-stage criticism of the earlier contract logic. Some causes both internal to the legal system and external to it can, speculatively, be suggested. Internally, one is reminded by the rather novel citation of new treatises in these opinions of the very late eighteenth century that the enlightenment's drive to collect and to systematize cases meant that very late eighteenth-century judges were more likely to notice anomalies in the law and to be moved to try to reduce them. Externally, the increased publicity surrounding criminal conversation trials, the appearance of racy gossip columns in magazines, the increased number of parliamentary divorces, and the increase of separate maintenance contracts themselves led to much public complaining about the decline of morality and family stability and to some clamor for more rigid controls. Also, and more generally, as Jamil Zainaldin has noted in tracing a somewhat similar development in the law of child custody, after the French Revolution English political and legal thought "underwent an extreme and conservative reaction." This reaction, he argues, was "more than merely a reinstatement of the pre-Mansfield doctrine": "The nineteenth-century English judges adopted a patriarchal paradigm of family relations and applied it to the law with such force and vigor that it had the effect of creating new paternal rights, the existence of which had only been vaguely hinted at by previous judges."[40]

Lord Ellenborough, whom Zainaldin singles out as the personification of reaction in the custody cases, followed *Marshall* with enthusiasm in *Wardell v. Gooch* (1806). There he found against a creditor who had sued a married woman with a separate maintenance.[41] Despite *Weedon v. Trimbell* (1792), which had disallowed a husband's claim to criminal conversation damages after he had entered into a separate maintenance contract, Lord Ellenborough then in *Chambers v. Caufield* (1805) discovered that another separate maintenance deed was not such an absolute renunciation of the husband's marital rights as to prevent his action for criminal conversation.[42]

Modified Reaffirmation of Contract Logic

The radical repudiation of the earlier contract logic in *Marshall*, however, was not in the long run found to be practical, so this second stage was succeeded by a third. In the third stage of the development of the legal theory of separate maintenance contracts the courts neither, as in the first stage, gave free play to contract ideas, nor, as in the second stage, attempted to overturn the earlier cases by insisting on the unity of husband and wife as an absolute rule. Instead, there was an agreement to give force to separate maintenance contracts, but only to those contracts which conformed to newly developed rules. These rules were presented as rules discovered in the earlier cases, but they were actually invented by an aggressive process of interpretation, not passively discovered. A few of the earlier cases were explicitly overturned, some were ignored, and most were interpreted to support the development of these new rules. What these new rules represented, I contend, was a reimposition of deep patriarchal structures on a field of law where those structures had been weakened by contract ideas.

Basically, the perception was that separate maintenance contracts negotiated and recognized on a pure contract logic allowed the parties to evade the obligations of marriage and worked to the detriment of society as a whole. Thus, in an opinion noted in my introduction, Lord Eldon in *Lord St. John v. Lady St. John* (1805) fulminated:

Independent of the effect of the contract of marriage itself, the rule upon the policy of the law is, that the contract shall be indissoluble, even by the sentence of the law: to a certain extent the Legislature thinking it for the interest of the community that it should not be dissolved except by the Legislature: upon the principle probably, that people should understand that they should not enter into these fluctuating contracts; and, after that sacred contract they should feel it to be their mutual interest to improve their tempers. . . . It is admitted every where, that by the known law, founded upon policy, for the sake of keeping together individual families, constituting the great family of the public, there shall be no separation *a mensa &* *thoro, except propter saevitiam aut adulterium* [that is, no separation from board and hearth except for cruelty or adultery].[43]

Despite such ideological objections to separate maintenance contracts, the fact was that these contracts had proven to be con-venient ways of controlling some of the problems of unhappy marriage and that they afforded advantages not only to women but also to men. The possibility of separation assuaged husbands' fears of being trapped with bad wives or ruined by spendthrift wives and fathers' fears of having their daughters made miserable by bad husbands or losing the property settled on them to feckless or coercive husbands. Moreover, it was thought socially desirable that the bad behavior of married persons, particularly upper-class married persons, not be too publicly aired. Consequently, despite ideological scruples, in this third stage ways were found to preserve the perceived advantages of separate maintenance contracts while limiting the effect of untrammeled party autonomy and limiting the more radical implications of husbands and wives trading away marital duties. As the judges invented and enforced the stage-three rules, they repeatedly asserted that the general rule was the indissolubility of marriage and that, were it not for previous de-cisions and dicta, they personally would never have permitted separate maintenance contracts to be the foundation of actions in their courts. Thus, in *St. John,* Lord Eldon insists that separate maintenance contracts are against public policy and that he per-sonally, "if this were *res integra*" would not have allowed them, yet he refuses a husband's request to have his separation deed delivered up as void as against public policy because he does not wish to shake settled law.[44] Also characteristic of the schizoid quality of this third stage is Roper's *Treatise of . . . Husband and*

Wife (1820), which explains the "difficulties" of current law regarding separation as rooted in the "evil" of allowing any separation between husband and wife and characterizes some of the current doctrines as setting "reason and principle at defiance," but simultaneously declares legal separation established by the decisions and prints standard forms for separate maintenance contracts.[45]

How exactly did the judges' newly developed and refined rules of this third stage reimpose patriarchal structures on a field of law where those structures had been weakened by contract? Basically, they declined to enforce a straight contract between husband and wife based simply on a mutual exchange of promises to live apart and not molest each other or to enforce any contract declaring that the wife was for all purposes a feme sole from the moment of separation. Instead, the judges required certain special conditions to be met before a separate maintenance contract was enforceable and also subjected the subsequent conduct of the parties to certain tests and restrictions derived from their marital status. Consider the following rules developed in this third stage:

1. Contracts between husband and wife alone are invalid, but contracts between husband and trustees for the wife are valid.
2. Simple mutual covenants to live apart and not molest each other are not valid, but contracts with some additional consideration are valid.
3. Contracts for future separation are void as against public policy, but contracts for immediate separation are valid.
4. Separate maintenance allowances contracted for but not actually paid do not bar the husband's liability for his wife's debts for necessaries.
5. A wife possessing an annuity under a separate maintenance contract cannot assign it to another.

Consider first how the new rule requiring that the agreement be between the husband and trustees for the wife entails a reimposition of patriarchal structure. This rule was certainly not derived simply from the earlier cases, as *Fitzer, Barwell,* and *Guth,* for example, all gave effect to contracts between the husband and wife alone.[46] What the rule accomplished was the erasure of the wife, converting the separation transaction into what was normally a male to male transaction between the husband and, usually, some male relative of the wife. A principal argument for this rule was that contracts between husband and wife alone were invalid for lack of consideration, the wife having nothing to exchange with the husband for his agreement to provide a separate maintenance so that the husband's promise was gratuitous. Trustees, in contrast, by covenanting to indemnify the husband against the wife's debts provided consideration. Although the advocates of this rule present it as forced by legal logic, they could alternatively have found adequate consideration in some other guise within the husband and wife relationship, as we shall see shortly in analyzing the second rule of this stage. Furthermore, of course, as is evident from Chapter 5, by this time many women had separate property of their own to which they could have given their husbands rights by way of consideration for separation.

The strangeness of a rule not allowing husbands and wives to contract with each other but allowing husbands to contract with trustees where the agreement of the wife to live separate and not molest the husband was a material element of the contract was commented upon by the same judges who proposed to enforce it. Grant, Master of the Rolls, said in *Worrall v. Jacob* (1816, 1817):

> I apprehend it now to be settled, that this Court will not carry into execution articles of separation between husband and wife. It recognizes no power in them to vary the rights and duties growing out of the marriage contract or to effect, at their pleasure, a partial dissolution of the contract. It should seem to follow, that the Court would not acknowledge the validity of any stipulation that is merely accessary to an agreement for separation. The object of the covenant between the husband and the trustees, is to give efficacy to the agreement between the husband and the wife; and it does seem rather strange, that the auxiliary agreement should be enforced, while the principal agreement is held to be contrary to the spirit, and the policy, of the law. It has, however, been held, that engagements entered into between the husband and a third party shall be held valid and binding although they originate out of, and relate to, that unauthorized state of separation, in which the husband and wife have endeavoured to place themselves.[47]

The judges here found a way to construe separate maintenance contracts as male to male transactions, agreements between husbands and trustees. In so doing, they looked away from the consequences of contract ideology and returned to an earlier property regime in which men alone appeared publicly as the owners of property. The agreement of the woman here was not capable of creating an enforceable contract, but men were enabled to agree among themselves to provide maintenance for the woman.

As we have seen, the rule that trustees were required to create a valid separate maintenance agreement rested in part on the idea that some consideration on the wife's side was required. Here, without a long discussion of the complex developments in the theory of contract in the early nineteenth century, I can only comment very briefly on certain aspects of the more general third-stage rule that simple mutual covenants by the husband and wife to live apart and not molest each other are not valid, but that contracts with some additional consideration on each side are valid. Basically, by refusing to recognize the simple exchange of promises to live apart as valid, the judges consoled themselves that they were not actually enforcing separation agreements but merely recognizing ancillary agreements concerning property made after couples had independently agreed to separate. In the separation agreement in *Logan v. Birkett* (1833) a wife had charged her separate property with a £400 annuity for her husband; he, in exchange, released his marital rights in any and all the property which she might acquire after their separation. When the validity of this agreement was challenged and *Marshall v. Rutton* invoked to claim that it was "against the policy of the law" for the husband so to constitute "himself the dissolver of the marriage contract," Sir John Leach, Master of the Rolls, nevertheless held "that the release of the husband of his marital right in the future-acquired property of the wife" was a sufficient consideration to support the annuity.[48]

In the third-stage turmoil over what the judges would count as legitimate consideration the most ideologically fraught area was that of promises not to litigate issues of the marriage in the ecclesiastical courts. In *Hobbs v. Hull* (1788) Kenyon had decided to count a wife's promise not to sue her husband for cruelty or adultery in the ecclesiastical court as sufficient valuable consideration to entitle her claim for separate maintenance to prevail over the claims of her husband's creditors.[49] Since a principal purpose of separate maintenance contracts was to resolve conflicts privately, without the scandal of publicity, and also without the costs and hazards of litigation, it is not surprising that many contracts had such clauses in them. Should one of the parties attempt to repudiate a promise not to sue in the ecclesiastical courts and begin litigation there, the remedy was for the other party to get

an injunction from the secular courts. But in the period of conservative reaction after the French Revolution, fear that the established church was in danger was one of the most vivid Tory
fears. Judges like Lord Eldon, who were also important Tory politicians, worked tirelessly and effectively in Parliament to resist
repeated efforts to repeal the Test and Corporation Acts and all
bills for Catholic relief. Given their sense of the crucial importance
of a strong state church, they were loath to collaborate in allowing
its jurisdiction over matrimonial causes to be reduced. Eldon, Lord
Chancellor for twenty-four of the years between 1801 and 1827,
was a dominating conservative figure both as the chief lawyer in
the land and as Speaker of the House of Lords. Reviewing his
own career as a sitting judge after his retirement, he claimed quite
plausibly: "I have been constantly engaged in a struggle to leave
all these matters about separation rather to the Ecclesiastical Court,
than to take them in any degree from that Court; and that the
contrary practice is in my judgment bad policy."[50]

Yet the effects of his judicial philosophy considerably muddied
the waters on questions of the effects of separate maintenance
contracts generally and on clauses not to litigate in the ecclesiastical
courts particularly. On the one hand, as he pointed out very cred-
ibly in retirement, he had great reverence for precedent and did
not like to deny the clearly stated doctrines of the earlier cases
giving effect to separation deeds. On the other hand, as he insisted
with equal credibility, and as his remarks in *St. John* quoted above
suggest, no one could read all his decisions enforcing separate
maintenance contracts and suppose that he could ever "originally
have been a party to such doctrine." The effects of his principles—
and his famous excessive dubitiveness—are clearly visible in the
horribly protracted and complex litigation arising from two separation agreements entered into by the Earl of Westmeath and the
Countess of Westmeath, litigation which dragged on in many
courts, including the ecclesiastical courts, from 1819 to 1831,
when the new Lord Chancellor Lord Brougham finally helped put
an end to it. Eldon as Lord Chancellor in 1820 was asked by the
husband to issue an injunction to restrain proceedings at law for
the wife to recover her separation allowance and to order her deed
delivered up as against public policy; he refused to do so and sent
the parties to law. The deed contained a covenant that the husband
would not sue for restitution of conjugal rights in the church

courts, a covenant he subsequently ignored. The wife also had covenanted not to sue in the ecclesiastical courts for a divorce *a mensa et thoro* on the ground of his cruelty; her counsel continuously argued in the secular courts that this covenant was a valuable consideration that went to making the agreement valid. Not surprisingly, the church courts seem to have decided that they would not permit private separation agreements to bar suits for the restitution of conjugal rights.[51] When the Marquess sued in 1821 for a restitution of conjugal rights, the Marchioness replied with a suit for divorce on the grounds of his adultery and cruelty. There was never at any time doubt that he did hit her on several occasions. After an initial victory for him, she won a divorce for cruelty on appeal to Arches (1827). The appellate Arches judge decided to accord the separate maintenance agreement some evidentiary value, commenting:

> As a deed of separation upon mutual agreement, on account of unhappy differences, though containing a covenant not to bring a suit for restitution of conjugal rights, these articles would offer no impediment to the husband's present suit, but as evidence against him, . . . they appear unanswerable, and are a strong acknowledgment that the casus foederis had occurred. On that confession alone, coupled with the character and temper of his former acts, if the case had even rested here . . . I should have entertained considerable doubt whether the husband was entitled to the aid of the Court to compel his wife to return; whether the Court would not, at least, dismiss the wife.[52]

Eldon's strong dislike of assuming jurisdiction over issues arising from separation agreements actually seems to have led in his period to the courts of law rather than the courts of equity taking the lead in formulating these doctrines. Despite Eldon and after much struggle, the earlier doctrine of *Hobbs v. Hull* that a promise not to sue on past matrimonial misconduct was a valuable consideration was established.[53]

These first two of our third-stage rules, the rules requiring trustees and consideration, did not survive into the twentieth century. It is now agreed that contracts for separate maintenance require neither trustees for the wife nor consideration beyond mutual promises to live apart. Our third rule, however, the rule declaring contracts for future separation void as against public policy but contracts for immediate separation valid, has endured to our own time. At first the desirability or even the theoretical possibility of making such a distinction was doubted. In *Rodney v. Chambers* (1802), the court had decided that it could not say future contracts were invalid without overturning present contracts, indeed, without calling into question the very concept of the wife's separate property. The losing side in *Rodney* had argued that "it is contrary to the policy of law and to good morals to enter into any contract which has a direct tendency to loosen the band of union between husband and wife," and that future contracts were more noxious than present ones because "it is of more evil consequence to facilitate the happening of a mischief than to provide for it after it has happened."[54] But Mr. Justice Le Blanc had rebutted this and insisted: "I cannot see how it can be more illegal to contract for separate maintenance in case of future than of present separation. Upon the same ground it might equally be objected, that every provision by will or deed making a permanent provision for a wife apart, from the control of her husband, with whom she was then living, was illegal; because by rendering her independent of him, it would facilitate their separation."[55] Yet the decision in *Rodney* began to be doubted, and *Rodney* was finally and firmly overturned by Lord Chief Justice of King's Bench Abbott and Lord Chief Justice of Common Pleas Dallas in *Durant v. Titley* (1819). The couple in *Durant* had in 1809 entered into a kind of deed that was particularly odious to patriarchal judges, one under which the wife was entitled at any future time in the marriage to leave her husband and "to take any one of her children by her husband which she should fix on, to reside and live with her, except the eldest."[56] She did, in fact, in 1817 leave her husband and tried to take one child, "named Anguish," with her. The agreement, it was complained, attempted to permit the wife "to separate herself from her husband whenever she pleased" and to make the husband "a tenant at will" to the wife of his marital and paternal rights. Here the husband succeeded in having his contract declared void.

The last two rules of this third stage reimpose patriarchal structures by insisting on the husband's continued economic responsibility for the wife, despite the efforts and intents of the parties to declare the wife no longer in the status of wife but, from the moment of the separation, "as if she were sole and unmarried," to use a common formula of the contracts. Just as now many husbands do not actually pay alimony or child support which they have agreed to pay or been ordered to pay, so in the eighteenth century many husbands who had agreed to pay separate maintenance allowances did not actually pay them. The straightforward contract solution to this problem was to say that since the parties had agreed the wife was to be henceforth "as if she were sole and unmarried" and the husband was no longer liable for her debts, her remedy was for her or her trustees to sue the husband on the contract just as any other contract creditor would have. Under the contract, the husband was liable to her or to her trustees for the allowance but not liable to third parties like merchants to whom she became indebted after the separation. In the leading case of *Nurse v. Craig* (1806) a tailor and his wife had executed a separation deed according to which he agreed to pay her £13 a year (5s. a week). When he failed to pay, her sister, who provided her with necessary food, washing, and lodging, sued the tailor. The husband produced the deed and Sir James Mansfield found for the husband. On appeal, Sir James pointed out that he knew no earlier case where payment had ever been considered an essential circumstance, that the wife "lives as a feme sole," and further that he had often heard Lord Mansfield say "that where a separate maintenance was agreed upon, it put the parties in a new situation, and that the husband was relieved from any common law obligation, being subject to no other than that which was contained in the deed of separation."[57] Yet on appeal, Mansfield was outvoted three to one by his brother judges, all of whom were struck by the virtual uselessness to a very poor woman of a remedy involving a long suit in equity. (Mansfield's decision was appealed to a group of judges including himself; this was not an uncommon occurrence in eighteenth-century appellate procedures.) "If [the husband] refuse to perform that covenant, the wife may be starved before redress can be obtained," said Heath: "To suppose that a woman who is parted from her husband under an agreement for separate maintenance is not by law entitled to charge her husband with payment for necessaries, when he withholds that stipulated allowance, shocks my humanity and revolts my reason."

A related expression of economic anxiety about separated women and also a repudiation of the contract logic in favor of public control of agreements may be seen in *Hodgkinson v. Fletcher* (1814), in which Lord Ellenborough held not only that a sum must be actually paid but also that its amount "must be sufficient according to the degree and circumstances of the husband." Proceeding by analogy to the common law liability of the husband for his wife's necessaries, as suited to his rank, where the necessity of the articles in question to a particular wife was left to be decided by a jury, Ellenborough directed the jury to determine whether the wife's allowance was sufficient. "The mere acquiescence of the wife" in a specific amount, he reasoned, does not establish adequacy: "She might be willing to accept a provision wholly inadequate because she could not get more."[58] It is worth noting that even twentieth-century English law does not permit husbands and wives to be the sole arbiters of what level of support shall be provided for the wife. A representative modern text instructs that "a wife's right to future maintenance is a matter of public concern which she cannot barter away."[59] The Matrimonial Causes Act of 1973 (s. 34) makes any contractual agreement between husband and wife purporting to restrict her right to apply to a court for a maintenance order a void provision.

Similarly, our fifth rule not permitting a wife with a separate maintenance allowance to assign it to another expressed economic anxiety about separated wives and denied the implications of contract logic. If Sir James Mansfield's view that a woman with a separate maintenance allowance had separate property in that allowance were followed, then she ought to have all the powers over that property that any owner has over his property, including the power of alienation. Just such a view was advanced in *Hyde v. Price* (1797) when Mary Price, a wife with a separate maintenance, had used it as security for a loan, granting an annuity to Hyde in exchange for £560 she used to buy her son an army commission.[60] Relying on *Corbett v. Poelnitz* and similar cases, counsel for Hyde insisted a wife with a separate maintenance must obviously be able to dispose of the fund, just as she could obviously dispose of savings from it in any way she liked. But Sir Richard Arden, Master of the Rolls, rejected this logic, deciding that a separated wife could not dispose of such a fund and risk being left without any maintenance. To follow the contract logic, he felt, would go against the intention of the husband and risk putting the husband in a kind of double jeopardy, once for paying the allowance and then again, if the wife disposed of the fund, if she became a pauper and the parish required him to pay maintenance.

Judges in the 1790s expressed considerable concern over mar-

ried women's separate property generally. They worried that wives
were not able to hang on to property intended for their maintenance and for the maintenance of their young children, being, as
contemporaries said, "kissed or kicked" out of it by husbands or
others. The remedy they invented first for separate property settled on women in marriage settlements was to permit restraints
on anticipation that barred the wife from sinking the fund. Arden's
decision in *Hyde* is thus congruent with a more general turn-of-
the-century effort to create a distinction between men's property,
which was alienable, and married women's property, which was
less alienable and more designed for maintenance.

By structuring the separate maintenance contract as a male to
male transaction and by imposing these third-stage restrictions on
party autonomy, judges partially returned to a property regime
that had prevailed before contract ideology, one in which men
alone appeared publicly as the owners of property, women functioning as transmitters of inheritance and being provided, by a
different order of transaction—one within the domestic sphere—
with maintenance. In the eighteenth century when this property, understood to be for the transmission of inheritance and
maintenance, was labeled "married women's property" and made
the subject of contract, judges were tempted to suppose that it
was actually just like men's property. In *Corbett* Mr. Justice Buller
had been able to imagine that if a woman had "a power of contracting" with respect to some particular piece of separate property
"it must be a general" power—that the "ownership" of "property"
by women must mean that they could alienate it in the same ways
men could.[61] Yet, married women's property—not only property
like pin money but also separate maintenance allowances—was a
"creature of equity," as Lord Chancellor Thurlow realized when
he invented the restraint on anticipation, which having been invented by equity could be and was molded by equity to perform
traditional transmission and maintenance functions.

Conveyancers and judges, having together created something
called "married women's property," then subsequently had to puz-
zle over whether to treat it as though it were like men's property—
called "property"—or whether to develop idiosyncratic rules for
it alone. For a time, before 1800, the property coming to married
women under marriage settlements as pin money or under separate
maintenance contracts as separate maintenance allowances en-

couraged an illusion of symmetry, of men's property and women's property, of men capable of contracting and women capable of contracting. But this illusion was dispelled by a confrontation with the realities of what happened when the disruptive logic of symmetry was followed, what happened when men and women rejected the traditional prepackaged matrimonial dish of rights and responsibilities set before them and began to be their own carvers.

7

Conclusion

A. W. B. Simpson has aptly characterized eighteenth-century English legal history as "a black hole."[1] Despite some excellent recent work by a small number of scholars, only now is eighteenth-century legal history beginning to receive a little of the attention earlier lavished on medieval English legal history and on nineteenth-century American legal history.[2] As a scholar of the eighteenth century who has on occasion sought the advice of law professors on specific points of law in some of the cases in this book, I have several times been urged to shift the subject of my inquiries into "more interesting" or "better understood" periods. Rejecting such advice, I have stubbornly pressed on, taking whatever consolation I could from the realization that those I had hoped might be informants were no more able to answer my questions than I was. Nevertheless, I am vividly aware that my account of the history of the rules of married women's separate property cannot be considered authoritative. While I believe that what I have written does increase our knowledge of the development of these rules, indeed, that the approach I have used not only sheds light on a previously murky area but also suggests ways to illuminate other dark areas in this period, I am also aware of many unsolved problems and subjects about which we are still quite strikingly ignorant.

One object of my exploration of the legal rules of married women's property has been to show how, despite their appearance as private law rules, these rules nevertheless express public ideologies. Although "public" and "private" are significantly and importantly defined as the opposites of each other, what has been understood as "public" and what has been understood as "private" have varied significantly over time. The now apparently obvious distinction between public law (constitutional, criminal, regulatory) and private law (property, tort, contract, commercial) was by no means always an obvious way of dividing things. As Morton Horwitz has pointed out, ideas of a distinct public realm only began to crystalize in the sixteenth and seventeenth centuries with the emergence of nation states and new theories of sovereignty. Then, in relation to the claims of monarchs and parliaments to an unrestrained power to make law, "there developed a countervailing effort to stake out a distinctively private sphere free from the encroaching power of the state." It was not really until the nineteenth century that the distinction between public and private "was brought to the center stage" of English and American legal and political thought.[3] Moreover, it is also possible to consider the category of "private law rules" oxymoronic since these rules are made by judges holding public office and enforced by the power of the state's courts to imprison, to set fines and civil damages, to decree specific performance, and so on.[4] Equally, we may suspect that assertions of "public interest," when there is in fact no unitary public interest but rather a diverse mixture of classes and genders, serve to mask and to legitimate the interests of a particular male private interest group.

The enterprise of making married women's property rules between 1660 and 1833 presents itself as a private law process. Individuals in the propertied classes with which I have here been concerned usually, although certainly not invariably, married after agreeing to various kinds of settlements or prenuptial agreements that stipulated how interests in what was to be marital property were to be divided during the marriage, after the death of one or the other of the spouses, and—often—in the next generation of children to be born of the marriage. As we have seen, conveyancers who drafted the settlements invented a variety of tactics designed to allow individuals to make private property arrangements other than those created by common law. Thus, they developed ways to avoid common law dower and inserted settlement clauses giving married women pin money or other separate property that they were to enjoy to their own separate use free from the debts of their husbands, as though they were feme sole. In the event that a marriage proved unhappy, lawyers were also ready to draw up separate maintenance contracts according to which the couple agreed to live apart and in which they bound themselves to new financial arrangements.

Whether any particular one of these new conveyancing innovations was to have the effect desired by client and conveyancer, however, was up to the judges; a new rule is not established until it receives judicial sanction. At this point in the process, public policy considerations enter. Historians, familiar with legislative enactments of public policy in the nineteenth and twentieth centuries, need to be more alert to the possibility of policy in earlier periods being made outside Parliament, as here, by the judges; consequently, they must be ready to look for evidence of change outside the legislative process, as we have found evidence of change in case law and treatises. There were three important public interests asserted in the married women's property cases discussed here: the public interest in having a system of property law that ensured secure titles to property, the public interest in maintaining the alienability of land, and the public interest in promoting families and good behavior within families. All of these interests are ideological.

About the development of these legal rules and about their ideological character I will, in this final chapter, draw some conclusions with confidence. However, the legal rules of married women's separate property in and of themselves could not determine women's experience. It is only natural to want to know how changes in the legal rules concerning married women's property affected women. Yet I must emphasize that certain commonsense assumptions about the relation of legal rules to social practice are not necessarily valid assumptions. What a woman's experience of the property regime actually was depended on at least five important variables: (1) the legal rules; (2) how, or even whether, the legal rules were applied in practice; (3) the particular forms of property at a given time; (4) the class to which she belonged; and (5) the social construction of gender. Over the period from 1660 to 1833 the interactions among these variables were very complex.

Nevertheless, let us at this point return to the four possible histories of married women's separate property suggested in Chapter 2—the sociological, the liberal, the neo-Marxist, and the feminist—in light of what we have learned about the legal ideology of married women's separate property and in light of the current historiography concerned with the rise of the great estate, strict settlement, and the condition of women. (Obviously, what I can say here about the actual condition of women is necessarily more derivative and more speculative than my conclusions about the legal ideology; it is intended more to respond to readers' curiosity about what connections might be made between this study of legal ideology and other work in social history than it is to make an original contribution to social history.)

Current Historiography and Legal Rules

Readers acquainted with the twentieth-century historiography of the early modern landed classes may, reasonably enough, want to know what implications this analysis of legal ideology has for the debates currently raging among scholars such as Sir John Habbakuk, Lawrence Stone and Jeanne Stone, Christopher Clay, Lloyd Bonfield, J. V. Beckett, and David Spring and Eileen Spring.[5] For almost fifty years this debate has been powerfully shaped by Habbakuk's two classic articles, "English Landownership, 1660–1740," and "Marriage Settlements in the Eighteenth Century," in which he argued that the development and use of strict settlements among landed families contributed to the rise of the great estate.[6] Since 1940 historians have been debating both whether anything that could fairly be called the rise of the great estate occurred in the eighteenth century and whether, if it did occur, strict settlement made an important contribution to it.

Habbakuk initially proposed a neat vision of the economic function of the strict settlement. According to Habbakuk in 1940 and 1950, strict settlement clearly promoted the growth of the great estates and advantaged larger land holders against smaller land holders. By keeping the current heir a life tenant only, the settlement protected against sales of settled land by cash-hungry or feckless heirs. In providing alternate male kin as heirs for the estate at moments when the family had not produced a surviving son, strict settlement clearly resisted the dispersal of these estates to sisters as coparceners, which would have occurred had the rules of common law been permitted to operate. By common law, land that went either to sisters or to a single heiress would, if the woman died without issue, at her death return to her family. But if she had issue, the land would descend through them, and, since her issue would normally bear their father's name, in that sense, the land would seem to go to the father's family.[7] More ingeniously, Habbakuk also proposed that, once mortgage money was reasonably available, the larger landowners as a group had been able to raise themselves by their own bootstraps.[8] The wealthiest landowners were in a position to attract the brides with the largest portions, but once a bride's land-rich father had good access to mortgage money, then he could mortgage land to pay his daughter's large portion, leaving himself no less land and giving his son-in-law cash with which to buy still more land. In a series of three recent articles, Habbakuk has continued to maintain that "marriage was the principal means by which landed families extended their estates" and that marriages with heiresses tended to result in a leveling up in size of estates and in disproportionate increases in the size of larger estates.[9]

Others have expressed considerable doubt that the strict settlement could have functioned so efficiently. Even in the wealthiest families, it was very unlikely that, at a given time, all the land belonging to the family was strictly settled. Most studies of settlement practice have recognized that there were some economic disincentives to strict settlement and that families tried to balance the advantages and disadvantages of strict settlement by settling some core land holdings, including the main house and surrounding land, and leaving other, remoter lands out of the settlement so that they could be dealt with more freely, even sold in case of need. Furthermore, Lloyd Bonfield has urged, contemporary demographic facts meant that a significant number of fathers did not live long enough to see their eldest sons come of age and marry; in such families the strict settlement was not likely to be renegotiated, and the heir would come into the estate not as a life tenant only but rather in tail male with power to alienate.[10]

Among the other more important objections that have been raised to Habbakuk's thesis is that portions, in fact, were frequently not spent on buying new land. Bonfield, studying more than 230 Kent and Northamptonshire settlements drawn between 1600 and 1740 observed that only very rarely did strict settlements stipulate that portions were to be spent on land and found "little evidence to suggest that portions were actually expended on the acquisition of land."[11] As noted in Chapter 4 in discussing the bargaining that occurred at the making of marriage settlements, families often entered into agreements that the bride's father would pay only interest on the capital sum supposed to be his daughter's portion. Moreover, even when capital sums were actually paid at marriage, they frequently went to pay off debts the groom or the groom's family had already incurred; sometimes such sums were used to provide portions for the groom's siblings or other family members. Thus, in the families of Yorkshire baronets Peter Roebuck studied, numbers of portions were not paid cash down and, among those that were, we find instances such as the £6,000 portion of Lady Gertrude Stanhope, eldest daughter of Philip, Earl of Chesterfield, being used entirely to pay off a mortgage debt of the fourth Baronet Hotham when she married the fifth Baronet.[12] Even had the bride's father mortgaged his land and had the cash been used to buy land for the groom, Christopher Clay has argued, a net loss would have resulted because in this period the yield from land was less than the rate of interest on mortgages.[13]

As a consequence of such criticisms and others, most historians seem to have backed away from both the claim that strict settlement succeeded in creating a virtual equivalent of perpetuities in tail male and the claim that, at least in any simple or monocausal sense, strict settlement caused the larger landowners to increase significantly the size of their holdings at the expense of smaller holders. While not finding the actual growth of great estates terribly pronounced, many have commented on the success of the larger landowners in maintaining their estates from generation to generation and on a movement of larger owners to consolidate holdings scattered in various counties into larger estates in a single county.[14] Landowners' interest in consolidation has been plausibly linked to the increased importance of parliamentary power in this period. Some participants in the debate have recently arrived at positions which admit that strict settlements did not, in fact, settle property so strictly as was once thought—but now add that this very "flexibility" made them all the more effective in practice. Thus Lawrence Stone, who in his earlier *The Family, Sex, and Marriage, 1500–1800* basically followed Habbakuk's suggestions, in his and Jeanne Stone's more recent *An Open Elite?* writes: "The central significance of the strict settlement was that it was in practice not very strict. Effective controls lay not in legal documents but in states of mind."[15]

Historians have increasingly appreciated the difficulty of reaching economic conclusions based on settlement documents. These documents usually describe the family holdings, particularly land, in ways that do not indicate its economic value. Bonfield observes that "settlements of the early eighteenth century rarely state the value of the patrimony," and he correctly concludes that using settlements alone, "it is therefore impossible to surmise the proportion of portions to estate value."[16] A. W. P. Malcomson puts the case nicely when he comments that a settlement "is apt to be as uncommunicative as the lawyer who drew it up."[17] Not only is it virtually impossible to state the quantitative value of an estate from the original marriage settlement, but testamentary devise cases of the kind described in Chapter 4 illustrate only one of several ways in which the provisions in a settlement might be subsequently altered. Another and happier occasion on which original settlement agreements might be altered is noted by Judith Lewis, who observes that aristocratic husbands often gave their wives "extravagant presents" (or, I may add, supplemented their pin money or jointures) when their wives gave birth to a son, particularly an heir.[18] Only in-depth studies of a single family's finances over some generations, like Ray Kelch's of the Duke of Newcastle or W. A. Maguire's of the Earls of Donegall, studies that use settlements along with other evidence of income and expense, really allow much sense either of the total amount of wealth that was distributed within the family or of the way or extent to which the provisions of a particular settlement ever came into effect.[19] Such studies are inevitably few and far between and are usually also of notably untypical families, so attempts to generalize from them would be hazardous.

From my point of view, it is striking how tightly focused this Habbakuk debate has remained on the landed wealth of the family as controlled by the heir. Since land was the basis of political power, it is not surprising or inappropriate that historians have been concerned with how land holdings were acquired, retained, or increased. Certainly we want to know what legal, political, social, and economic arrangements made it possible for an individual like George Granville Leveson-Gower, second Duke of Sutherland, to control thousands of acres in Staffordshire and

Shropshire.[20] Yet most male historians seem to me oddly identified with the perspective of the male heir and even with his supposed drive for accumulation. The eighteenth-century lawyer's characterization of women's common law right to dower as a "clog to alienability" is echoed by the twentieth-century male historian's frequent characterization of jointure as a drain on the estate. Women figure in this historiography as bearers or sources of assets (when their portions can be "captured" by an heir in need) or dependents whose needs take assets away from the heroic job of accumulation. Quite sharp distinctions are made between the interest of the "family," understood as economic interests, and the interests of women, who seem to be individuals competing against the "family" interest rather than integral and necessary parts of the "family"—perhaps even sharper distinctions than those made by eighteenth-century patriarchs themselves. Thus, Bonfield writes: "Likewise widows were detrimental to the family interest because they required the estate to support a second, somewhat more modest household for a varying period. A wife who had the courtesy to waive her demographic 'right' to survive her husband by upwards of fifteen years after having dutifully brought a substantial portion that had been intended to provide for her widowhood might likewise contribute to painless retrenchment."[21] That, even in the wealthiest families most amply provided with servants, women's reproductive work was critical to the "success of the family" gets little attention, perhaps because childbearing has been thought of as a part of nature outside history.[22] Even biographies of important eighteenth-century politicians or in-depth studies of particular families tend to consider wives very cursorily, once at the moment of marriage and again at the moment of death. To try to gain an accurate picture of the real economic situation even of women in these famous families from such accounts is an exercise in frustration since the authors ask so few relevant questions. Among the questions that this book has shown need to be asked before we can conclude that a provision made in a settlement was the provision a particular woman actually enjoyed are: whether the portion a bride was supposed to have had according to newspaper accounts or settlement documents actually got paid, whether the couple quarreled over the payment of pin money, whether there were additional postnuptial financial agreements in the family, whether the wife subsequently agreed to relinquish all or part of her jointure, whether the wife subsequently agreed to waive the provisions made for her in the settlement in favor of acquiescing in provisions made in her husband's will, whether if the wife were widowed adequate jointure payments were actually made, or whether the widow enjoyed dower or free bench in land left out of the family settlements and trusts. Historians have frequently used settlement documents—and settlement documents alone—as evidence for stating the portion or jointure sums of individual women or as evidence for calculating general portion/jointure ratios, and so on. Although these documents do offer valuable evidence of bargains agreed to at one point, it should be understood that until such questions as I have raised are asked and answered, we cannot know for certain what income a wife actually enjoyed.

Common sense would seem to dictate that there must be a relationship between the legal rules concerning married women's property and the real wealth and condition of married women, yet caution is required in attempting to infer practice from theory. Some of the sharpness and apparent irreconcilability of the historiographical debate on the eighteenth-century landed family has probably resulted from historians, fallaciously, inferring social practice and social consequences from their knowledge of legal rules and legal arrangements. Thus, Stone and Stone in *An Open Elite?* offer what seems to me a rather idyllic view of the strict settlement, whereby it

> preserved the patrimony for the eldest son of the marriage, and failing a son for the next or closest male relative; safeguarded the bride's jointure or pension if she became a widow; and guaranteed adequate financial provisions for daughters or younger sons. Flexibility was also achieved by provisions allowing the current owner to raise capital, and by the use of private Acts of Parliament in exceptional cases to change the settlement in order to remedy any gross injustices which might have arisen. The device was thus in principle satisfactory to all parties.[23]

Certainly, this is what strict settlements were supposed to do. In *An Open Elite?* the Stones consider seriously whether the patrimony was, in fact, usually preserved for the eldest son and find that it was. The Stones, however, do not explore with equal seriousness whether, in fact, brides' jointures were "safeguarded" and whether provisions for daughters were "adequate"; nor do they look for information as to whether women (or younger sons, for that matter) thought the arrangements made for them were satisfactory. They do not, for instance, look for the kind of contemporary comment (quoted in Chapter 3) suggesting that opposition to the establishment of registration of titles was in part based on owners' desires to keep settlements secret from dependent family members and owners' fears that, were other family members to know how family property had been divided, their discontent would disrupt family harmony.

Legal rules can fail to have what one might suppose were their obvious social effects for a wide variety of reasons. In the early modern period, one reason some legal rules failed to shape social practice was that people who were presumed to be applying them or whose lives they were intended to affect simply did not know what they were. A modern scholar working on the London legal elite soon enough has the unsettling experience of comparing notes with a colleague working with some provincial archive where archaic, muddled, or otherwise "invalid" (from the London elite's perspective) rules are the rules practically applied. For example, in 1769, decades after London legal intellectuals thought burning women for petty treason had been abolished, a newspaper reported that near Maidstone, one Susannah Lott had been convicted of petty treason for poisoning her husband; she "was drawn on a hurdle . . . , and fixed to a stake, with an iron chain around her middle, and her body burned to ashes."[24] My study of dower has suggested that in some quarters the common law right to dower was simply "forgotten" considerably before the Dower Act of 1833. Although some early modern women took an interest in their legal entitlements to marital property, and there are a few examples of individual women consulting counsel to discover their legal rights to property, most women appear to have been quite ignorant of the subject and inhibited about becoming informed or asserting legal entitlements of which they were aware. The business of negotiating settlements and enforcing rights under them seems generally to have been left to men. Men themselves, as is clear from the election cases discussed in Chapter 4, were also capable of forgetting settlement provisions when, many years later, they came to draw up their wills. Even legal professionals made a significant number of mistakes. That they should have done so is unsurprising given the rather poor law reporting available to them and the extreme difficulty of the law of real property in this period. Their reliance on customary conveyancing practices also contributed to mistakes when practice tradition was from time to time disrupted by strikingly bold innovations. Hence, we have Blackstone's explanation that private acts were needed to establish titles hopelessly clouded "by the ingenuity of some, and the blunders of other practitioners"; and we find the problems W. A. Maguire has noted bedeviling the Earl of Donegall and many other Irish landowners who, when they needed to sell land to raise cash, sometimes had such extreme difficulty establishing clear title to land they wanted to sell that the land was practically inalienable.[25] Hence, also, the plausibility of the decisions we have encountered based on the maxim *communis error facit jus*.

Another reason why particular legal rules can fail to shape social practice is that the rules apply to nonexistent or virtually nonexistent entities. Householders in modern Cambridge, Massachusetts, may be legally entitled to certain pasturage rights on Cambridge Common, yet, since no householders now have cows (indeed, since by other legal rules no householder is permitted to have a cow), no cows are presently visible chomping grass on the common. Eighteenth-century widows were entitled to dower in freehold land of which their husbands had been legal owners at any time during the marriage, but, as we have seen, gentry and aristocratic husbands used trusts to avoid being legally seized of freehold land. Some such rules are principally archaic, the leftover rubbish of the legal system, and perform no social function. Others may perform important ideological functions, as I have argued the common law dower rules did—after a large-scale disappearance of dower—in justifying the fairness of jointure as freely selected by wives in exchange for dower.

Still another and crucial reason why a particular legal rule can fail to shape social practice is that—sometimes unbeknownst to the historian—people have developed effective avoidance practices. Or, to put this another way, one rule seems to require or to prohibit a certain behavior, but somewhere, elsewhere in the total rule system, another rule allows avoidance of the first. In early modern English law, the gulf between obvious statutory and judge-made rules, on the one hand, and practice, on the other hand, appears to have been very wide indeed. For example, by the usury statutes in this period contracts to lend money at more than 5 percent were invalid as usurious contracts. Yet in the late eighteenth century many people borrowed money at rates far above this, rates roughly equivalent to our credit card rates today. This was done through an unusual form of annuity contract.[26] Instead of, as earlier and as in the annuity sales familiar to us today, the seller of the annuity contracting to make annual payments for the buyer's life, in these late eighteenth-century annuities the buyer got a capital sum in return for his promise to make annual payments to the seller over a defined period, conventionally six years. Sellers of annuities regularly took advantage of the new life insurance offices to insure the life of the buyer for about 5 percent. Thus, the debt-ridden or otherwise cash-hungry buyer got money at about 18 percent and the seller, subtracting for his insurance cost, got a secured debt paying about 12 percent interest. Naturally, questions were raised as to whether such annuity contracts were usurious. But in *Murray v. Harding* (1773), Chief Justice De Grey decided (taking no official cognizance of the seller's practice of insuring the buyer's life) that, since the buyer could die at any point during the contract and have no further obligation to make payments, the capital sum was at risk and the contract not usurious. Contemporary critics of this traffic in annuities complained that men they characterized as "dirty little monied rascal[s]" were taking advantage of "young noblemen . . . of first rank and fortune," and lamented also that the lenders' promises of secrecy were so regularly broken that such noblemen's names were tarnished and "made cheap." Yet, as historian after historian working on a particular segment of the upper classes in this period has discovered, the eighteenth-century upper classes were net debtors, people living above their means and in constant need of credit in one form or another. Parliament wished to stigmatize lending money at more than 5 percent as a way of acquiring money practiced by bad people, in contrast to acquiring money through inheritance or in the form of rents, supposed to be the way of acquiring money practiced by good people, so they kept the usury statutes. But upper-class people also needed cash which prudent persons refused to lend them at 5 percent, so Parliament also continued to tolerate the traffic in annuities, merely establishing a register of transactions and making void annuity contracts with minors. Interestingly, Thomas Erskine, himself a younger son of the aristocracy famed as an eloquent barrister, commented that purchasing such annuities "was the only way younger children, especially females, of the first families could make their portions maintain the decencies of their stations."[27]

Much of my study of married women's property might be regarded as a study of effective avoidance practices and of judicial sanction of avoidance practices. Trusts, of course, have long been and still are mechanisms to avoid the operation of common law and statutory rules. We have seen how trusts were used to avoid common law dower—although not common law curtesy. We have also observed other avoidance tactics such as the mortgage tacking used to subvert even the limited registration of titles to land and to postpone doweress's interests to those of commercial purchasers. The development of the doctrine of equitable jointure, I would argue, countenanced avoidances of the security requirements of the Statute of Uses and so made jointures less secure than they would otherwise have been.

The Sociological Story

Despite the necessity of such preliminary caution about the relation between legal rules and practice, let us now see what can be said about the four stories of married women's separate property we have earlier suggested: the sociological, the liberal, the neo-Marxist, and the feminist. According to the sociological story, each society makes some provision for women; when larger social structures change, provisions for women change to fit the new structures. If the largely agricultural society of the early seventeenth century becomes the commercial, imperial society of 1833, the provisions made for women will have to change; changes are "adaptations" rather than "improvements" or "detriments." The emphasis here is on the function of each local social practice in the larger social universe. Certainly, by a rough, low-level test of functionality, we must say that both the system of married women's property in 1660 and the system in 1833 were functional: at both points provision for women was adequate enough so that massive numbers of women were not starving in the streets and so that the nation survived.

Clearly it is reasonable to say that some "adaptations" had to be made to the reality that there were newer forms of wealth in addition to land. In the seventeenth century land was both a more important and a more exclusive form of wealth than it later came to be in the nineteenth century. At the very end of the seventeenth century and in the early eighteenth century the development of the mortgage market and the invention of government funds began to provide significant competition to land for investors. Unlike stocks, which earned themselves a very bad reputation at the time of the South Sea Bubble in 1722, mortgages and government funds increasingly were considered safe, passive investments suitable for women's money. I have explained in Chapter 3 how the judicial treatment of the equity of redemption encouraged mortgagors and made it easier to treat land as a capital asset.

During the eighteenth century, moreover, there was a sea change in the understanding of the purpose of property in all its forms, a change from considering property a stable resource in a fixed form for the purpose of maintaining human life (Model I), to considering property a more abstract, unstable asset easily transformable into whatever its highest economic use might be at a given time (Model II). In Model I, to "own" a piece of arable land means to be able to enjoy the produce of the fields year after year. If this arable is turned into something else—if the "owner" turns it into a forest or opens up new mines on it, for instance—he forfeits it for waste. In Model II, there is no impeachment for waste; "owners" expect to be able to turn arable land into forest, if forests are more profitable at the moment, or to be able to level forests to build factories. In Model I land is to be used, not sold, whereas in Model II alienability is maximized.

Nevertheless, the sociological claim that the rules for married women's separate property had to change between 1660 and 1833 to "adapt" to these transformations in the forms of property has to be viewed with some suspicion. While the general rules of real property were becoming Model II rules, Model I rules were in significant ways retained, and invented, for the landed property of the governing classes. Thus, the rationales of property law at the end of the eighteenth century were massively contradictory. The retention of the rule insulating landed property from contract debts was one old Model I rule benefiting the governing classes; the rules enabling strict settlement in tail male were important new Model I rules for their benefit. The various anti-alienation provisions conveyancers and judges invented for new forms of married women's separate property were also Model I rules, for example, the restraint on anticipation and the rule prohibiting the beneficiary of a separate maintenance allowance from assigning the fund from which her maintenance was to come. Similarly, the rule in *Peacock* that real property purchased with cash that was the wife's separate property is to be treated as real property descending to her heirs and not as her separate property was a Model I rule. Yet all forms of married women's separate property were not treated according to Model I rules. Most dramatically, jointure gave wives a kind of property more alienable than dower. Also, the development of the doctrine of equitable jointure, as we have seen, depended upon treating as interchangeable entities like freehold, copyhold, and personal property, which the older law had insisted on treating according to distinct rules and as not interchangeable. The election cases reviewed in Chapter 4 also show confusion arising from competing ideas of treating the testator's property as a set of immiscible species of property and of treating it as a mixed general fund. Thus, in some contexts the traditional categories of property were virtually fetishized, judges and even Parliament behaving as though to transgress against them would be to make chaos come again; in other contexts these traditional categories were quite blithely ignored.

Against the sociological story's notion of functional "adaptation" we also must observe that, in some important respects, the eighteenth-century system of property law exhibited considerable apparent dysfunction. Despite the complexity of settlements and despite the best efforts of conveyancers to plan for future generations, what Peter Roebuck has so aptly called "demographic roulette" time and time again frustrated the intentions of planners.[28] The archaic procedures of land transfer, so dear to Blackstone, also produced very high transaction costs. As for settlements and women, when we are told that settlements "guaranteed adequate financial provisions" for daughters that enabled them to marry, we must wonder why, then, roughly 25 percent of the daughters of peers remained celibate in 1800 (a problem to which I will return later in this chapter).

Even the most fundamental and obvious function of a system

of real property law, to guarantee security of title, was quite imperfectly accomplished. Despite the apparently nonideological character of the public interest in having a system of property law that ensures secure titles to property, the belief that judges ought to act so as to promote security of title was ideological, and like any ideological principle was—in Marx's phrase—an "empty generality torn away from the facts." We have seen how this principle was used selectively in ways that promoted some interests and not others. On the one hand, in a variety of married women's property cases, including *Chaplin,* the public interest in security of title was asserted to be so important that it ought to prevail over what the judges themselves characterized as technical correctness. On the other hand, the judges and Parliament certainly did not always act as though promoting security of title were a paramount interest. Judicial permissiveness toward complex conveyancing tactics, including the multiplication of contingent future interests, the manipulation of terms of years, and the multiplication of equitable interests separate and distinct from legal interests, actually contributed to making titles insecure. Nor did Parliament believe security of title was important enough to accept various proposals for a national system of registration of titles to land. Thus, judicial assertions that particular decisions in married women's property cases were forced by a paramount public interest in security of title cannot be accepted at face value.

Nor can we concede, at least for the landed elite of the eighteenth century, that a Model I forced share of land would have been hopelessly maladaptive. For this elite, land continued to be the principal source of wealth. It is also worth observing that an important irony of this history of married women's property is that, although the shift from Model I to Model II ideas of property normally also entails a shift from qualitative distinctions (for example, forest versus meadow, freehold versus copyhold, life tenant versus term of years) to quantitative valuation (equivalency in numerical cash terms), when judges considered women's entitlements they both abandoned qualitative standards (allowing "equitable jointures" in base estates or of personal property to replace dower) and refused to consider issues of quantitative equivalence—on the ground that marriage bargains were too private and too subjective for such public scrutiny.

The Liberal Story

If the sociological story thus seems weak in its explanatory power, is the liberal story any more convincing? Like the sociological story, the liberal story highlights what we have admitted to be the reality of change from a world of relatively stable landed property to a world in which land increasingly becomes a commodity like others and a world in which newer forms of wealth like government funds and East India stock begin to replace land as significant forms of wealth. Unlike the sociological story, the liberal story also emphasizes the benefits of a general increase in wealth as a consequence of this transformation, stresses the importance for this purpose of promoting alienability, and points to what it heralds as improvements, including improvements in the condition of women. By itself, the transformation in the forms of property might suggest the reasonableness of replacing women's entitlement to land with entitlements to other and newer forms of property. At least as far as the end of our period is concerned, however, we cannot accept at face value the liberal interpretation that dower rights had to be defeated because of a general policy in favor of promoting alienability.

Assertions of public interest in promoting alienability were more obviously ideological than assertions of public interest in promoting security of title, and contemporaries like Blackstone understood that whether alienability was limited or promoted was a political issue. There have been two conventional histories of alienability, one that might be called the lawyers' history and one that might be called the more general history. Within the lawyers' history of property, alienability has traditionally been seen as a grand longitudinal theme: private owners and their lawyers struggle to control the ownership of their land after their deaths, hoping to make the original owner's dead hand reach from the grave to control and shape future uses, but periodically the king or the state reaches out to slap down the dead hand and to resist the owner's attempts to create perpetuities. Within the more general history, the story of alienability is told not so much as the story of a see-saw back and forth between owners' desire for mortmain and the state's hostility to perpetuities as the story of a single shift from medieval minimal alienability to modern maximized alienability, the shift described above as from Model I to Model II. This shift, as Robert Gordon's discussion of adaptation theory shows, has generally been represented as progress and a good thing.

But the rationales of property law at the end of the eighteenth century were profoundly contradictory with respect to alienability. On the one hand, the general rules of property with respect to alienability were becoming Model II rules. Since the Statute of Wills (1540) landowners had had the legal power to dispose of freeholds by will, and throughout the early modern period entails could be barred by common recovery. Under the bankruptcy statutes traders' lands could be sold to pay their debts. During the Restoration and the eighteenth century Parliament acted aggressively on the older relation of landlord and leaseholder to create something much more like the modern landlord tenant relationship. Landlords to whom rent was due were for the first time permitted not merely to seize and hold chattel property for unpaid rent but to change the form of such property by selling it and keeping the cash. Toward the end of the eighteenth century also, the mortgagor's ability to retain land after default of payment was lessened by the practice of inserting an express power of sale for the mortgagee in the mortgage deed. Public interest in promoting alienability, as we have seen, was invoked to justify the erosion of women's dower rights. In *Radnor* and related cases the courts permitted the assignment of satisfied terms of years to purchasers or mortgagees to defeat dower.

On the other hand, the alleged public interest in promoting freedom of alienation did not stop the judges from accepting conveyancing tactics which promoted strict settlement on the male heir or their acceptance of restraints on anticipation of married women's separate property. Nor did it interfere with the invention of new rules that afforded landowners further protection against their own bad behavior—the new gambling statutes, which made conveyances of land to satisfy gambling debts void, for instance. Clearly, alienability was by no means a necessary incident of property by the early nineteenth century, and assertions of public interest in promoting freedom of alienability, said to motivate decisions like that in *Radnor* and judicial willingness to see doweress's rights defeated by the interests of purchasers, were very selectively applied.

Another strand of a liberal history of the transformations in married women's property in this period is more affective than economic. Historians have not drawn much attention to the point made earlier that the substitution of jointure and other forms of contractual separate property for women, property not forfeitable for adultery and elopement, meant freedom for women from some of the customary status constraints that required dower and free bench to be forfeited for such behavior. The number of adulterous women living apart from their husbands and enjoying legal support from their husband's estates, although very disturbing to contemporaries, was small. Living husbands who wished to discipline their straying wives retained the legal power to do so, the power exercised by Lord Belvedere when, suspecting Lady Belvedere had committed adultery with his brother, he locked her up from 1744 until her death in 1774 at his second seat, Gaulston Park.[29]

Most historians have been more interested in the idea that the condition of daughters whose parents married with settlements improved because those daughters had "guaranteed" portions that allowed them the freedom to choose their own marriage partners without the fear of being disinherited by disapproving parents. Lawrence Stone has pressed this claim forcefully, stating that "patriarchal authority . . . was only undermined after 1660, when 'strict settlement' deprived the father of his power to give or withhold, by stipulating the provision allocated to each unborn child at the time of the parents' marriage."[30] Similarly, Randolph Trumbach, in *The Rise of the Egalitarian Family,* sees portions in aristocratic families as making "greater allowance for romantic rather than arranged marriages, for domesticity over patriarchy."[31]

Perhaps, though, not too much weight ought to be given to this purported liberation of daughters to enjoy portions with the men of their choice. Some settlements did fix the portions of individual daughters, others did not. Trumbach himself in the set of aristocratic settlements he studied found that after 1720 it became the predominant practice to provide a lump sum for all younger children, leaving it "at a parents' discretion to decide what share each child should receive" and providing "that it was to be equally shared only if no disposition had been made before the parents' death."[32] Other settlements provided that a daughter who married without the permission of a named relative was not to have her portion, and the Marriage Act of 1753 required parental consent for the marriage of a minor. Well-known upper-class women who were coerced into marriages with men they did not like for financial reasons that made sense to their relatives are easy enough to bring to mind, as, for example, Mary Granville (later Mrs. Delany), who at eighteen was married to Alexander Pendarves when he was nearly sixty, or Hester Salusbury (later Mrs. Piozzi), who was married to the brewer Henry Thrale. Of greater practical importance than explicit denials of portions or clear coercion, daughters in the classes that married with settlements had little opportunity to meet and form relationships with men of whom their parents would not have approved, and in this way the socialization of daughters itself effectively and severely limited misalliances.[33]

A good example of the difficulty of extrapolating from either a particular settlement scheme or demographic data (or both together) to a conclusion about an improvement in the actual condition of women is, I believe, to be found in two arguments Lawrence Stone and Jeanne Stone make in *An Open Elite?* They begin by charting a dramatic decline in the rate of remarriage of widows to inheritors of great estates during the early modern period. I have adapted their table to show the experience of widows only (they also show a decline in the rate of marriage to heiresses) in Table 2. This decline appears to them evidence of the transformation to the companionate marriage and the affective family about the mid-eighteenth century, a transformation described in Lawrence Stone's earlier *The Family, Sex, and Marriage in England, 1500–1800.* If marriages for dynastic and economic motives were increasingly supplanted by marriages based on personal affection, "one would expect to find," they write, "a decline in the number of wealthy squires or above who pursued and captured widows or heiresses"—precisely what they have now found here in *An Open Elite?* "Marriage with a widow or an heiress," they comment, "is always fraught with the not unjustified suspicion that the motive is mercenary rather than emotional."[34]

Table 2. Proportion of all marriages by inheritors to widows

Period of birth	Marriages to widows (%)	All marriages (N)
1549	22	95
1550–1599	11	237
1600–1649	11	292
1650–1699	8	278
1700–1749	5	261
1750–1799	6	265
1800–	3	231

Yet, surely, there are several possible explanations for this apparent decrease in the attractiveness of widows to inheritors other than an increase in marriages for affection. The Stones' account seems to make certain assumptions they do not explicitly state: first, that in purely economic terms widows were conspicuously more valuable than unmarried women, and consistently so from 1549 to 1800; second, that a widow was a less attractive object for personal affection than an unmarried woman; and, third, that the level of widows' desire for remarriage with inheritors was roughly constant from 1549 to 1800. None of these assumptions, it seems to me, are self-evident. Instead of implying that, in the later eighteenth century, inheritors increasingly turned away from rich but personally unappealing old crones, sacrificing some economic advantage to personal desire for an attractive partner, one might venture to explain the same table by suggesting that widows generally became poorer. Indeed, subsequently the Stones do suggest that "the growing sophistication of the trustee system . . . gave a widow greater ability to protect her property from being squandered by her second husband for his own benefit," in which case the widow would have been poorer as far as the second husband was concerned.[35] (The reader will recall, however, my account in Chapter 2 of the rules permitting such widows to make only certain "unselfish dispositions" without the consent of their subsequent husbands.) Perhaps the total assets available not only to a second husband but to a widow herself should she remarry decreased. As we have seen, if a widow in 1549 had a life estate in her dower or jointure, she brought that life estate to a second or subsequent marriage; if a widow in 1800 had a jointure contingent on her remaining a widow, then she had neither a portion nor a jointure to bring to a second marriage and so might have been less rather than more economically desirable than a single woman. I have suggested that such clauses may have become more common over this period, although I certainly cannot demonstrate that they did. My point at the moment is simply that evidence such as that provided by the Stones does not allow us to reach so quickly the conclusion they suggest about an increase in marriages for affection.

Alternatively, if widows were making out like the bandits some seem to think them, then perhaps they simply could afford to live independently and increasingly preferred not to remarry. The

Stones, in fact, make an argument of this sort about the never-married daughters of the elite. Observing that the celibacy rate of elite daughters was unusually high and got higher over the course of the eighteenth century, rising to about 25 percent for daughters of peers in 1800, they suggest that the size and security of daughters' portions, coupled with the fact that portions commonly came to be payable at majority rather than at marriage, meant that these women were not forced by necessity to marry and that they elected to please themselves by remaining single. This argument is probably more plausible as an explanation of declining remarriage rates for widows than it is as an explanation for a high female celibacy rate in the eighteenth century. To marry once is to escape the social dysfunction and social opprobrium attached to spinsters; twice is unnecessary for this purpose. Even absent such powerful social constraints to marry once, anyone convinced of the optimism of youth and the greater caution of experience is inclined to suspect a widow with a "competence" is likely to be more risk-averse to marriage than a single girl. The celibacy rates ranging from 20 to 27 percent for daughters of peers during the eighteenth century were very high, much higher than the 5 percent celibacy rate for English women in 1986, women now possessed of many more viable economic and social alternatives to marriage than were available to aristocratic women in the eighteenth century.[36] Instead of reflecting that the settlement system, as the Stones claim, "guaranteed [daughters] substantial cash sums to enable them to marry," why not consider that a significant number of these celibate young women were too underfunded to compete on the marriage market, either because their portions were too small to attract suitable husbands or because the assets that were supposed by the settlement to be made available for their portions were not, in fact, available when needed, or, in a few cases, because their parents had married without a conventional settlement? I certainly do not wish to argue that the Stones' conclusions on this matter in *An Open Elite?* are clearly wrong; rather I am suggesting that more explanations for the phenomena they observe must be considered than they do consider, and that, in the current state of our knowledge about the settlement system in practice—especially as it affected women—we cannot reach these particular conclusions as expeditiously as they do or, indeed, reach them at all. We can say that changes in married women's separate property rules were not required by a thoroughgoing liberal policy of promoting alienation with more confidence than we can say that changes in either the rules or in social practice significantly liberated women from family control.

The Neo-Marxist Story

While the liberal story tells of "improvements" in the condition of women, the neo-Marxist story recounts deterioration in their condition. Not surprisingly, neo-Marxist stories have been told mainly by women who have been more interested in poor women than in rich ones.[37] The experience of any particular woman, of course, was crucially dependent on what class she happened to be born into, and a very wide gulf was fixed between, on the one hand, those women who labored in the fields or at domestic service, and, on the other, those daughters of the middling, gentry, and aristocratic classes with whom we have been concerned. In so far as upper-class women shared significantly in the profits extracted from the labor of the poor by their fathers and husbands, and in the imperial wealth extracted by English oppression of Ireland, the West Indies, and India, it may be hard for a Marxist to have too much sympathy for them. It is probably true that class divisions among women became greater and that the lives of women in the different classes were more sharply separated in 1833 then they were in 1660. Studying the diaries of Stuart women, Sara Heller Mendelson reports that they "reveal fewer class variations in women's daily round than might have been expected," that "the differences appear to lie more in the scale of their responsibilities than in the essential nature of their duties."[38] In the male historians' treatment of upper-class women and in the claims that their conditions were improved by portions or jointures, it is striking that mention is not made of the value of earlier dower rights. Social historians have simply not seriously asked the question of whether the loss of dower and free bench was fully compensated by the gains of portions and jointure.[39]

A neo-Marxist complaint that the liberal story masks the selectivity with which the ruling classes applied such principles as the promotion of security of title to advance its own interests at the expense of the interests of others seems to me justified. Furthermore, a neo-Marxist may well question the frequent praise of

English law as notably fair because "of the almost total absence of the complex hierarchy of legal privilege which separated status groups from one another . . . in Continental Europe" and because the laws passed by the ruling elite "in fact served to protect not only their own property but also that of the expanding mass of lower-middle-class shopkeepers, artisans, small manufacturers, and small holders."[40] It is true enough that it was (and is) a convention of English law that rules should be general, not class-specific—or gender-specific, for that matter. In the period 1660–1833, however, the rules of property law continued to be heavily formulated in terms of categories (or sometimes, amounts) of property, and the ownership of particular categories (or amounts) of property was quite class-specific. As we have seen, freehold land was hedged about with very special protections tending to prevent its loss. Owners of commercial property, by contrast, throughout this period inhabited a legal world in which the limited liability company was unknown, and so their personal fortunes were at risk for liabilities incurred by their businesses. To the extent that men in the privileged class continued to own land as their preferred form of property while their sisters and wives were given wealth in the form of personal property, the property of their wives and sisters was more vulnerable to loss.

The poor laws, while often honored more in the breach than in the observance, nevertheless at least in theory quite sharply limited the freedom of those with very small amounts of property or no property at all. (The poor laws, of course, were intended to provide work and subsistence to the poor.) For example, an Elizabethan poor law, still in force in the eighteenth century, set a property threshold of "an estate of 40s. clear yearly value freehold" or £10 in goods; individuals falling below this threshold could be compelled by the justices to work at wages set by the justices.[41] Unmarried individuals or individuals under thirty knowing particular listed trades could be bound apprentice upon the request of a master in their trade; unskilled men between the ages of twelve and sixty not employed or "gentlemen born" or "scholars" could be compelled to agricultural labor on pain of imprisonment for refusal. Unmarried poor women between twelve and forty could alternatively be obliged by two justices to enter into service "by the year, week, or day."

Throughout the century, those whose only valuable property

was their labor were also prohibited by the Combination Acts from attempting to join with one another to bargain with their masters to raise wages, lessen hours, or alter working conditions on pain of criminal penalties, including imprisonment. Individual workers were prosecuted either under particular Combination Acts concerned with specific trades or in common law prosecutions for criminal conspiracy.[42] Eighteenth-century legal intellectuals saw no relation between married women's property and labor contracts; indeed, the early categories of legal thought make such a connection unlikely. Nevertheless, there are some interesting parallels and differences between the history of married women's property and the history of labor contracts. Most obviously, the earlier relations between workers and employers (or servants and masters, to use the older language) and the earlier relations between wives and husbands were conceptualized as status relationships over which some communal control was exercised, the magistrates (at least in theory) setting fair wages for workers and common law providing forced fair shares of marital property for wives. The shift from status to contract seems to have occurred earlier in the domestic sphere than in the sphere of contracts for employment, but both the effect of contract thinking and a larger movement toward thinking in terms of legal categories at higher levels of abstraction affected both subjects. No doubt the idea of contractual bargaining among elite families over marriage settlements was easier for conservative legal intellectuals to accept than the idea of contractual bargaining between masters and groups of servants; at no time during this period was anyone haunted by the specter of a raucous married women's union.

We have observed that at the end of the eighteenth century in the field of married women's property the judges cut back somewhat from contract models, for example, in *Marshall v. Rutton* (1800) declaring separate maintenance contracts invalid as against public policy. At the same time, earlier English combination acts, specific to particular trades, were generalized into the Combination Acts of 1799 and 1800 making void all contracts of all workmen for raising wages, lessening hours, and criminalizing the making of such contracts or the combining to attempt to make them. (The 1799 act, read literally, outlawed even contracts between a master and an individual workman; the 1800 act permitted such contracts between individuals.) When qualified journeymen refused to work for "reasonable wages" or for particular employers, employers could apply for licenses to use otherwise unqualified and illegal labor. The Combination Act of 1800 added a binding arbitration section to settle disputes over work done under existing contracts. As John Orth has argued, in 1800 "the paradigmatic employment contract was between individuals: one employer contracting for the services of one workman. The Tudor-Stuart policy of wage regulation by the justices of the peace was ending. . . . Regulation was abandoned; in its place was offered arbitration concerning existing contracts."[43] Then, in the early nineteenth century, the absolutism of the Combination Acts became increasingly unpopular; in 1824 they were repealed in an effort to improve industrial relations.[44] Similarly, in the early nineteenth century, we saw the courts draw away from the absolutist position that separate maintenance contracts were invalid by developing categories of valid separate maintenance contracts. In both the relations between employer and laborer and the relations between husband and wife the supposed fairness of a bargain arrived at by negotiation between autonomous individuals was used to legitimate the results. Yet, in the early nineteenth century, a neo-Marxist is entitled to complain, neither the supposed bargainers in labor relations nor those in domestic relations were playing on a level field.

The Feminist Story

In their development of contract doctrines as well as in most of real property law, English legal intellectuals normally used gender-neutral language; yet attention to gender, a feminist storyteller would insist, is necessary if we are to understand the development of the law of married women's property. As should be clear, one defect of the liberal history of married women's separate property is that the legal changes allowing married women to become "autonomous" owners of property did not—as liberal theory would predict—notably empower married women. Our study of the legal rules has already suggested two reasons why this should be so. First, the inventors of the new legal rules were motivated more by desires to facilitate the transmission of significant property from male to male and to ensure a level of basic protection for women and young children than they were by any interest in increasing the autonomy of married women. Second, in keeping with these aims of the inventors, the very rules that conferred ownership on women gave them a kind of ownership different from that imagined in a liberal property regime—entitlement to profit from capital, but not control over capital itself or the power to alienate capital. Moreover, the more complex the system of property law grew and the more abstract and remote the newer forms of property, the more difficult women, in the absence of appropriate education and socialization, were likely to find understanding their entitlements or controling their assets.

But a full answer to the crucial question of why the legal changes allowing women to become autonomous owners of property did not empower married women cannot be given without considering the changes in gender roles that occurred between 1660 and 1833. In 1660 the subordination of women to men was secured, to a significant extent, by the public authority of the church and the state, an authority articulated from the pulpit and enforced by church and state courts. Women were taught and—for the most part—believed that they had religious and moral obligations to obey their husbands. As Mendelson observes in her study of Stuart women's diaries, "those diarists who took their piety seriously felt obliged to confess and repudiate all manifestations of marital insubordination."[45] While religion continued to play an important role in convincing women of the legitimacy of their subordination, the eighteenth century witnessed an efflorescence of relatively new secular sources of pronouncements of right conduct in the family. Conduct and advice books, domestic novels and dramas, and newspapers and magazines depicted idealized domestic families and gave rules about appropriate behavior in the family. In these more secular, indeed, more "private" sources we see a new ideological formulation that also legitimates the subordination of women, but on new, more sentimental, grounds.

Trumbach and Stone have each offered a different, more liberal analysis. What Trumbach calls "domesticity" and Stone "companionate marriage" they believe to have bettered the condition of women, making them "more equal" with men. The idea that women were "freer" to make a choice of marriage partner and that dynastic and economic motives for marriage were subordinated to personal choice and personal affection has appeared to both Trumbach and Stone an obvious improvement for women.

Yet, it seems to me, both historians have succumbed to a bourgeois illusion that there can be a clear separation between, on the one hand, a public and economic sphere, and, on the other, a private domestic sphere of true feeling and personal authenticity. In this aspect of their work, they have accepted the very ideological formulation created by eighteenth-century advocates of domesticity.

Instead of imagining that in the eighteenth century the family suddenly became a protected enclave where true individual feeling could be expressed, independent of public ideologies and economic motivation, it seems to me more accurate to suppose that bourgeois ideology masked state and economic forces bearing on the family (rather than that such forces were purged from the family). It is certainly true that the new bourgeois ideology insisted that the family was a private sphere and liked to deny that the state or economic realities were or ought to be powerful in its construction; indeed, bourgeois ideology generally denigrated public actions and celebrated private feeling.[46] The new ideal bourgeois man excelled in the private sphere, which, in any case, was a more likely sphere for demonstrations of bourgeois superiority. Part of the schizophrenia of bourgeois culture was to repress the importance of the very market achievements that gave the bourgeoisie its wealth and power, to insist on nonmonetary motives for action and nonmonetary sources of value, and to cry up the worth of psychic achievements. (Hence the odd phenomenon of the heroes of bourgeois drama like Belcour in Richard Cumberland's popular play, *The West Indian*, showing no interest in accumulation and signing their worth by compulsively giving away money to worthy unfortunates.) In the realm of the family, especially, bourgeois ideology insisted that the right basis was not economic but affective. As the character of the ideal bourgeois individual was constructed, the individual was supposed very powerful in determining his life; morality consisted in making the right choices. One of those crucial choices was made in courtship—and courtship was imagined as proceeding in a perfect open market, absent any barriers to free trade. Thus, the *Spectator* instructed its readers, "The happy marriage is where two Persons meet and voluntarily make Choice of each other," and waxed rhapsodic over: "Marriage . . . an Institution calculated for a constant Scene of as much Delight as our Being is capable of. Two Persons who have chosen each other out of all the Species, with Design to be each other's mutual Comfort and Entertainment, have in that Action bound themselves to be good-humour'd, affable, discreet, forgiving, patient, and joyful, with Respect to each other's Frailties and Imperfections, to the End of their Lives."[47] In reality, of course, an eighteenth-century woman hardly made her choice "out of all the Species"; yet the rhetoric of free choice was apt to give her an added sense of personal responsibility for the consequences, and to make her more psychologically dependent on her relationship with her husband.

A striking feature of the new domestic family—one insufficiently commented upon—was that responsibility for good order and happiness within the family moved away from the husband, who as sovereign of the older family had responsibility for its governance, and toward the wife, who became a more specialized expert on the home. Women, for example, were inundated with advice on how to behave and how to feel in the common circumstance of the husband's sexual infidelity. Although the husband's adultery was generally considered a positive evil by moralists and writers of advice literature, wives were advised that they had the power and the responsibility to transform their adulterous husbands into models of chastity. If husbands' private conduct fell below the standards of decency, wives had only themselves to blame.

In a very recent and revealing study of middle-class families in and around Birmingham and in Essex and Suffolk, Lenore Davidoff and Catherine Hall describe some of the complex interactions of gender and class at the beginning of the nineteenth century.[48] Just as middle-class men struggled to free themselves from dependence on patricians and began to define themselves against aristocratic men as competent and fiscally responsible managers and manipulators of the newer forms of property, they also made their own claims to gentility increasingly dependent on having wives who were not engaged in productive work outside the home and wives who had leisure to engage in amusements like reading, music, and shopping. Gentility, now a possible aspiration for many manufacturers and retail tradesmen, required the separation of the household economy from the business and so increasingly excluded the female members of the household not only from knowledge about the business but even from the place where business was conducted. Consequently, Davidoff and Hall argue, "the same forces which favoured the rise of the private company and ultimately the business corporation, the development of public accountability and more formal financial procedures also shifted the world of women even further from the power of the active market."[49] These middle-class sons were given land and cash and expected to treat both as capital assets; these middle-class daughters, like their aristocratic and gentry sisters, were given income from property in trust. In such middle-class circles, however, Davidoff and Hall report, trusts for women were structured with an eye to giving the male trustees, normally relatives, "access to the woman's capital to use in the pursuit of their own economic interests."[50] Also, as I have noted earlier, they observe that these trusts for women "had the subsidiary advantage of keeping part of the family assets safe from creditors even under unlimited liability." Men normally served as trustees for female relatives and then, with the development of new charitable and friendly societies, as trustees for the affairs of these societies as well, through such experience gradually building up "the personal competence in business affairs which was part of a masculine persona"—and not part of a feminine persona. At this social level, a woman's contribution to the family enterprise and to economic development more generally was "hidden": she produced personnel for the family enterprise; helped maintain relationships among male family members, some of whom were likely to be partners in the enterprise; helped make contacts and connections; and watched "her" money lent for investment purposes by her trustees. Yet, Davidoff and Hall interestingly suggest, since the new forms of property were innately as manipulable by women as by men and since developing markets offered opportunity, it is possible that the concerted attack on female *sexual* independence in the early nineteenth century "may have much to do with fears about new opportunities for their *economic* activity."[51]

Be that as it may, not only in the middle classes but also in the gentry and the aristocracy, genteel femininity increasingly became dissociated from active and direct personal involvement in household management and household production and increasingly became associated with the possession of leisure time for amusement, consumption, and travel away from the home. When femininity is so constructed, indeed, when femininity is, at long last, finally associated with honored virtue instead of with a special propensity to vice, few women will be willing to forgo the honor and to risk the social sanctions attached to transgressing the bounds of passive womanhood by appearing actively to assert their own economic interests against those of their male kin.

Instead of seeing the late eighteenth-century domestic or "sentimental" family as particularly liberating for women, Susan Okin has argued that sentimental ideology "acted rather, as a *reinforcement* for the patriarchal relations between men and women that had temporarily been threatened by seventeenth-century individualism."[52] Okin, whose field is political theory, addresses herself particularly to the question of why such philosophers as Locke, Rousseau, Kant, and Bentham were not willing to consider women citizens. Just when "the freedom, individuality, and rationality of men was coming to be recognized as the foundation of their political and legal equality," she observes, women were increasingly characterized "as creatures of sentiment and love rather than of the rationality that was perceived as necessary for citizenship." (And, I would add, because of this contemporary construction of femininity as sentiment and feeling, Mary Wollstonecraft in *A Vindication of the Rights of Women,* 1792, struggles with particular fervor to insist, against what she understands to be prevailing assumptions, that women are capable of full rationality.) Despite the contemporary stress on representation and the consent of the governed as the grounds legitimating the authority of the state, given the sentimental family model in which the interests of the family are supposed to be "totally united" and "family relations, unlike those outside, are [supposed to be] based only on love," the male philosophers were content to suppose that husbands and fathers could be trusted with "the right of representing their families in the political realm." Women, relegated to a domestic sphere where they were free to influence their families in emotional ways, were assumed to lack "both the need and the capacity to participate in public life."

Women, thus sentimentalized, were seen to lack not only the rationality required for citizenship but also the rationality required for the active management of property. One can see that the generalizations historians customarily make about the special value of land are quite true, so long as one also makes, as usually they do, the tacit assumption that the owner of land is male. So long as the owner was male, to own even a moderate-sized estate meant not only to be entitled to use the land as a capital resource but also to be entitled to a degree of social prestige and a degree of political power. John Cannon has remarked in *Aristocratic Century: The Peerage of Eighteenth-Century England:* "Since land was prized, not only as an investment, but for the political and social position it gave, it was an expensive commodity and purchasers were often willing to pay above the strict economic rate for it."[54] With an explicit sense of the relevance of gender, A. P. W. Malcomson nicely expresses the contemporary sense that land "needed" a man to own it: "In the male oriented and dominated world of this period, an estate needed a man: it needed one to reside upon it at least periodically; to provide employment for, and otherwise to spend money among, some of its inhabitants; to protect its interests as a loyal magistrate and perhaps county grand juryman; and, if it was big enough, to represent in parliament the county constituency in which possession of it conferred electoral influence."[55] Not only were women supposed unfit "to meddle with the land," in the phrase of the lawyer I quoted testifying before the Commissioners for Real Property, but, as nonland properties became increasingly important, women were also supposed to lack the business sense that their active management required.

The most complex public interest we have considered is perhaps the public interest in promoting families and good behavior in families. In so far as the secular courts dealt with what we would call family law, the common law courts enforced the common law obligations and rights of spouses and the equity courts represented themselves as what might be called back-up or safety net protectors of those wives and minor children who, for one reason or another, were not adequately protected by common law. In furtherance of this public interest in promoting families and good behavior in families, judges acted to enforce the duties imposed on husbands and wives by the traditional patriarchal paradigm that defined marriage as a reciprocal exchange of the husband's support and protection for the wife's services and chastity. Thus, in Chapter 6 we saw Blackstone, as a King's Bench judge, rebut the argument that commercial creditors would be defrauded if neither adulterous wives with separate maintenance nor their husbands were to be liable for the wives' debts by insisting on the public policy benefits of his position: "And I see no hardship in a man's losing his money, that avows upon the record, that he furnished a coach to [a] wife

... whom he knew to be run away from her husband. If this were universally known to be law, it would be difficult for such women to gain credit, and this would consequently reduce the number of wanderers."

Nevertheless, it certainly was not true that the courts were prepared to enforce the obligations of spouses in a thoroughgoing way. While judicial regulation of family relations was justified on the ground that the great family of the public was made up of individual families, judges also proclaimed that individual families were private and resisted scrutinizing very closely what went on in them. Each husband and father was in important ways to be the judge of what went on in his own family, and public judges disliked interfering with his jurisdiction. Mr. Justice Buller, in a case where he was about to refuse to decree specific performance on a separate maintenance contract, began his opinion by confessing: "Dissensions existing between man and wife are in all events very unfortunate: when they become the subject of consideration to third persons, they are very unpleasant, and if the case requires that the conduct of each party should be commented upon in public, it is a most painful task to those whose lot it falls to judge on them."[56] Reluctance to expose behavior in private families was one reason why the judges developed their extremely idiosyncratic contract rule that a wife could not sue her husband for arrears of pin money beyond a year. Indeed, judicial conduct in this period contributed to making the family a more private place, one more insulated from public scrutiny and one in which individual husbands gained more discretion in dealing with their wives and children.

That the public interests in promoting families and in enforcing the husband's duty to support his wife were selectively applied is evident in judicial refusals to scrutinize the adequacy or fairness of provisions made for wives. The substitution of jointure for dower and the development of doctrines of equitable jointure most clearly show how the public interests in forcing husbands to provide for their wives and in legitimating patriarchal rights by requiring equivalent responsibilities were defeated by assertions that the family ought to be a sphere for private contract.

Finally, at the conclusion of my history of the development of married women's property law between 1660 and 1833, I confess that in an important sense the subject almost has no history—if by "history" we mean to imply important change. As soon as I lift my eyes from the relatively short time span of the early modern period and look at the longer time from the middle ages to the present, the same struggles appear to be repeated over and over again with only minor variations of vocabulary, depending on what particular forms of property were important at different historical moments. To describe the pattern with brutal simplicity: first there are forced share rules, socially enforced rules which entitle wives to some fixed share of marital property; next, husbands, usually with the help of lawyers, figure out how to evade those rules; then the evasion reaches such proportions that too many women who are or have been married and their minor children become public charges; then the legislature intervenes with new forced share rules that are supposed to protect women and keep them from becoming public charges; then husbands and their lawyers get to work perfecting new evasions. And so on and on. Forced share rules are tolerated by men in economic circumstances where the wife's forced share of the husband's property affords subsistence for a woman (not a man) of the husband's rank, but when individual husbands accumulate sufficient property to make a forced share significantly more than subsistence for a woman of that rank, then forced share schemes are evaded or repealed.

At the deepest level, in patriarchal society rules concerning married women's property have always functioned to facilitate the transmission of significant property from male to male; entitlements of women have been to provide them with subsistence for themselves and minor children dependent upon them. Although contract ideology did penetrate the field of married women's property in the mid-eighteenth century, and challenged older models of patriarchal protection, these challenges were turned back in the later eighteenth century. Thus, while the surface forms of Restoration married women's property rules appear to differ significantly from the surface forms of the rules at the beginning of the nineteenth century, at a deeper level both share an underlying patriarchal structure. Parliament, in earlier and in later periods concerned to intervene to protect the interests of dependent women and children from the contrivances of lawyers and their male clients, if only to prevent women and children from becoming public charges, in this period remained passive. As I have shown, the judges had very considerable room for maneuver despite the supposed importance of precedent in the system. They were comparatively free to reimpose patriarchal structures after those structures had been challenged by contract, and reimpose them they did.

Or at least that's the story you might get—not from Blackstone—but from Blackstone's sister. Whether this patriarchal history is a nightmare from which Blackstone's sisters may one day awake, I do not know. It certainly is not over yet.

Glossary
Bibliography
Notes
Case Index
General Index

Glossary

Aequitas erroribus medetur. A Latin maxim meaning "equity corrects the law" or "equity corrects errors."

Aequitas sequitur legem. A Latin maxim meaning "equity follows the law."

Bar. Used as a noun, that which defeats, annuls, cuts off, or puts an end to. Also used as a verb. A provision, such as a limitation in a deed, "in bar of dower," is one which has the effect of defeating or cutting off the dower rights to which a wife would otherwise become entitled in the particular land.

Bargain and sale. In conveyancing, the transferring of the property in a thing from one to another, upon valuable consideration, by way of a sale. A contract or bargain by the owner of land, in consideration of money or its equivalent paid, to sell land to another person, called the "bargainee," whereupon a use arises in favor of the latter, to whom the seisin is transferred by force of the Statute of Uses. One objective was to avoid some of the formalities and expenses associated with conveying real property at law.

Baron and feme. Husband and wife.

Cestuy que trust. The beneficiary of a trust. He who has a right to a beneficial interest in and out of an estate the legal title to which is vested in another.

Chancery. Also called, "equity." The court having jurisdiction of suits in equity and in which equitable remedies are administered. Said to be a court of "conscience" in which the rigors of the common law were mitigated, considering the intention rather than the words of the law, equity being the correction of that wherein the law, by reason of its universalities, is deficient.

Chattels. Movable property not so connected to the land as to become a part of real estate. See "Personal property."

Chattels real. Interests in real property considered lesser interests than freehold. The category includes estates for terms of years (as a lease for two years), from year to year, and at will. Chattel interests devolve on the personal representative of the owner, rather than on the heir.

Chose in action. Literally, a thing in action. A personal right not reduced into possession but recoverable by a suit at law. For example, a right of proceeding in a court of law to procure payment of a sum of money.

Church courts. See "Ecclesiastical courts."

Common law. The rules and practices of law supposed to be derived from the immemorial customs of the English people, ascertained and expressed by the judgments of the national courts of law, and as distinguished from manorial law, regional customary law, and statute law. Also distinguished from equity and from the canon law of the English ecclesiastical and admiralty courts. Common law courts include King's Bench, Common Pleas, and Exchequer.

Common recovery. In conveyancing, a fictitious action at law ending in the recovery of the lands against the tenant of the freehold, which recovery, being a supposed adjudication of the right, bars all persons and vests a fee simple in the recoverer. Like bargain and sale, a way of conveying real property to avoid the formalities and expense of older methods of conveyancing at law. (2 Black. Comm. 357.)

Communis error facit jus. A Latin maxim meaning "common error makes right."

Contingent remainder. See "Remainder."

Conveyance. The transaction of passing the title to property, usually real property; also the instrument or deed in writing by which this is done.

Conveyancer. One whose business is to write conveyances, deeds, bonds, mortgages, wills, and other legal papers and to examine titles to real estate.

Coparcener. One who, with others, holds an estate in any case where the ownership is in heirs who take from the same ancestor, for example, sisters who take from the same father. Coparceners are regarded as one heir joined together by unity of interest, unity of title, and unity of possession.

Copyhold. An estate by copy of the court roll, at the will of the lord of the manor and according to the custom of the manor. The term has sometimes been used in a general sense to include every customary tenure, as distinguished from freehold, but I avoid that use.

Coverture. The condition or state of a married woman.

Criminal conversation. A tort action for money damages by a plaintiff husband against another man who has had adulterous intercourse with the plaintiff's wife.

Curtesy. At common law, the legal right or interest which the husband acquires in the real estate of his wife. A life estate in all the lands and tenements in fee simple or fee tail of which she was seised at any time during the marriage. Four things are required to give an estate by curtesy: marriage, seisin of the wife, issue, and the death of the wife.

Devise. A gift of real property by the last will and testament of the donor. When used as a noun, a testamentary disposition of real property. When used as a verb, to dispose of real property by will.

Distrain. To take by distress; see "Distress."

Distress. A common law right of a landlord to seize a tenant's goods and chattels in a nonjudicial proceeding to satisfy an arrears of rent. More generally, the seizure and detention of the goods of another in order to obtain satisfaction of a claim (as for rent, taxes, or an injury) by the sale of the goods seized.

Distributive share. The share or portion which a given distributee receives on the legal distribution of an intestate estate. The most important formulas for such distribution are laid down in the Statute of Distribution (1670), 22 & 23 Car. 2, c. 10.

Dower. At common law, the legal right or interest which the wife acquires by marriage in the real estate of her husband. A life estate in one-third of all the lands and tenements of which the husband was beneficially seised in fee simple or fee tail at any time during the marriage, and which the heirs born of the marriage, if any, could have inherited.

Ecclesiastical courts. Also called "church courts" and "courts Christian." A system of courts held by authority of the sovereign having jurisdiction over matters pertaining to the religion and ritual of the Church of England, including marriage.

Ejectment. Originally an action by which a leaseholder could recover his possession from an ejector. In the eighteenth century, a fictitious action in which a nominal plaintiff, Doe, supposedly a leaseholder, alleges a lease by the genuine claimant, an entry under the lease on the land in dispute, and an ejection by Roe, the casual ejector. Roe informs the occupant of the land, the real defendant, that he plans to let the judgment go against him by default and advises the real defendant to defend the action. Ejectment became the common way of trying titles to land.

Entail. As a noun, an estate in fee limited to a person and the heirs of his body, or to certain classes of the heirs of his body; also called an "estate in tail" or a "fee tail." As a verb, to settle property upon a person in "fee tail."

Entry. Right of entry. The right of taking or resuming possession of land by entering on it peaceably.

Equitable estate. An estate cognizable in courts of equity, as distinguished from courts of law; governed by the rules and principles of equity, in contradistinction to the rules of law.

Equity. Cf. "Chancery." (1) The mitigating principles, by the application of which substantial justice is supposed to be attained in particular cases where the prescribed or customary forms of common law seem inadequate. (2) A system of law administered by the Chancery court. A system of jurisprudence collateral to, and in some respects independent of "law," the object of which is to render the administration of justice more complete, by affording relief where the courts of law are incompetent to give it, or to give it with effect, or by exercising certain branches of jurisdiction independent of them.

Equity of redemption. The right of a mortgagor, after nonpayment or a breach of the condition of the mortgage, to redeem property from forfeiture by discharging the obligation within a reasonable period. An equity of redemption was conceptualized as an equitable estate in land; it could be devised or descend to heirs.

Escheat. Upon failure of heirs or corruption of the tenant's blood by reason of crime, reversion of an estate to the original grantor, or lord of the fee. An escheat might be to an inferior lord or to the king himself.

Estate. The fundamental term of the law of real property. Technically, the degree, quantity, nature, and extent of the interest a person has in real property.

Estate of inheritance. An estate which will descend to the owner's heirs, and descend infinitely as long as he has heirs.

Fee. Alternatively called "fee," "fee simple," or "fee simple absolute." An estate in real property, which is an estate of inheritance clear of any condition, limitation, or restriction to particular heirs; it includes the right of alienation. In the doctrine of estates, the largest estate known to the law, the highest in dignity and most ample in extent, since every other estate is derivable thereout and mergeable therein. After the death of the owner, the fee descends to the heir at law, unless the course of descent has been altered by settlements or will.

Fee tail. A legal or equitable estate in real property, limited to a person and the heirs of his body. The statute *De donis conditionalibus* (13 Edw. 1, c. 1) took away from the holders of such estates the power of alienation, thus dividing the estate into the estate tail and the reversion or remainder in fee expectant upon the failure of the estate tail. By 1660, means of evading the statute to bar the entail and change the fee tail into a fee simple had been developed. "Fines" and "common recoveries" were both used for this purpose.

Fee tail female. An estate in real property, limited to a person and to the female heirs of that person's body.

Fee tail male. An estate in real property, limited to a person and to the male heirs of that person's body.

Fee tail special. An estate in real property, limited to a person and to certain specified heirs of his body, as the heirs of his body begotten of a certain wife.

Feme sole. An unmarried woman.

Fine. Originally, a final agreement concerning lands. Then a fictitious suit by the party to whom land was to be conveyed, the buyer, claiming that the possessor of the land had promised to convey it; the object was to produce a public record of the new owner's title. Thus, a species of conveyance. So called because it puts an *end (fine)* not only to the suit thus commenced but also to all other suits and controversies concerning the same matter. At common law fines were conclusive not only upon the parties thereto, but also upon all persons who, not being under any disability, neglected to put in a claim within a year and a day. Fines were often used to bar entails and to convey the real property of married women.

Free bench. The legal interest a widow acquired at the death of her husband in a fixed share of the copyhold land of which he died seised. Shares varied according to the custom of the manor in which the copyhold was; half was common, but one-third or all are also found. Sometimes a widower's share of copyhold of which his wife died seised was also called free bench.

Freehold. An estate in real property, either for life or of inheritance, and thus of uncertain duration, which may possibly last for the life of the tenant at least. Freehold estates of inheritance are the fee simple absolute, fee simple conditional, fee simple determinable or defeasible, and estates in fee tail.

Gavelkind. A species of socage tenure common in the county of Kent but also sometimes attached to land in other counties. In gavelkind the lands descend to all the sons, or heirs of the nearest degree, together, share and share alike; the lands may be disposed of by will, do not escheat for felony, and may be aliened by the heir at the age of fifteen; and dower and curtesy are given of half the land.

Heir at law. At common law, he who, after his ancestor dies intestate, has a right to all lands, tenements, and hereditaments which belonged to the ancestor or of which the ancestor was seised. The eldest son, if there is one.

Hereditament. Any property which may be transmitted by the law of descent; not only that which has come to its owner by descent, but anything of such nature that it may descend.

Impeachment of waste. Liability for waste committed or a demand or suit for compensation for waste committed upon lands or tenements by a tenant thereof who has no right to commit waste. A tenure "without impeachment of waste" signifies that the tenant cannot be called to account for waste committed. See "Waste."

Incident. A privilege, burden, custom, etc., commonly or inevitably attaching to an office, estate, or the like.

Infant. A minor. A person under the age of twenty-one, the age of legal competence.

Inter vivos conveyance. Conveyance from one living person to another living person, as distinguished from transfer by succession or devise.

Intestate. Without making a will. A person is said to die intestate when he dies without making a will. The word is also used to signify the person himself.

Jointure. According to Coke (1628), "a competent livelihood of freehold for the wife of lands or tenements, &c to take effect presently in possession or profit after the decease of her husband for the life of the wife at the least." Normally a provision of land or income made in the marriage settlement for the wife should she survive her husband. A substitute for dower.

Legal estate. An estate cognizable in courts of law, as distinguished from courts of equity; governed by the rules and principles of law, in contradistinction to the rules of equity.

Life estate. Alternatively, an "estate for life." A freehold estate in lands, not of inheritance, which is held by the tenant for his own life, or for the life or the lives of one or more other persons. Common law dower is an estate for the life of the widow; at her death, the land goes to her husband's heir, not to her heir.

Livery of seisin. An early form of conveyance of land requiring a transfer of ownership to occur on the land in question; the donor and the donee in person or by attorney must come on the land, and the donor must say the words of gift.

Merger. When a greater estate and a lesser estate coincide and meet in one and the same person, without any intermediate estate, the lesser estate is immediately annihilated, or merged, or sunk or drowned, in the greater. For example, if a tenant for years (the holder of a lesser estate) inherits a fee simple (a greater estate) in the same land, the term of years is merged with the inheritance and no longer exists.

Mesne incumbrance. An incumbrance prior in right to one incumbrance and subsequent in right to another ("mesne" means intermediate or intervening), for example, a second mortgage prior in right to a third mortgage and subsequent in right to the first mortgage.

Mortgagee. One who lends money to a landowner who has put up his land as security.

Mortgagor. A landowner who offers his land or property as security for a loan.

Paraphernalia. Those goods which a wife is allowed to have, after the death of her husband, besides her dower or jointure, consisting of her apparel and ornaments, suitable to her rank and degree. These goods she could also devise.

Personal property. Movable things—such as money, bonds, furniture, cattle—which may be transported by the owner wherever he thinks proper to go, and may therefore be said to attend his person. All objects and rights which are capable of ownership other than those which constitute real property.

Pin money. Money paid by a husband to a wife according to the terms of a contract, the contract usually being the marriage settlement.

Portion. The share of the parent's estate, often expressed as a lump sum of money, to which a younger son or a daughter was entitled under the marriage settlement of his or her parents.

Puisne judge. An inferior or junior judge in the superior courts of common law.

Purchaser. In ordinary language, one who obtains land or another thing of value by paying money. As a technical term of real property law, a person to whom land is granted or devised as distinguished from a person who takes land as an heir by descent.

Real property. Land; lands, tenements, and hereditaments. An interest in land, immovable things, and things of the nature of land or issuing from land (e.g., an advowson, the right to appoint a clergyman to a benefice). But leases for terms of years are chattels, not real property.

Remainder. A future interest in real property in someone other than the grantor which according to its terms may become possessory upon the natural termination of some particular estate of freehold. A remainder is "vested" if it is subject to no condition precedent to its becoming possessory other than the termination of the particular estate of freehold. A remainder is "contingent" if to become possessory it is subject to some additional condition precedent other than the termination of the prior particular estate. Thus, a remainder to a son as yet unborn is necessarily a contingent remainder, contingent on his birth.

Remainderman. One who is entitled to the remainder of an estate after a particular estate carved out of it has expired.

Rent charge. Originally, a rent granted out of lands by deed for the payment of a sum due periodically, constituting a hereditament which passes to the heirs or devisees of him in whose favor it was created, unless disposed of by him in his lifetime. Originally, the grantee had no power to distrain, but express powers of distress came to be inserted in grants. A rent for the recovery of which no power of distress was given either by common law or the agreement of the parties was called a "rent-seck" or a "barren rent." By 4 Geo. 2, c. 28, a power of distress was made incident to both rents-charge and rents-seck.

Restraint on anticipation. A provision in an instrument of conveyance that prohibits the grantee from selling or transferring the property which is the subject of conveyance, thus limiting the grantee to enjoyment of the income from the property only.

Reversion. A future interest in real property, that part of the grantor's estate still retained by him when he conveys away an estate smaller than he has.

Reversioner. A person who is entitled to an estate in reversion.

Rule against Perpetuities. No interest is valid, unless it must vest, if at all, within twenty-one years after lives in being at the creation of the interest.

Rule in Shelley's Case. Whenever a person, either by deed or will, takes an estate for life and, in the same instrument, there is a remainder limited, either immediately or otherwise, to his heirs in fee, that person takes the whole estate in fee. Thus, a rule concerning "merger."

Seisin. Possession of real property under claim of freehold estate; most simply, possession plus freehold title. "Livery of seisin" is delivery of possession, the formal and actual passing of ownership of land on the land.

Separate maintenance contract. A written agreement between husband and wife, and frequently others, particularly trustees for the wife, that the husband and wife shall live apart, and—usually—that the husband or some other party shall pay fixed sums of money toward the wife's support. Particular additional provisions of these contracts varied widely.

Severalty. The character of a holding of land by one person in his own right only, without any other person being joined or connected with him in point of interest during the continuance of his estate in the land. It is thus opposed to holding in joint tenancy, coparcenary, and in common.

Tacking. To unite or join securities given at different times so as to prevent a person having intermediate securities or rights from claiming a title to redeem or otherwise discharge one or more prior ones without also redeeming or discharging one or more subsequent ones.

Term of years. An estate or interest in land to be enjoyed for a fixed period, a chattel interest. When a person holds an estate for a specified number of years, it is called his "term," and the person is called, with reference to the term he holds, the "termor," or "tenant of the term."

Trust. The legal relationship between one person having an equitable interest in property and another person having legal title to such property, the equitable ownership of the former entitling him to the performance of certain duties and the exercise of certain powers by the latter, which performance can be compelled in a court of equity. The person from whom the property is derived is generally called the "donor" and the beneficiary "cestuy que trust." See "Equitable estate" and "Legal estate."

Use. The equitable right to receive the profit or benefit of real property divorced from the legal ownership thereof. The person from whom the property is derived is generally called the "donor" and the beneficiary "cestuy que use." The Statute of Uses, 27 Hen. 8, c. 10, converted the interest of cestuy que use into a legal interest, that is, made the beneficiary of the use the legal owner. But uses were succeeded by "trusts," which accomplished roughly the same ends.

Vested remainder. See "Remainder."

Void. Having no legal force or binding effect; unable, in law, to support the purpose for which it was intended. A contract is null and void from the beginning if it seriously offends law or public policy, in contrast to a contract which is merely voidable at the election of one of the parties to the contract.

Waste. An abuse or destructive use of property by one in rightful possession, but not the owner in fee simple. Spoil or destruction, done or permitted, to lands, houses, gardens, trees, or other corporeal hereditaments, by the tenant thereof, to the prejudice of the heir, or of him in reversion or remainder. See "Impeachment of waste."

Selected Bibliography

Addison, Joseph, and Richard Steele. The *Spectator,* ed. Donald F. Bond, 5 vols. Oxford: Clarendon Press, 1965.

Ashton, John. *The History of Gambling in England.* London, 1898.

Atherley, Edmond Gibson. *A Practical Treatise on the Law of Marriage and Other Family Settlements.* London, 1813.

Babcock, Barbara Allen, Ann E. Freedman, Eleanor Holmes Norton, and Susan C. Ross. *Sex Discrimination and the Law: Causes and Remedies.* Boston: Little, Brown, 1975.

Baker, J. H. *An Introduction to Legal History,* 2d ed. London: Butterworth, 1979.

Baker, J. H., ed. *Legal Records and the Historian: Papers Presented to the Cambridge Legal History Conference . . . .* London: Royal Historical Society, 1978.

Baker, Rt. Hon. Sir George Gillespie, and Joseph Jackson, "Husband and Wife." In *Halsbury's Laws of England,* 4th ed., 56 vols., 22:565–717. London: Butterworth, 1979.

[Ballow, Henry]. *A Treatise of Equity.* Dublin, 1756.

Baron and Feme: A Treatise of Law and Equity, 3d ed. Savoy, 1758.

Baron and Feme: A Treatise of the Common Law Concerning Husbands and Wives. London, 1700.

Beckett, J. C. *The Making of Modern Ireland, 1602–1923.* London: Faber and Faber, 1981.

Beckett, J. V. "English Landownership in the Seventeenth and Eighteenth Centuries: The Debate and the Problems." *Economic History Review,* 2d ser., 30 (1977):567–581.

Berkovits, Bernard. "Towards a Reappraisal of Family Law Ideology." *Family Law* 10 (1980):164–172.

Blackstone, William. "An Argument in the Exchequer-Chamber on Giving Judgment in the Case of Perrin and Another against Blake." In *A Collection of Tracts Relative to the Law of England,* ed. Francis Hargrave, 487–510. London, 1787.

——*Commentaries on the Laws of England: A Facsimile of the First Edition of 1765–1769,* ed. Stanley N. Katz, 4 vols. Chicago: University of Chicago Press, 1979.

Bleakley, Horace. *Life of John Wilkes.* London: John Lane, 1917.

Blunt, Reginald. *Thomas, Lord Lyttleton: The Portrait of a Rake, with a Brief Memoir of His Sister Lucy Valentia.* London: Hutchinson, 1936.

Boardwell, Percy. "Alienability and Perpetuities." *Iowa Law Review* 22 (1937):437–460.

Bond, Richmond P. "Mr. Bickerstaff and Mr. Wortley." In *Classical, Mediaeval, and Renaissance Studies in Honor of Berthold Louis Ullman,* ed. Charles Henderson, Jr. Rome: Edizioni di Storia e Letteratura, 1964.

Bonfield, Lloyd. "Marriage Settlements and the 'Rise of Great Estates': The Demographic Aspect." *Economic History Review,* 2d ser., 32 (1979):483–493.

——"Comment: Family Law Section." Paper presented at the annual meeting of the Northeast Society for Eighteenth-Century Studies, Syracuse, N.Y., October 1983.

——"Marriage, Property, and the Affective Family." *Law and History Review* 1 (1983):297–312.

——*Marriage Settlements, 1601–1740: The Adoption of the Strict Settlement.* Cambridge: Cambridge University Press, 1983.

——"Affective Families, Open Elites, and Strict Family Settlements in Early Modern England." *Economic History Review,* 2d ser., 39 (1986):355–370.

Bramwell, George. *An Analytical Table of the Private Statutes Passed between the 1st Geo. 2 A.D. 1727, and 52nd Geo. 3 A.D. 1812.* London, 1812.

A Breefe Discourse, Declaring and Approving the Necessarie and Inviolable Maintenance of the Laudable Custemes of London: Namely, of That One, whereby a Reasonable Partition of the Goods of the Husbands among Their Wives and Children Is Provided. London, 1584, Short Title Catalogue Film.

Bromley, P. M. *Family Law,* 5th ed. London: Butterworth, 1976.

Cairns, John W. "Blackstone, an English Institutist: Legal Literature and the Rise of the Nation State." *Oxford Journal of Legal Studies* 4 (1984):318–360.

Campbell, Sybil. "Usury and Annuities of the Eighteenth Century." *Law Quarterly Review* 44 (1928):473–491.

Cannon, John. *Aristocratic Century: The Peerage of Eighteenth-Century England.* Cambridge: Cambridge University Press, 1984.

Casner, A. James, and W. Barton Leach. *Cases and Text on Property,* 2d. ed. Boston: Little, Brown, 1969.

Chesterman, M. R. "Family Settlements on Trust: Landowners and the Rising Bourgeoise." In *Law, Economy, and Society, 1750–1914: Essays in the History of English Law,* ed. G. R. Rubin and David Sugarman, 124–167, i-xii. Abingdon, Oxon.: Professional Books, 1984.

Chused, Richard H. "Married Women's Property Law: 1800–1850." *Georgetown Law Journal* 71 (1983):1359–1425.

Cioni, Maria Lynn. *Women and Law in Elizabethan England with Particular Reference to the Court of Chancery.* Ph.D. diss., Cambridge University, 1974, reprinted in Garland Economic History Series, ed. Peter Mathias and Stuart Bruchy, New York: Garland, 1985.

Clark, J. C. D. *English Society, 1688–1832: Ideology, Social Structure, and Political Practice during the Ancien Regime.* Cambridge: Cambridge University Press, 1985.

Clay, Christopher. "Marriage, Inheritance, and the Rise of Large Estates." *Economic History Review,* 2d ser., 21 (1968):508–518.

———"Property, Settlement, Financial Provisions for the Family, and Sale of Land by the Great Land Owners, 1660–1790." *Journal of British Studies* 21 (1981):18–38.

Coke, Sir Edward. *The First Part of the Institutes of the Laws of England; or, A Commentary upon Littleton* (annotated by Francis Hargrave and Charles Butler), 19th ed., 2 vols. London, 1832; reprint, New York: Garland, 1979.

Corish, Patrick J. "Catholic Marriage under the Penal Code." In *Marriage in Ireland,* ed. Art Cosgrove, 66–77. Dublin: College Books, 1985.

Cretney, Stephen. "The Maintenance Quagmire." *Modern Law Review* 33 (1970):662–683.

———*Principles of Family Law,* 2d. ed. London: Sweet and Maxwell, 1976.

Davidoff, Lenore, and Catherine Hall. *Family Fortunes: Men and Women of the English Middle Class, 1780–1850.* London: Hutchinson, 1987.

Dicey, A. V. *Lectures on the Relation between Law and Public Opinion in England during the Nineteenth Century,* 2d ed. 1914; reprint, New Brunswick, N.J.: Transaction Books, 1981.

Dickson, P. G. M. *The Financial Revolution in England: A Study in the Development of Public Credit, 1688–1756.* London: Macmillan, 1967.

Duman, David. *The Judicial Bench in England, 1727–1825: The Reshaping of a Professional Elite.* London: Royal Historical Society, 1982.

Enever, F. A. *History of the Law of Distress for Rent and Damage Feasant.* London: Routledge and Sons, 1931.

English, Barbara. "The Family Settlements of the Sykes of Sledmere, 1792–1900." In *Law, Economy, and Society, 1750–1914: Essays in the History of English Law,* ed. G. R. Rubin and David Sugarman, 209–240. Abingdon, Oxon.: Professional Books, 1984.

Fearne, Charles. *An Essay on the Learning of Contingent Remainders and Executory Devises,* ed. John Joseph Powell, 2 vols. London, 1791–92.

First Report Made to His Majesty by the Commissioners Appointed to Inquire into the Law of England Respecting Real Property. House of Commons, 1829.

Fisher, Richard Barnard. *A Practical Treatise on Copyhold Tenure.* London, 1794.

Fonblanque, John. *A Treatise of Equity, Revised and Edited by John Fonblanque.* 1793–94; reprint, 2 vols. in 1, New York: Garland, 1979.

Foss, Edward. *The Judges of England, with Sketches of Their Lives . . . ,* 9 vols. London, 1848–1864.

Fraser, Antonia. *The Weaker Vessel.* New York: Knopf, 1984.

Fuller, Lon F., and Melvin Aron Eisenberg. *Basic Contract Law,* 3d ed. St. Paul, Minn.: West Publishing, 1972.

George, M. Dorothy. "The Combination Laws Reconsidered." *Economic History* 1 (1927):212–228.

Gordon, Robert. "Critical Legal Histories." *Stanford Law Review* 36 (1984):57–125.

[Gore, Mrs. Catherine]. *Pin Money, a Novel,* 3 vols. London, 1831.

Gore-Browne, Robert. *Chancellor Thurlow: The Life and Times of an Eighteenth Century Lawyer.* London: Hamish Hamilton, 1953.

Greenberg, Janelle. "The Legal Status of the English Woman in Early Eighteenth-Century Common Law and Equity." *Studies in Eighteenth-Century Culture* 4 (1975):171–181.

Habbakuk, H. J. "English Landownership, 1680–1740." *Economic History Review* 10 (1940):2–17.

——"Marriage Settlements in the Eighteenth Century." *Transactions of the Royal Historical Society,* 4th ser., 32 (1950):15–30.

——"The Rise and Fall of English Landed Families, 1600–1800." *Transactions of the Royal Historical Society,* 5th ser., 29 (1979):187–207; 30 (1980):199–221; 31 (1981):195–217.

Halsband, Robert. *The Life of Lady Mary Wortley Montagu.* Oxford: Clarendon Press, 1956.

Hamilton, Roberta. *The Liberation of Women: A Study of Patriarchy and Capitalism.* London: George Allen and Unwin, 1978.

The Harleian Miscellany; or, A Collection of Scarce, Curious, and Entertaining Pamphlets and Tracts, ed. J. Malham, 12 vols. (London, 1808–1811).

The Harleian Miscellany: A Collection of Scarce, Curious, and Entertaining Pamphlets and Tracts, ed. William Oldys and Thomas Park, 10 vols. (London, 1808–1813).

Hart, Walter G. "The Origin of the Restraint upon Anticipation." *Law Quarterly Review* 40 (1924):221–226.

Haskins, George L. "Extending the Grasp of the Dead Hand: Reflections on the Origins of the Rule against Perpetuities." *University of Pennsylvania Law Review* 126 (1977):19–46.

Hay, Douglas. "The Criminal Prosecution in England and Its Historians." *Modern Law Review* 47 (1984):1–29.

Henley, Robert, Lord Henley. *A Memoir of the Life of Robert Henley, Earl of Northington, Lord High Chancellor of Great Britain.* London, 1831.

Hodgkin, John. *Observations on the Proposed Establishment of a General Register.* London, 1829.

Holcombe, Lee. *Wives and Property: Reform of the Married Women's Property Law in Nineteenth-Century England.* Toronto: University of Toronto Press, 1983.

Holdsworth, William. *A History of English Law,* 16 vols. London: Methuen, 1922–1966.

———"The Movement for Reforms in the Law (1793–1832)." *Law Quarterly Review* 56 (1940):33–48, 208–228, 340–353.

Hollingsworth, T. H. "The Demography of the British Peerage," supplement to *Population Studies* 18 (1964):i-iv, 1–108.

Homans, George Caspar. *English Villagers of the Thirteenth Century.* Cambridge, Mass.: Harvard University Press, 1941.

Horsman, Gilbert. *Precedents in Conveyancing, Settled and Approved by Gilbert Horsman,* 2d ed., 2 vols. Savoy, 1757; 3rd. ed., 2 vols., London, 1768.

Horwitz, Henry. "Testamentary Practice, Family Strategies, and the Last Phases of the Custom of London." *Law and History Review* 2 (1984):223–239.

Horwitz, Morton J. *The Transformation of American Law, 1780–1860.* Cambridge, Mass.: Harvard University Press, 1977.

———"The History of the Public/Private Distinction." *University of Pennsylvania Law Review* 130 (1982):1423–28.

Howell, David W. *Patriarchs and Parasites: The Gentry of South-West Wales in the Eighteenth Century.* Cardiff: University of Wales Press, 1986.

Ives, E. W. "The Genesis of the Statute of Uses." *English Historical Review* 82 (1967):673–697.

Jacob, Giles. *A New Law Dictionary,* 7th ed. London, 1756.

Johnston, Edith M. *Great Britain in Ireland, 1760–1800: A Study in Political Administration.* Edinburgh: Oliver and Boyd, 1963.

Kahn-Freund, O. "Inconsistencies and Injustices in the Law of Husband and Wife." *Modern Law Review* 16 (1953):34–49, 148–173.

——— "Law Reform (Husband and Wife) Act, 1962." *Modern Law Review* 25 (1962):695–697.

Keate, E[dith] M[urray]. *Nelson's Wife: The First Biography of Frances Herbert, Viscountess Nelson.* London: Cassell, 1939.

Keeton, George W., and L. A. Sheridan. *The Law of Trusts,* 10th ed. London: Professional Books, 1974.

Kelch, Ray A. *Newcastle, a Duke without Money: Thomas Pelham-Holles, 1693–1769.* Berkeley: University of California Press, 1974.

Kenney, Courtney Stanhope. *The History of the Law of England as to the Effects of Marriage on Property and on the Wife's Legal Capacity.* London, 1879.

Ketcham, Michael C. *Transparent Designs: Reading, Performance, and Form in the Spectator Papers.* Athens: University of Georgia Press, 1985.

Keysar, Alexander. "Widowhood in Eighteenth-Century Massachusetts: A Problem in the History of the Family." *Perspectives in American History* 8 (1984):89–119.

Lawson, F. H., and Bernard Rudden. *The Law of Property,* 2d ed. Oxford: Clarendon Press, 1982.

Lewis, Judith Schneid. *In the Family Way: Childbearing in the British Aristocracy, 1760–1860.* New Brunswick, N.J.: Rutgers University Press, 1986.

MacDonald, William D. *Fraud on the Widow's Share.* Ann Arbor: University of Michigan Law School, 1960.

Maguire, W. A. "The 1822 Settlement of the Donnegall Estates." *Irish Economic and Social History* 3 (1976):17–32.

Makower, Felix. *The Constitutional History and Constitution of the Church of England.* New York, 1895.

Malcomson, A. P. W. *The Pursuit of the Heiress: Aristocratic Marriage in Ireland, 1750–1820.* Antrim: Ulster Historical Foundation, 1982.

McCahill, Michael. *Order and Equipoise: The Peerage and the House of Lords, 1783–1806.* London: Royal Historical Society, 1978.

McCree, Griffith J. *Life and Correspondence of James Iredell,* 2 vols. New York, 1858.

McDowell, Banks. "Contracts in the Family." *Boston University Law Review* 45 (1965):43–62.

McKillop, Alan Dugald. "Charlotte Smith's Letters." *Huntington Library Quarterly* 15 (1952):237–255.

McMurtry, John. *The Structure of Marx's World-View.* Princeton, N.J.: Princeton University Press, 1978.

Mellows, Anthony P. *The Law of Succession,* 3d ed. London: Butterworth, 1977.

Mendelson, Sara Heller. "Stuart Women's Diaries and Occasional Memoirs." In *Women in English Society, 1500–1800,* ed. Mary Prior, 181–201. London: Methuen, 1985.

Miles, Michael. "'Eminent Practitioners': The New Visage of Country Attorneys, c. 1750–1800." In *Law, Economy, and Society, 1750–1914: Essays in the History of English Law,* ed. G. R. Rubin and David Sugarman, 470–503, i-xii. Abingdon, Oxon.: Professional Books, 1984.

Milsom, S. F. C. "Inheritance by Women in the Twelfth and Early Thirteenth Centuries." In *On the Laws and Customs of England: Essays in Honor of Samuel E. Thorne,* ed. Morris S. Arnold et al., 60–89. Chapel Hill: University of North Carolina Press, 1981.

———"The Nature of Blackstone's Legal Achievement." *Oxford Journal of Legal Studies* 1 (1981):1–12.

Mingay, G. E. *English Landed Society in the Eighteenth Century.* London: Routledge and Kegan Paul, 1963.

Montagu, Lady Mary Wortley. *The Complete Letters of Lady Mary Wortley Montagu,* ed. Robert Halsband, 3 vols. Oxford: Clarendon Press, 1965–1967.

Nelson, William. *Lex Maneriorium; or, The Law and Customs of England, Relating to Manors and Lords of Manors. . . .* Savoy, 1726.

O'Donovan, Katherine. "Should All Maintenance of Spouses Be Abolished?" *Modern Law Review* 45 (1982):424–433.

Okin, Susan Moller. "Women and the Making of the Sentimental Family." *Philosophy and Public Affairs* 11 (1982):69–88.

———"Patriarchy and Married Women's Property in England: Questions on Some Current Views." *Eighteenth-Century Studies* 17 (1983–84):121–138.

Oldham, James. "Law Reporting in the London Newspapers: 1756–1786." *American Journal of Legal History* 31 (1987):177–206.

Olsen, Alison Gilbert. "Parliament, Empire, and Parliamentary Law, 1776." In *Three British Revolutions: 1641, 1688, 1776,* ed. J. G. A. Pocock, 289–322. Princeton, N.J.: Princeton University Press, 1980.

Orth, John V. "English Combination Acts of the Eighteenth Century." *Law and History Review* 5 (1987):175–211.

Park, John James. *A Treatise on the Law of Dower, Particularly with a View to the Modern Practice of Conveyancing.* London, 1819.

Park, Patrick. "The Combination Acts in Ireland, 1727–1825." *Irish Jurist* 14, n.s. (1979):340–359.

Phipps, Oval A. *Titles in a Nutshell: The Calculus of Interests.* St. Paul, Minn.: West Publishing, 1968.

Pike, Luke Owen. *A Constitutional History of the House of Lords.* London, 1894.

Pollock, Sir Frederick, and Frederic William Maitland. *The History of English Law before the Time of Edward I*, ed. S. F. C. Milsom. Cambridge: Cambridge University Press, 1968.

Prosser, William L. *Handbook on the Law of Torts*, 4th ed. St. Paul, Minn.: West Publishing, 1971.

Reed, Joseph W., Jr. "A New Samuel Richardson Manuscript." *Yale University Library Gazette* 42 (1968):215–231.

Rivers, Theodore John. "Widow's Rights in Anglo-Saxon Law." *American Journal of Legal History* 19 (1975):208–215.

Roebuck, Peter. *Yorkshire Baronets, 1640–1760: Families, Estates, and Fortunes*. Oxford: Oxford University Press, 1980.

Roper, R. S. Donnison. *A Treatise on the Revocation and Republication of Wills and Testaments: Together with Tracts upon the Law Concerning Baron and Feme*. London, 1800.

———*A Treatise on the Law of Property Arising from the Relation between Husband and Wife*, 2 vols. London, 1820.

Rubin, G. R., and David Sugarman, eds. *Law, Economy and Society, 1750–1914: Essays in the History of English Law*. Abingdon, Oxon.: Professional Books, 1984.

Russell, Elmer Beecher. *The Review of American Colonial Legislation by the King in Council*. New York, 1915.

Salmon, Marylynn. *Women and the Law of Property*. Chapel Hill: University of North Carolina Press, 1986.

Schoenfeld, Maxwell P. *The Restored House of Lords*. The Hague: Mouton, 1967.

Schwoerer, Lois. "Seventeenth-Century English Women: Engraved in Stone?" *Albion* 16 (1984):389–403.

Shannon, R. W. "The Countess of Strathmore *versus* Bowes." *Canadian Bar Review* 1 (1923):425–427.

Simms, J. G. "The Making of a Penal Law (2 Anne, c. 6), 1703–4." *Irish Historical Studies* 12 (1960):105–118.

Simpson, A. W. B. *An Introduction to the History of the Land Law*. Oxford: Oxford University Press, 1961.

———"The Rise and Fall of the Legal Treatise: Legal Principles and the Forms of Legal Literature." *University of Chicago Law Review* 48 (1981):632–679.

———*Biographical Dictionary of the Common Law*. London: Butterworth, 1984.

Smith, Warren Hunting. *Originals Abroad: The Foreign Careers of Some Eighteenth-Century Britons*. New Haven, Conn.: Yale University Press, 1952.

Spring, Eileen. "The Family, Strict Settlement, and the Historians." *Canadian Journal of History* 18 (1983):379–398.

————"Law and the Theory of the Affective Family." *Albion* 16 (1984):1–20.

Staves, Susan. *Players' Scepters: Fictions of Authority in the Restoration.* Lincoln: University of Nebraska Press, 1979.

————"Pin Money." *Studies in Eighteenth-Century Culture* 14 (1985):47–77.

————"Separate Maintenance Contracts." *Eighteenth-Century Life* 11, n.s. 2 (1987) : 78–101.

Stone, Lawrence. *The Family, Sex, and Marriage in England, 1500–1800.* New York: Harper and Row, 1977.

Stone, Lawrence, and Jeanne C. Fawtier Stone. *An Open Elite? England, 1540–1880.* Oxford: Clarendon Press, 1984.

Stone, O. M. "Ninth Report of the Law Reform Commission (Liability in Tort between Husband and Wife)." *Modern Law Review* 24 (1961):481–486; 25 (1962):695–697.

————"Married Women's Property Act, 1964." *Modern Law Review* 27 (1964):576–580.

Sugden, Sir Edward. *A Treatise on the Law of Property as Administered by the House of Lords.* London, 1849.

Todd, Barbara J. "The Remarrying Widow: A Stereotype Reconsidered." In *Women in English Society, 1500–1800,* ed. Mary Prior, 54–92. London: Methuen, 1985.

A Treatise of Feme Coverts; or, The Lady's Law. 1732; reprint, New York: Garland, 1978.

Trial for Adultery, &. the Rt. Hon. Hugh Baron Percy v. the Right Hon. Anne Baroness Percy, Libel Given in the 27th of May 1778. [London? 1778?].

Trumbach, Randolph. *The Rise of the Egalitarian Family: Aristocratic Kinship and Domestic Relations in Eighteenth-Century England.* New York: Academic Press, 1978.

Turberville, A. S. "The House of Lords as a Court of Law, 1784–1837." *Law Quarterly Review* 52 (1936):189–219.

Turner, Richard. *The Equity of Redemption: Its Nature, History, and Connection with Equitable Estates Generally.* Cambridge: Cambridge University Press, 1931.

Turner, Thomas. *The Diary of Thomas Turner, 1754–65,* ed. David Vaisey. Oxford: Oxford University Press, 1985.

Twiss, Horace. *The Public and Private Life of Lord Chancellor Eldon, with Selections from His Correspondence,* 2d ed., 3 vols. London, 1844.

Viner, Charles. *A General Abridgment of Law and Equity,* 2d ed., 23 vols. London, 1791–1795.

Walpole, Horace. *The Yale Edition of Horace Walpole's Correspondence,* ed.

W. S. Lewis et al., 48 vols. New Haven, Conn.: Yale University Press, 1937–1983.

Watkins, Charles. *Treatise on Copyholds,* 2 vols. London, 1797–1799; 4th ed., ed. Thomas Coventry, London, 1825.

Wilkes, John. *The Correspondence of John Wilkes, with Memoirs of His Life,* ed. John Almon, 5 vols. London, 1805.

Wilmot, Sir John Eardley. *Notes of Opinions and Judgments Delivered in Different Courts.* London, 1802.

Winnett, Arthur Robert. *Divorce and Remarriage in Anglicanism.* London: Macmillan, 1958.

Wood, W[illiam] P. *A Letter to His Majesty's Commissioners for an Inquiry into the State of the Laws of Real Property* . . . . London, 1829.

Wordie, J. R. *Estate Management in Eighteenth-Century England: The Building of the Leveson-Gower Fortune.* London: Royal Historical Society, 1982.

Zainaldin, Jamil S. "The Emergence of a Modern American Family Law: Child Custody, Adoption, and the Courts, 1796–1856." *Northwestern University Law Review* 73 (1979):1038–89.

Notes

1. Introduction

1. Katherine O'Donovan, "Should All Maintenance of Spouses Be Abolished?" *Modern Law Review* 45 (1982):433.
2. Bernard Berkovits, "Towards a Reappraisal of Family Law Ideology," *Family Law* 10 (1980):164–172.
3. A comprehensive and authoritative account which displays the modern legislation on this subject can be found in the section "Husband and Wife" by the Rt. Hon. Sir George Gillespie Baker, President of the Family Division of Her Majesty's High Court of Justice, and Joseph Jackson, Esq., M.A., Ll.M., one of her Majesty's Counsel, in Halsbury's *Laws of England*, 4th ed. (London: Butterworth, 1979), 22:565–717.
4. See, e.g., "A Congress of Men Asks Equality for Both Sexes," *New York Times*, June 15, 1981.
5. 1970 Matrimonial Proceedings and Property Act, c. 45. Cf. Stephen Cretney, "The Maintenance Quagmire," *Modern Law Review* (1970) 33:662–683.
6. See, e.g., Janelle Greenberg, "The Legal Status of the English Woman in Early Eighteenth-Century Common Law and Equity," *Studies in Eighteenth-Century Culture* 4 (1975):171–182.
7. 12 Car. 2, c. 24.
8. Richard Francis, *Maxims of Equity*, cited in Sir William Holdsworth, *A History of English Law*, 16 vols. (London: Methuen, 1922–1966), 12:188.
9. Holdsworth, 5:309–315.
10. 3 & 4 Will. 4, c. 105.
11. Real Property Limitation Act (1833), 3 & 4 Will. 4, c. 27; Fines and Recoveries Act (1833), 3 & 4 Will. 4, c. 74.
12. The quoted phrase is from John McMurtry's *The Structure of Marx's World-View* (Princeton, N.J.: Princeton University Press, 1978), 124. I have generally found McMurtry's discussion of ideology very helpful, although I treat his account as suggestive rather than authoritative.

13. *The Iliad of Homer,* trans. Richmond Lattimore (Chicago: University of Chicago Press, 1961), 266.
14. Lord St. John v. Lady St. John (1805), 11 Ves. Jun. 526, at 532, 530.
15. Fletcher v. Fletcher (1788), 2 Cox 99, at 103.
16. Strathmore (Countess of) v. Bowes (1789), 2 Cox 28, at 33.
17. Michael M. v. Superior Court of Sonoma County, 101 S. Ct. 1200, 450 U.S. 464, 67 L. Ed. 2d 437.
18. Corbett v. Corbett [1970], 2 All E.R. 331.
19. McMurtry, 136, citing *The German Ideology.*
20. McMurtry, 138.
21. McMurtry, 137.
22. Drury v. Drury (1760–61), 2 Eden 39, at 65–66. Cf. Mansfield's history of the transformation of the use into the trust: "Great inconvenience arose from so narrow and contracted a system" (Burgess v. Wheate, 1 Black. W. 157).
23. Robert W. Gordon, "Critical Legal Histories," *Stanford Law Review* 36 (1984): 59.
24. E.g., A. C. Dicey, *Lectures on the Relation between Law and Public Opinion in England during the Nineteenth Century* (1914, 2d ed.; reprint, New Brunswick, N.J.: Transaction Books, 1981), 293–295; Lee Holcombe, *Wives and Property: Reform of the Married Women's Property Law in Nineteenth-Century England* (Toronto: University of Toronto Press, 1983), 46–47.
25. See Morton J. Horwitz, "The History of the Public/Private Distinction," *University of Pennsylvania Law Review* 130 (1982):1423–28.
26. Holdsworth; A. W. B. Simpson, *An Introduction to the History of the Land Law* (Oxford: Oxford University Press, 1961); Lloyd Bonfield, *Marriage Settlements, 1601–1740: The Adoption of the Strict Settlement* (Cambridge: Cambridge University Press, 1983).
27. J. H. Baker, ed., *Legal Records and the Historian: Papers Presented to the Cambridge Legal History Conference . . .* (London: Royal Historical Society, 1978).
28. Willoughby v. Willoughby (1756), 1 T. R. 763, at 769. Cf. his complaints about Musgrave v. Dashwood in Hinton v. Hinton (1755), 2 Ves. Sen. 634, at 638.
29. Curtis v. Curtis. For another example, see Day v. Leman (1789), 2 Bro. C. C. 620, at 631, 632.
30. Gordon, 120.
31. A more sophisticated critical attention is just beginning to be paid to the most famous of all eighteenth-century legal treatises: see John W. Cairns, "Blackstone, An English Institutist: Legal Literature and the Rise of the Nation State," *Oxford Journal of Legal Studies* 4 (1984):318–360.
32. Maitland, *Collected Papers* (1911), 2:484, quoted in Baker.
33. J. H. Baker, *Introduction to Legal History,* 2d ed. (London: Butterworth, 1979), 159.
34. Baker, *Introduction to Legal History,* 159, citing *Legal History Studies* 1972, 7.
35. S. F. C. Milsom, "The Nature of Blackstone's Achievement," *Oxford Journal of Legal Studies* 1 (1981):1–12.
36. A. W. B. Simpson, "The Rise and Fall of the Legal Treatise: Legal Principles

and the Forms of Legal Literature," *University of Chicago Law Review* 48 (1981):652.

37. William Blackstone, *Commentaries on the Laws of England: A Facsimile of the First Edition of 1765—1769*, 4 vols. (Chicago: University of Chicago Press, 1979), 1:Preface [i], ii, [3].

38. Blackstone, 1:31, [3].

39. Blackstone, 1:33, 30.

40. Charles Watkins, *A Treatise on Copyholds*, 2 vols. (London, 1797—1799), Preface, vii—viii, and 2:82.

41. Marylynn Salmon, *Women and the Law of Property in Early America* (Chapel Hill: University of North Carolina Press, 1986), 216, n. 21.

42. Felix Makower, *The Constitutional History and Constitution of the Church of England* (London, 1895); Arthur Robert Winnett, *Divorce and Remarriage in Anglicanism* (London: Macmillan, 1958).

43. Susan Staves, *Players' Scepters: Fictions of Authority in the Restoration* (Lincoln: University of Nebraska Press, 1979).

44. Westmeath v. Westmeath (1827), 2 Hagg. Ecc. (Supp.) 61, at 131.

45. David Vaisey, ed., *The Diary of Thomas Turner: 1754—65* (Oxford: Oxford University Press, 1985), 293.

46. David Duman, *The Judicial Bench in England, 1727—1825: The Reshaping of a Professional Elite* (London: Royal Historical Society, 1982), is a most useful study of the social origins and career patterns of the judges appointed to the bench in this period.

47. Robert Gore-Browne, *Chancellor Thurlow: The Life and Times of an Eighteenth Century Lawyer* (London: Hamish Hamilton, 1953), 61—74.

48. Horace Twiss, *The Public and Private Life of Lord Chancellor Eldon, with Selections from His Correspondence*, 2d ed., 3 vols. (London, 1844).

49. Duman, 118.

50. Michael W. McCahill, *Order and Equipoise: The Peerage and the House of Lords, 1783—1806* (London: Royal Historical Society, 1978), 71, and cf. chap. 6, "The Lord's Leadership."

51. Duman, 84.

52. In addition to McCahill, see Luke Owen Pike, "The Judicature of the House of Lords in General," in *A Constitutional History of the House of Lords: From Original Sources* (London, 1894), 279—309; Maxwell P. Schoenfeld, *The Restored House of Lords* (The Hague: Mouton, 1967), esp. chaps. 6 and 7; A. S. Turberville, "The House of Lords as a Court of Law, 1784—1837," *Law Quarterly Review* 52 (1936):189—219.

53. Alison Gilbert Olson, "Parliament, Empire, and Parliamentary Law, 1776," in *Three British Revolutions: 1641, 1688, 1776*, ed. J. G. A. Pocock (Princeton, N.J.: Princeton University Press, 1980), 289—322.

54. Salmon, 61.

55. J. C. Beckett, *The Making of Modern Ireland, 1603—1923* (London: Faber and Faber, 1981), 51, 150—166, 225.

56. 6 Geo. 1, c. 5.

57. 6 Geo. 1, c. 5; 39 & 40 Geo. 3, c. 67.

58. 9 Wm. 3, c. 3 (1697); Patrick J. Corish, "Catholic Marriage under the Penal

Code," in *Marriage in Ireland,* ed. Art Cosgrove (Dublin: College Press, 1985), 71.

59. Antonia Fraser, *The Weaker Vessel* (New York: Knopf, 1984), 12–19.

2. Dower and the Rule of No Dower of a Trust

1. On older dower rights see Theodore John Rivers, "Widow's Rights in Anglo-Saxon Law," *American Journal of Legal History* 19 (1975):208–215; George Caspar Homans, *English Villagers of the Thirteenth Century* (Cambridge, Mass.: Harvard University Press, 1941), chap. 13; Sir Frederick Pollock and Frederic William Maitland, *The History of English Law before the Time of Edward I,* ed. S. F. C. Milsom, 2 vols. (Cambridge: Cambridge University Press, 1968), 2:407–427; S. F. C. Milsom, "Inheritance by Woman in the Twelfth and Early Thirteenth Centuries," in *On the Laws and Customs of England: Essays in Honor of Samuel E. Thorne,* ed. Morris S. Arnold, et al. (Chapel Hill: University of North Carolina Press, 1981), 60–89.

2. An Act for the Amendment of the Law Relating to Dower, 3 & 4 Will. 4, c. 105 (1833). One of the provisions of this act, s. 6, was "that a Widow shall not be entitled to Dower out of any Land of her Husband when in the Deed by which such Land was conveyed to him, or by any Deed executed by him, it shall be declared this his Widow shall not be entitled to Dower out of such Land."

3. Courtney Stanhope Kenny, *The History of the Law of England as to the Effects of Marriage on Property and on the Wife's Legal Capacity* (London, 1879), 56, 58, 57.

4. 27 Hen. 8, c. 10 (1535).

5. See Chapter 4 for a more detailed discussion of these statutory provisions and their subsequent history.

6. Maria Lynn Cioni, *Women and Law in Elizabethan England with Particular Reference to the Court of Chancery* (Ph.D. diss., Cambridge University, 1974, reprinted in Garland Economic History Series, ed. Peter Mathias and Stuart Bruchey, New York: Garland, 1985), 289. Cioni has interesting archival material about the kinds of litigation brought, but a number of her statements about points of law seem to me confused or inaccurate.

7. Janelle Greenberg, "The Legal Status of the English Woman in Early Eighteenth-Century Common Law and Equity," *Studies in Eighteenth-Century Culture* 4 (1975):177. Cf. Lawrence Stone, *The Family, Sex, and Marriage in England: 1500–1800* (New York: Harper and Row, 1977), 330–331. Most writers also add that the benefits of equitable doctrines were not enjoyed by lower-class women.

8. Kenny, 15; A. V. Dicey, *Lectures on the Relation between Law and Public Opinion in England during the Nineteenth Century* (1914, 2d ed.; reprint, New Brunswick, N.J.: Transaction Books, 1981), chap. 1, n. 23.

9. Robert W. Gordon, "Critical Legal Histories," *Stanford Law Review* 36 (1984):68, 62.

10. William Blackstone, *Commentaries on the Laws of England: A Facsimile of the First Edition of 1765–1769,* 4 vols. (Chicago: University of Chicago Press, 1979), 2:136.

11. John James Park, *A Treatise on the Law of Dower, Particularly with a View to the Modern Practice of Conveyancing* (London, 1819), 3.

12. Morton J. Horwitz writing of American dower rights at the beginning of the nineteenth century has argued that in a leading Massachusetts case, the court, motivated by a desire to defeat dower as a clog on alienability, "was prepared to use any method to cut off the widow's share, including reliance on dubious assumptions about the relation between market price and productive value" (*The Transformation of American Law, 1780–1860,* Cambridge, Mass.: Harvard University Press, 1977, 58). "Any method" seems to be an overstatement; other contemporary and later Massachusetts cases were decided in favor of doweresses. In Connor v. Shepherd (1818) one issue which Horwitz does not mention was that the forest lands in question were a liability rather than an asset because taxes had to be paid on them; if a widow lacked either motive or ability to pay such taxes the estate might be sold to the loss of the reversioner. Alexander Keysar's work on Massachusetts widows gives some support to the idea that even dower in improved lands was frequently not much of an asset for these widows at this time ("Widowhood in Eighteenth-Century Massachusetts: A Problem in the History of the Family," *Perspectives in American History* 8, 1974:89–119). Blackstone says that one of the signs of the law's favor toward dower is that tenants in dower are "subject to no tolls or taxes," but this particular sign of favor seems not to have crossed the Atlantic (Blackstone, 2:138).

13. E. P. Thompson, *Whigs and Hunters: The Origin of the Black Act* (London: A. Lane, 1975).

14. Homans, 188.

15. Drury v. Drury (1760–61), 2 Eden 39, at 65–66.

16. *First Report Made to His Majesty by the Commissioners Appointed to Inquire into the Law of England Respecting Real Property* (House of Commons, 1829), 258.

17. William D. MacDonald, *Fraud on the Widow's Share* (Ann Arbor: University of Michigan Law School, 1960), 23.

18. *A Breefe Discourse, Declaring and Approving the Necessarie and Inviolable Maintenance of the Laudable Customes of London: Namely, of That One, whereby a Reasonable Partition of the Goods of Husbands among Their Wives and Children Is Provided* (London, 1584, Short Title Catalogue Film), 45.

19. 11 Geo. 1, c. 18 (1724), so the preface to the statute claims. Henry Horwitz, in a study of 290 wills of wealthy Londoners probated before this statute, finds that a majority of the testators "ignored the custom or made explicit provision to circumvent it." See his "Testamentary Practice, Family Strategies, and the Last Phases of the Custom of London, 1660–1725," *Law and History Review* 2 (1984):239.

20. *Breefe Discourse,* 31.

21. Anthony R. Mellows, *The Law of Succession,* 3d ed. (London: Butterworth, 1977); chaps. 14 and 15 are useful in showing the current state of the English law.

22. Chaplin v. Chaplin (1737), 3 P. Wms. 229. For general accounts of the law of dower in this period, see Edward Coke, *The First Part of the Institutes of the Laws of England; or, A Commentary upon Littleton* (annotated by Francis Hargrave and Charles Butler), 19th ed., 2 vols. (London, 1832; reprint, New York: Garland, 1979), 31a–41a; Giles Jacob, *A New Law Dictionary,* 7th ed. (London, 1756); 2 Eq. Ca. Abr. 382–392; Charles Viner, *A General Abridgment of Law and Equity,* 2d ed. (London, 1792), 9:209–304; Park, *A Treatise on the Law of Dower.*

23. 3 P. Wms. 232, 234.

24. Burgess v. Wheate (1759), 1 Black. W. 123, at 138–139.

25. 1 Black. W. 160–162. Cf. Charles Butler's remark, "though *curtesy* out of a *trust* is allowed, yet *dower* has been refused; a partiality not easy to be reconciled with reason, however settled by the current of authorities" (Coke, *First Part of the Institutes,* 299, n. 6).

26. Dixon v. Saville (1783), 1 Bro. C. C. 326, at 327–328.

27. D'Arcy v. Blake (1805), 2 Sch. & Lefr. 389.

28. Viner, 9:223: "But before the statute [of Uses] she was not dowable of land conveyed to uses" and citations there.

29. Kenny, 59, referring to the assignment of terms of years, discussed in the next chapter.

30. 6 Co. Rep. 66; quoted in J. H. Baker, *An Introduction to Legal History,* 2d ed. (London: Butterworth, 1979), 240.

31. Watts v. Ball (1708), 1 P. Wms. 109.

32. 1 Black. W. 160, 162.

33. Oldham v. Hughes (1742), 2 Atk. 452.

34. 1 Black. W. 123, at 178.

35. Tullet v. Armstrong (1839), 4 My. & Cr. 390, at 406. See also Walter G. Hart, "The Origin of the Restraint upon Anticipation," *Law Quarterly Review* 40 (1924):221–226.

36. D'Arcy v. Blake (1805), 2 Sch. & Lefr. 389 ; cf. Park, 127.

37. John Bell on *viva voce* examination, *First Report of the Commissioners,* 232.

38. Sir William Holdsworth, *A History of English Law,* 16 vols. (London: Methuen, 1922–1966), 12:265–266.

39. Fletcher v. Robinson, 2 P. Wms. 709–712, 3 P. Wms. 231–232; Otway v. Hudson, 2 Vern. 584; Dudley v. Dudley, Prec. Ch. 241; Ambrose v. Ambrose, 1 P. Wms. 321; Banks v. Sutton, 2 P. Wms. 700.

40. *Ballentine's Law Dictionary* (Rochester, N.Y.: Lawyer's Co-Operative Publishing Company, 1969), s.v. "equity of redemption."

41. Banks v. Sutton (1732), 2 P. Wms. 700, at 712.

42. 2 P. Wms. 702–703.

43. 2 P. Wms. 709.

44. 2 Vern. 583, at 585.

45. Godwin v. Winsmore (1742), 2 Atk. 525. Cf. Hinton v. Hinton (1755), in which father contracts with son for valuable consideration to sell a copyhold estate but dies before surrender. This is a constructive trust and the widow must surrender her free bench to the son (2 Ves. Sen. 631).

46. Foder v. Wade (1794), 4 Bro. C. C. 520. Foder was partially a complicated

case of mistake about the correct heir by the custom of Borough English in which the youngest instead of the eldest is supposed to inherit.

47. 4 Bro. C. C. 525, 526.
48. E.g., Jekyll in Banks v. Eldon in D'Arcey, Sch. & Lefr. 389.
49. Marylynn Salmon, *Women and the Law of Property in Early America* (Chapel Hill: University of North Carolina Press, 1986), 148.
50. 9 Geo. 3, c. 29 (1769); 6 Anne, c. 8 (1706); 2 Will. & Mary, c. 5 (1689); 8 Anne, c. 14 (1709); 11 Geo. 2, c. 19 (1737); F. A. Enever, *History of the Law of Distress for Rent and Damage Feasant* (London: Routledge and Sons, 1931), 293.
51. Hansard, *Parliamentary Debates,* 3d ser., 15 (1833), 657.
52. Hansard, *Parliamentary Debates,* 3d ser., 3 (1832), 561.
53. Radnor v. Vandebendy (1697), Shower 69, at 71.
54. Howard v. Hooker (1672–73), 2 Chan. Rep. 81, at 84; 1 Eq. Ca. Abr. 59. Cf. Lance v. Norman (1672–73), 2 Chan. Rep. 79; 1 Eq. Ca. Abr. 59.
55. Quoted in George W. Keeton and L. A. Sheridan, *The Law of Trusts,* 10th ed. (London: Professional Books, 1974), 119.
56. Hunt v. Matthews (1686), 1 Vern. 408 ; King v. Cotton (1732), 2 P. Wms. 674.
57. Strathmore (Countess of) v. Bowes (1789), 2 Cox 29, at 33.
58. See Chapter 5 for discussion of this reciprocity.
59. King v. Cotton (1732), 2 P. Wms. 674, at 675.
60. See discussion of husband's obligation to pay for "necessaries" for his wife in Chapter 6.
61. Pitt v. Hunt (1681), 1 Vern. 18.
62. 2 Cox 33–34.
63. *Dictionary of National Biography,* s.v. "Bowes, Mary Eleanor, Countess of Strathmore"; R. W. Shannon, "The Countess of Strathmore *versus* Bowes," *Canadian Bar Review* 1 (1923):425–427.
64. Goddard v. Snow (1826), 1 Russ. 485.

3. *Avoidance of Dower by More Complex Conveyancing Techniques*

1. William Holdsworth, *A History of English Law,* 16 vols. (London: Methuen, 1922–1966), 7:384.
2. Holdsworth, 7:386.
3. F. H. Lawson and Bernard Rudden, *The Law of Property,* 2d ed. (Oxford: Clarendon Press, 1982), Preface, v.
4. Lawson and Rudden, 17.
5. Lawson and Rudden, 78–79.
6. A. James Casner and W. Barton Leach, *Cases and Text on Property,* 2d ed. (Boston: Little, Brown, 1969), 362–363. Lloyd Bonfield (*Marriage Settlements, 1601–1740: The Adoption of the Strict Settlement,* Cambridge: Cambridge University Press, 1983) has shown that Bridgeman was not the sole inventor of the device of trustees to preserve contingent remainders.

7. Holdsworth, 7:385.
8. Holdsworth, 7:385, n. 3, quoting the report of the Real Property Commission.
9. Lawson and Rudden, 17.
10. Holdsworth, 7:384.
11. Ray A. Kelch, *Newcastle, a Duke without Money: Thomas Pelham-Holles, 1693–1768* (Berkeley: University of California Press, 1974), 102.
12. Michael Miles, " 'Eminent Practitioners': The New Visage of Country Attorneys, c. 1750–1800," in *Law, Economy, and Society, 1750–1914: Essays in the History of English Law,* ed. G. R. Rubin and David Sugarman (Abingdon, Oxon.: Professional Books, 1984), 491.
13. Barbara English, "The Family Settlements of the Sykes of Sledmere, 1792–1900," in Rubin and Sugarman, 231.
14. Miles, 476, 491.
15. Holdsworth, 7:382, 384.
16. George L. Haskins, "Extending the Grasp of the Dead Hand: Reflections on the Origins of the Rule against Perpetuities," *University of Pennsylvania Law Review* 126 (1977):31.
17. G. E. Mingay has pointed out that such settlements "reached down and influenced the lives of wealthy freeholders to a remarkable extent," *English Landed Society in the Eighteenth Century* (London: Routledge and Kegan Paul, 1963), 85.
18. Joseph W. Reed, Jr., "A New Samuel Richardson Manuscript," *Yale University Library Gazette* 42 (1968):215–231.
19. Kelch, 96–100.
20. Edward Coke, *The First Part of the Institutes of the Laws of England; or, A Commentary upon Littleton* (annotated by Francis Hargrave and Charles Butler), 19th ed., 2 vols. (London, 1832; reprint, New York: Garland, 1979), S.720.
21. Holdsworth, 7:91.
22. Reeve v. Long (1695), 3 Lev. 408.
23. "To enable posthumous children to take estates, as if born in their fathers life-time," 10 & 11 W. 3, c. 16 (1699).
24. Purefoy v. Rogers (1671), 2 Wms. Saund. 380.
25. An earlier formulation of the rule was: where the ancestor takes an estate of freehold, and in the same gift or conveyance an estate is limited, either mediately or immediately, to his heirs, either in fee or in tail, the heirs are words of limitation of the estate and not words of purchase. Shelley's Case, 1 Co. Rep. 93b, cf. 104b. One of the more historically informed and intelligible accounts of this rule, a famous and hated legal quagmire, is to be found in Percy Boardwell, "Alienability and Perpetuities," *Iowa Law Review* 22 (1937):437–460.
26. Holdsworth, 7:111.
27. Bonfield, 92.
28. Plunket v. Holmes (1662), 1 Lev. 11, at 12; 1 Sid. 47.
29. Duncomb v. Duncomb (1695), 3 Lev. 437.
30. Parkhurst v. Smith d. Dormer (1740), 6 Brown 351, at 355.

31. Bonfield, 75; and see his discussion of Duncomb and Parkhurst, 72–81.
32. Bonfield, 75.
33. M. R. Chesterman, "Family Settlements on Trust: Landowners and the Rising Bourgeoisie," in *Law, Economy and Society, 1750–1914: Essays in the History of English Law,* ed. G. R. Rubin and David Sugarman (Abingdon, Oxon.: Professional Books, 1984), 136–137.
34. Quoted in Chesterman, 137.
35. William Blackstone, "An Argument in the Exchequer Chamber on Giving Judgment in the Case of Perrin and Another against Blake," in *A Collection of Tracts Relative to the Laws of England,* ed. Francis Hargrave (London, 1787), 500.
36. 2 Wms. Saund. 382, n. 1.
37. See Richard Turner, *The Equity of Redemption: Its Nature, History, and Connection with Equitable Estates Generally* (Cambridge: Cambridge University Press, 1931). Besides a history of mortgage, Turner also has a chapter (8) exploring the analogy of mortgages to trusts and the limitations of that analogy. See also Giles Jacob, *New Law Dictionary,* 7th ed. (London, 1756), s.v. "mortgage," for a sample eighteenth-century mortgage deed.
38. Noel v. Jevons (1678), 2 Freem. 43.
39. Turner, 52.
40. Casborne v. Scarfe (1737), 1 Atk. 603, at 606.
41. Dixon v. Saville (1783), 1 Bro. C. C. 326, at 327–328.
42. An exceptionally lucid account of the term of years is given in Oval A. Phipps, *Titles in a Nutshell: The Calculus of Interests* (St. Paul, Minn.: West Publishing, 1968), chap. 6.
43. William Blackstone, *Commentaries on the Laws of England: A Facsimile of the First Edition of 1765–1769,* 4 vols. (Chicago: University of Chicago Press, 1979), 4:424.
44. Bodmin v. Vandebenden (1685), 2 Chan. Cas. 172.
45. The Countess of Radnor v. Vandebendy (1697), Shower 69.
46. Butler's report of Hardwicke's MS. "argument, on making his decree" in Hill v. Adams, 2 Atkyns 208 & Amb. 6 as Swannock v. Lynford, in Coke, *First Part of the Institutes,* 208a, n. 1.
47. The phrase is Butler's in the note cited above, and the briefest, most coherent statement of the rules I have found is his, given in this same note. I cite it here by way of a demonstration of the point for the curious or skeptical:

> . . . with respect to mortgages for terms of years. It may be observed here, 1st. That, at common law, if a lease be made for a term of years, rendering rent, the wife is entitled to her dower of a third part of the reversion by metes and bounds, and to a third part of the rent; and execution will not cease during the term. 2dly. If the husband makes a gift in tail, rendering rent, as the rent is payable out of, or in respect of, an estate of inheritance, the wife shall be endowed of a third part of the rent. 3dly. If the husband makes a lease for life, rendering rent, the wife is not entitled to her dower of the rent, because it is not payable, in this case, out of, or in respect of, an estate of inheritance.

4thly. If the husband makes a lease for years, reserving no rent, then judgment will be given for the wife, with a *cesset executio* during the term. This, if the term be of long duration, deprives her, virtually, of her dower. 5thly. If a person purchases an estate of inheritance which is in mortgage for a term of years, the wife of the vendor will not be entitled to her dower in equity, if the term was created before the marriage of the vendor, and actually assigned to a trustee for the purchaser, to attend the inheritance. 6thly. If a person dies seised in fee, subject to a term of years, if the term be a term in gross, for securing the payment of a sum of money, the widow, by discharging the money secured by it, or paying one third of the interest, will be entitled to dower. 7thly. If the term be an outstanding satisfied term, she will also be entitled to her dower against the heir.

48. W[illiam] P. Wood, *A Letter to His Majesty's Commissioners for an Inquiry into the State of the Laws of Real Property* . . . (London, 1829), 18.
49. Radnor v. Vandebendy (1697), Shower 69, at 71.
50. Lord Dudley and Ward v. The Lady Dowager Dudley (1705), Prec. Ch. 241, at 244.
51. There is an important discussion of when terms attendant upon the inheritance can be used to bar dower in Maundrell v. Maundrell (1802). Lord Chancellor Eldon commented on Radnor: "In *Lady Radnor* . . . one thing is clear; that the purchaser had notice, that the individual, from whom he purchased, was married; and, therefore, that her inchoate title, as dowress, had attached upon the inheritance. . . . If this were *res integra,* the proposition would be monstrous, that the purchaser, having notice of this right, and, of the use that is made of a term outstanding by a Court of Equity, should buy in the term; and with full notice, not squeeze out any other incumbrance, but effectually displace the dower" (10 Ves. Jun. 246, at 271). Again, the practice of conveyancers, rather than the principles of equity, is said to be the basis for the rule.
52. In Swannock v. Lynford.
53. *First Report Made to His Majesty by the Commissioners Appointed to Inquire into the Law of England Respecting Real Property* (House of Commons, 1829), 17.
54. Drury v. Drury (1760–61), 2 Eden 39, at 42.
55. For an expression of the neo-Marxist view, see Roberta Hamilton, "The Transition from Feudalism to Capitalism: A Marxist Perspective on the Changing Role of Women," in *The Liberation of Women: A Study of Patriarchy and Capitalism* (London: George Allen and Unwin, 1978), 23–49.
56. John Hodgkin, *Observations on the Proposed Establishment of a General Register* (London, 1829), [5].
57. Blackstone, 2:344.
58. William Pierepoint, "Treatise Concerning Registers to be made of Estates, Bonds, Bills, &. with Reasons against Such Registers," in *The Harleian Miscellany: A Collection of Scarce, Curious, and Entertaining Pamphlets and Tracts* (London, 1809), 3:322.
59. Blackstone, 2:338.

60. 2 & 3 Anne, c. 4 (1703), and 6 Anne, c. 20 (1707), West Riding; 6 Anne, c. 62 (1707), East Riding; 7 Anne, c. 20 (1707), Middlesex. Noted in P. G. M. Dickson, *The Financial Revolution in England: A Study in the Development of Public Credit, 1688–1756* (London: Macmillan, 1967), 7.

61. Brace v. Duchess of Marlborough (1728), 2 P. Wms. 491; Wortley v. Birkhead (1754), 2 Ves. Sen. 571; Morret v. Paske (1740), 2 Atk. 52; Willoughby v. Willoughby (1756), 1 T. R. 763.

62. Wood, 22.

63. Haskins, 19–46.

64. "An Act for the better preventing of excessive and deceitful Gaming," 9 Anne, c. 14 (1710); "An Act for the more effectual preventing of excessive and deceitful Gaming," 12 Geo. 2, c. 28 (1739); "An Act to explain, amend, and make more effectual the Laws in being, to prevent excessive and deceitful Gaming; and to restrain and prevent the excessive Increase of Horse Races," 18 Geo. 2, c. 34 (1745).

65. John Ashton, *The History of Gambling in England* (London, 1898).

66. J. C. D. Clark, *English Society, 1688–1832: Ideology, Social Structure, and Political Practice during the Ancien Regime* (Cambridge: Cambridge University Press, 1985), 108.

67. 9 Anne, c. 14, s. 1.

68. William Holdsworth, "The Movement for Reforms in the Law (1793–1832)," *Law Quarterly Review* 56 (1940):33–48, 208–228, 340–353.

69. Horace Twiss, *The Public and Private Life of Lord Chancellor Eldon, with Selections from His Correspondence,* 2d ed., 3 vols. (London, 1844), 2:256–266 (p. 266 misnumbered 66).

70. "An Act for taking lands in execution for the payment of Debts" (1700), cited in Marylynn Salmon, *Women and the Law of Property in Early America* (Chapel Hill: University of North Carolina Press, 1986), 164.

71. A major dispute over the issue of where Irish appeals lay arose when the Irish House of Lords attempted to assert its own right to final jurisdiction in Ireland, and the English Parliament responded by affirming the appellate jurisdiction of the English House of Lords in "An Act for the better securing the dependency of the kingdom of Ireland on the crown of Great Britain" (1720), commonly known as "Sixth of George I," and "one of the standing grievances of Ireland." J. V. Beckett, *The Making of Modern Ireland, 1603–1923* (London: Faber and Faber, 1981), 164.

72. Edith M. Johnston, *Great Britain in Ireland, 1760–1800: A Study in Political Administration* (Edinburgh: Oliver and Boyd, 1963), 235–240.

73. Beckett, 150–181.

74. J. G. Simms, "The Making of a Penal Law (2 Anne, c. 6), 1703–4," *Irish Historical Studies* 12 (1960):105–118.

75. Quoted in William Henry Curran, *The Life of the Right Honourable John Philpot Curran, Late Master of the Rolls in Ireland,* 2 vols. (London, 1819), 1:163.

76. Henry Parnell, *A History of the Penal Laws against the Irish Catholics: From the Treaty of Limerick to the Union* (London, 1803), 20, 46.

4. Equitable Jointure

1. Edward Coke, *The First Part of the Institutes of the Laws of England; or, A Commentary upon Littleton* (annotated by Francis Hargrave and Charles Butler), 19th ed., 2 vols. (London, 1832; reprint, New York: Garland, 1979), 36b. Cf. William Blackstone, *Commentaries on the Laws of England: A Facsimile of the First Edition of 1765–1769*, 4 vols. (Chicago: University of Chicago Press, 1979), 2:137.
2. Ray A. Kelch, *Newcastle, a Duke without Money: Thomas Pelham-Holles, 1693–1768* (Berkeley: University of California Press, 1974), 187.
3. Peter Roebuck, *Yorkshire Baronets, 1640–1760: Families, Estates, and Fortunes* (Oxford: Oxford University Press, 1980), 60.
4. "An Act for Confirming a Jointure made by John Martin, Esq., under a Power contained in the Will of *James Martin,* deceased, and rendering the same Power more effectual," Private Act, 10 Geo. 3, c. 79 (1770).
5. E.g., £14 in Vizard v. Longden (1718–19), at 2 Eden 66–67.
6. G. E. Mingay, *English Landed Society in the Eighteenth Century* (London: Routledge and Kegan Paul, 1963), 30, 226.
7. Mingay, 35.
8. H. J. Habbakuk, "Marriage Settlements in the Eighteenth Century," *Transactions of the Royal Historical Society,* 4th ser., 32 (1950):29. See Chapter 7 for further discussion of the debate over Habbakuk's position.
9. Mingay, 35–36.
10. Coke, *First Part of the Institutes,* 36b, 37a.
11. Blackstone, 2:139.
12. 27 Hen. 8, c. 10, s. 6–9. E. W. Ives, "The Genesis of the Statute of Uses," *English Historical Review* 82 (1967):673–697. For eighteenth-century accounts of the statute and its effect on jointure, see, e.g., *Baron and Feme: A Treatise of the Common Law Concerning Husbands and Wives* (London, 1700), 113–114; Blackstone, 2:137–138.
13. "An Act for the better settling of intestates estates," 22 & 23 Car. 2, c. 10 (1670); Davila v. Davila (1716), 2 Vern. 724.
14. E.g., in a settlement of 1771, copyhold in trust with remainder to the wife for jointure "to take the rents for life (in case she should so long continue a widow), remainder to the children of the marriage." Caruthers v. Caruthers (1791), 4 Bro. C. C. 500, at 502.
15. Case 103 (1560), Moore (K.B.), 31.
16. Vernon's Case (1572), 4 Co. Rep. 3a.
17. It would appear that a widow had a right to waive an estate so conditioned and elect dower if she did so immediately upon the death of her husband before taking any benefit from the jointure. In order to do so, however, she would have to be aware of such a right and be psychologically and socially able to insist on a right to remarry immediately on the death of her husband. See comments on election below.
18. In a study of 622 widows of Abingdon, Berkshire, based on probate records from 1540 to 1720, Barbara J. Todd has observed that only about 10 percent of these husbands' wills referred to remarriage. In the mid-sixteenth-century

wills she studied, it was very unusual to make a widow's share of the estate contingent on continued widowhood, but after about 1570 it appears that testators penalized their widows for remarriage. Todd finds this "first in the wills of men of greater wealth and social standing, and later, in the seventeenth century, of men of all ranks." See Barbara J. Todd, "The Remarrying Widow: A Stereotype Reconsidered," in *Women in English Society, 1500–1800*, ed. Mary Prior (Methuen: London, 1985), 72–73. Some of these wills may recite prenuptial jointure provisions as well as make independent testamentary devises; how testamentary devises are related to jointure will be discussed later in this chapter.

19. Drury v. Drury (1760–61), 2 Eden 65–66.
20. R. W. Donnison Roper, *A Treatise of the Law of Property Arising from the Relation between Husband and Wife*, 2 vols. (London, 1820), 1:481.
21. Gilbert Horsman, *Precedents in Conveyancing, Selected and Approved by Gilbert Horsman*, 3d. ed., 2 vols. (London, 1768), 1:445–449. Cf. *A Treatise of Feme Coverts, or, The Lady's Law* (1732; reprint, New York: Garland, 1978), which prints both "A common *Marriage-Settlement, or Jointure* of Lands" (209–217) and "*Articles of Marriage* for settling a Wife's Estate, and paying the Wife a Sum of Money, in Lieu of a Jointure" (248–251), the lump sum being £500.
22. Davila v. Davila (1716), 2 Vern. 724.
23. Vizard v. Longden (1718–19), at 2 Eden 66.
24. Drury v. Drury, 2 Eden 39, at 49.
25. Drury v. Drury, 2 Eden 68.
26. Blackstone, 2:147–150, although most of the stigma of servile tenure had gone.
27. Richard Barnard Fisher, *A Practical Treatise on Copyhold Tenure* (London, 1794), chap. 6, "of Customs," and chap. 10, "of Fines"; Charles Watkins, *Treatise on Copyholds*, 2 vols. (London, 1797–1799), vol. 2, chap. 3, "Of Freebench."
28. Blackstone, 2, chap. 6, "Of the Modern English Tenures," where gavelkind and burgage are discussed as tenures and as species of socage tenure.
29. Walker v. Walker (1747), 1 Ves. Sen. 54, at 55. That this was not a trivial issue is suggested by William Nelson, *Lex Maneriorum; or, The Law and Customs of England, Relating to Manors and Lords of Manors . . .* (Savoy, 1726), where his preface says the greatest part of land in England was held by copy, [A2].
30. Bushe's Case (1560), 2 Dyer 220a. See Coke's discussion of this issue in the report of Vernon's Case, 4 Co. Rep. 1a, at 4. Coke seems to say, however, that a jointure made before marriage, when the woman is not the husband's wife, and a jointure made after the husband's death, when again the women is not the husband's wife, are equally jointures within the equity of the statute, which does strain credulity. One would think, at the least, that a testamentary jointure would have to be treated as a jointure after marriage permitting election, and that seems to have been the rule in this period.
31. Lawrence v. Lawrence (1717), 2 Vern. 365, 3 Brown 483.
32. Arnold v. Kempstead (1764), 2 Eden 237. Cf. Villareal v. Galway (1769), Amb. 682, 1 Bro. C. C. 292, n.; Jones v. Collier (1773), Amb. 730. For

cases that permit the widow to have both the devise and dower, see Lawrence v. Lawrence (1717), 3 Brown 483; Thompson v. Nelson (1788), 1 Cox 447; Strahan v. Sutton (1796), 3 Ves. Jun. 249; and French v. Davies (1795), 2 Ves. Jun. 572. French has an important discussion, implying criticism of Arnold, and gives a nice and elaborate example of how a man in trade divided control of his assets among his widow and children. Sir Richard Arden strongly suspected that this tradesman testator was not aware of his wife's dower right, but decided for the widow on the ground that dower was not expressly barred.

33. Villareal v. Gallway (1769), 1 Bro. C. C. 293, n. 2.; Amb. 682.

34. 1 Bro. C. C. 293, n. 2.

35. Broughton v. Errington (1773), 7 Brown 461.

36. E.g., Kenyon, Devise v. Pontet (1785), Prec. Ch. 240, and Thompson v. Nelson, 1 Cox 447; Loughborough, Pearson v. Pearson (1783), 1 Bro. C. C. 293; Thurlow, Foster v. Cook (1791), 3 Bro. C. C. 347.

37. Foster v. Cook (1791), 3 Bro. C. C. 347, at 351.

38. French v. Davies (1793), 2 Ves. Jun. 572, at 587.

39. In theory, "a party is always entitled to a clear knowledge of the funds between which he is to elect, before he is put to his election." See Pusey v. Sir Edward Desbouvrie (1734), 3 P. Wms. 315, at n. 4. This case involved a daughter's election between her orphan's part and a legacy from her father. The issues concerning election are well aired, though the case was settled by compromise.

40. *The Complete Letters of Lady Mary Wortley Montagu,* ed. Robert Halsband, 3 vols. (Oxford: Clarendon Press, 1965–1967), 3:254–255; Robert Halsband, *The Life of Lady Mary Wortley Montagu* (Oxford: Clarendon Press, 1956), 275–277.

41. *Tatler* 223, September 12, 1710; on attribution, Richmond P. Bond, "Mr. Bickerstaff and Mr. Wortley," in *Classical, Mediaeval, and Renaissance Studies in Honor of Berthold Louis Ullman,* ed. Charles Henderson, Jr., 2 vols. (Rome: Edizioni di Storia e Letteratura, 1964), 2:257–274.

42. Horace Walpole to Sir Horace Mann, December 16, 1756, in *The Yale Edition of Horace Walpole's Correspondence,* ed. W. S. Lewis et al., 48 vols. (New Haven, Conn.: Yale University Press, 1937–1983), 21:32.

43. David Duman, *The Judicial Bench in England, 1727–1825: The Reshaping of a Professional Elite* (London: Royal Historical Society, 1982), 171.

44. Dobson v. Dobson and Others (1734), Cas. T. Hard. 19.

45. The quoted phrase is from Lloyd Bonfield, "Comment: Family Law Section," a written response to an earlier version of this chapter I presented at a meeting of the Northeast American Society for Eighteenth-Century Studies, Syracuse, New York, October 1983.

46. Roebuck, 301.

47. Samuel Butler, *Hudibras,* ed. John Wilders (Oxford: Clarendon Press, 1967), Part III, canto i, ll. 1189–92; Part III was first published in 1677.

48. Alan Dugald McKillop, "Charlotte Smith's Letters," *Huntington Library Quarterly* 15 (1952):239.

49. Roebuck, 118–119, 329.

50. Sir Horace Mann to Horace Walpole, July 19, 1755, in *Correspondence*, 20:486.

51. J. H. Baker, *An Introduction to English Legal History*, 2d ed. (London: Butterworth, 1979), 321–322.

52. Bonfield, "Comment: Family Law Section."

53. Harvey v. Ashley (1748), 3 Atk. 607, at 612. From the statement of the settlement in Hardwicke's opinion, it appears that Dorothy's jointure was a conditional jointure not guaranteed to take effect presently on the death of the husband (jointure land was to go to the survivor of husband and wife only "in default of issue"); thus, it was not a good legal jointure. Hardwicke did not address this issue; since argument of counsel is not reported, one cannot tell whether it was raised.

54. Roebuck, 330.

55. A. P. W. Malcomson, *The Pursuit of the Heiress: Aristocratic Marriage in Ireland, 1750–1820* (Antrim: Ulster Historical Foundation, 1982), 9, 6.

56. Caruthers v. Caruthers (1794), 4 Bro. C. C. 500, at 513.

57. Roper, 2:481.

58. Cannel v. Buckle (1724), 2 P. Wms. 243, at 244.

59. Jordan v. Savage (1732), 2 Eq. Ca. Abr. 101.

60. Price v. Seys (1740), Barn. C. 117, at 122.

61. Harvey v. Ashley, 3 Atk. 607, at 612. He added, "I will not say how far a mere elusory jointure might be relieved against, but if it is not adequate to what she would have had in dower, it is no reason to set it aside." In this case, Lord Hardwicke attached weight to the fact that the wife had a money portion, arguing that unless she could make a valid agreement concerning that, the husband would be entitled to it absolutely on her marriage.

62. North v. Ansell (1731), 2 P. Wms. 618. Cf. Harvey v. Ashley, 3 Atk. 607, at 610: "As soon as the marriage is had, the principal contract is executed, and cannot be set aside, or rescinded, the estate and capacities of the parties are altered, the children born of the marriage are equally purchasers under both father and mother, and therefore it has been truly said that marriage contracts ought not to be rescinded, because it would affect the interest of third persons, *the issue*."

63. Drury v. Drury (1760–61), 2 Eden 39, at 48.

64. Hardwicke in Harvey v. Ashley, 3 Atk. 607, at 612.

65. Durnford v. Lane (1780), 1 Bro. C. C. 106, at 112.

66. Drury v. Drury, 2 Eden 57.

67. Daly v. Lynch (1715), 3 Brown 478, at 481.

68. Cray v. Willis (1734), 2 Eq. Ca. Abr. 389.

69. Glover v. Bates (1739), 1 Atk. 439. He ruled against the widow on the ground that she had accepted property under the settlement, and hence had elected to take under the settlement.

70. "An act for empowering *Esther Hanmer,* an infant, to settle her estates, pursuant to articles entered into in consideration of a marriage agreed upon between *Asheton Curzon* esquire, & the said Esther Hanmer," Private Act, 29 Geo. 2, c. 5 (1756).

71. "An act to enable *Sir Watkin Williams Wynn* baronet, a minor, to make a

settlement on his intended marriage with the Lady *Henrietta Somerset*," Private Act, 9 Geo. 3, c. 11 (1769). Cf. "An act for vesting the estate of *William Forrester* esquire, Brook Forrester his son and heir apparent, in the country of *Salop*, in trustees, to settle the same, pursuant to an agreement previous to the marriage of the said *Brook Forrester* with *Elizabeth* his wife, notwithstanding the minority of the said *Brook Forrester*," Private Act, 8 Geo. 2, c. 11 (1735).

72. George Bramwell, *An Analytical Table of the Private Statutes Passed between the 1st Geo. 2 A.D. 1727, and 52nd Geo. 3 A.D. 1812* (London, 1812). Between 1760 and 1812, for which Bramwell gives an analytic table, there are fourteen acts to enable infants to make marriage settlements or to settle their estates pursuant to marriage settlements, four of them for females. The period 1727–1760 seems similar.

73. Drury v. Drury, 2 Eden 39. Her jointure was £600 a year; without the settlement, assuming that the land of which her husband died seised was subject to dower, her dower would have yielded £876 a year, and her share of the personal estate would have been a lump sum of £20,000.

74. Drury v. Drury, 2 Eden 52. And: "we are told that men are become too sordid to marry on these terms, and that she would otherwise be compelled to live unmarried to twenty-one" (2 Eden 56).

75. Drury v. Drury, 2 Eden 46.

76. Drury v. Drury, 2 Eden 58–59.

77. Drury v. Drury, 2 Eden 70. Not fully reported here is the opinion of Sir John Eardly Wilmot, who argued for barring, presenting a rather good historical argument that the statute had intended to bar infants. See his *Notes of Opinions and Judgments Delivered in Different Courts* (London, 1802), 177–227.

78. Drury v. Drury, 2 Eden 73.

79. Drury v. Drury, 2 Eden 70.

80. Robert Lord Henley, *A Memoir of the Life of Robert Henley, Earl of Northington, Lord High Chancellor of Great Britain* (London, 1831), 36–37.

81. Horace Twiss, *The Public and Private Life of Lord Chancellor Eldon, with Selections from His Correspondence*, 2d ed., 3 vols. (London, 1844), 1:319–320.

82. See, Slocombe v. Glubb (1789), 2 Bro. C. C. 545, where Lord Chancellor Thurlow carefully avoids deciding the question of the infant male.

83. Caruthers v. Caruthers (1794), 4 Bro. C. C. 500, actually for part of her jointure, which was another issue in the case.

84. Milner v. Lord Harewood (1811), 18 Ves. Jr. 259.

85. Henry Ballow, *A Treatise of Equity*, revised and ed. John Fonblanque (1793–94; reprint, 2 vols. in 1, New York: Garland, 1979), 69. Williams v. Williams (1782), 1 Bro. C. C. 152.

86. Edmund Gibson Atherley, *A Practical Treatise on the Law of Marriage and Other Family Settlements* (London, 1813), 13–23, 41–45, 86.

87. Roper, 1:479.

88. Sidney v. Sidney (1734), 3 P. Wms. 269.

89. "An Act to enable Infants, with the Approbation of the Court of Chancery,

to make binding settlements of their Real and Personal Estate on Marriage," 18 & 19 Vict., c. 43 (1855).

90. "An Act for the better preventing clandestine marriages," 26 Geo. 2, c. 33 (1753).
91. Wilmot, 213.
92. Wilmot, 206.

5. Pin Money and Other Separate Property

1. John Vanbrugh, "The Relapse," in *British Dramatists from Dryden to Sheridan*, ed. George H. Nettleton, Arthur E. Case, and George Winchester Stone, Jr. (Carbondale: Southern Illinois University Press, 1969), 301–302.
2. *The Oxford English Dictionary*, s.v. "pin-money," gives as its first citation, "1542. *Test. Ebor.* (Surtees) VI. 160, I give my said doughter Margarett my lease of the parsonadge of Kirkdall Churche . . . to buy her pynnes withal." Also cited there is Addison's comment, "The Doctrine of Pin-money is of a very late Date, unknown to our Great Grandmothers, and not yet received by many of our Modern Ladies" (*Spectator* no. 295, 1712). For speculation on the origin of the term, see Sir Edward Sugden, *A Treatise on the Law of Property as Administered by the House of Lords* (London, 1849), 165, n. 1.
3. Richard Brinsley Sheridan, "The School for Scandal," in *British Dramatists*, 863.
4. Bennet v. Davis (1725), 2 P. Wms. 316. The wife's father had devised land to her separate use without establishing a trust. Especially since the husband had not consented to her having a separate estate in this property acquired after their marriage, it might well have been considered simply his property. But equity ruled that the husband's assignees in bankruptcy had no claim on the wife's property and construed the husband as the wife's trustee.
5. Thus, in the briefly reported case of Cornwall and Earl of Mountague (1701), 1 Eq. Ca. Abr. 66: "The Plaintiff's Relation (to whom he was Heir) allowed his Wife Pin-Money, which being in Arrear, he gave her a Note to this Purpose; I am indebted to my Wife £100, which became due to her such a Day; after, by his Will, he makes Provision out of his Lands for Payment of all his Debts, and all Monies which he owed to any Person in Trust for his Wife; and the Question was whether the £100 was to be paid within this Trust; and Ld K. decreed not, because in Point of Law it was no Debt, because a man cannot be indebted to his Wife; and it was not Money due to any Trust for her." Cf. Lady Tyrrell's Case (1674), discussed later in this chapter.
6. Gilbert Horsman, *Precedents in Conveyancing, Settled and Approved by Gilbert Horsman*, 2d ed., 2 vols. (Savoy, 1757), 1:33–39. For a form showing pin money secured to the wife by a penal bond, the payments to come directly from the husband with no mention of trustees, see "Condition of a Bond, made by an intended Husband to the Woman's Father, to pay her Pin-Money," Horsman, 1:199.

7. Horsman, 1:557.

8. Milles v. Wikes (1694), 1 Eq. Ca. Abr. 66.

9. More v. Scarborough, 2 Eq. Ca. Abr. 156 (no date, but the only Earl of Scarborough who married was created Earl in 1690 and died in 1721).

10. Sidney v. Sidney (1734), 3 P. Wms. 269, at 276. Talbot reasoned: "But the articles being, that the husband shall settle such and such land in certainty on his wife the plaintiff, for her jointure, this is pretty much in the nature of an actual and vested jointure; in regard what is covenanted for good consideration to be done is considered in equity in most respects as done; consequently, this is a jointure, and not forfeitable either by adultery or elopement."

11. Moore v. Moore (1737), 1 Atk. 272.

12. Blount v. Winter (1781), 3 Cox's P. W. 276. After Lord Hardwicke's term as Lord Chancellor, Lord Keeper Henley decided Lee v. Lee (1758), Dickens 321, 806, a case similar to Moore, differently, declining to give a separated wife an injunction against her husband's receiving the rents of her separate estate and basing his decision on the kind of arguments used by the losing side in Moore. A treatise writer might attempt to reconcile these cases by stressing Lord Hardwicke's sense that the husband in Moore had not made timely or convincing appeals to his wife to return and that the husband's early payments to his separated wife created a "presumption that he thought at least she was excusable in separating herself from him."

13. Powell v. Hankey and Cox (1722), 2 P. Wms. 82, at 84. Cf. Offley v. Offley (1691), 1 Eq. Ca. Abr. 66.

14. Ridout v. Lewis (1738), 1 Atk. 269. Cf. Countess of Warwick and Edwards (1728), 1 Eq. Ca. Abr. 140, where one and three-quarters years' arrears of pin money were allowed to the widow as a debt against her husband's estate.

15. *The Spectator,* ed. Donald F. Bond, 5 vols. (Oxford: Clarendon Press, 1965), 3:51.

16. Lon E. Fuller and Melvin Aron Eisenberg, *Basic Contract Law,* 3d ed. (St. Paul, Minn.: West Publishing, 1972), 101.

17. In England, the restrictions on interspousal tort claims were altered by statute. See O. M. Stone, "Ninth Report of the Law Reform Commission (Liability in Tort between Husband and Wife)," *Modern Law Review* 25 (1962):695–697. For the United States, where the rules vary from state to state, see William L. Prosser, *Handbook of the Law of Torts,* 4th ed. (St. Paul, Minn.: West Publishing, 1971), 554–555, 860–864, 868.

18. Miller v. Miller (Iowa, 1887), in Fuller and Eisenberg, 106.

19. Thomas v. Bennet (1725), 2 P. Wms. 341.

20. Howard v. Digby (1834), 2 Cl. & Fin. 634, at 655.

21. *Spectator,* 3:53.

22. Moore v. Moore, 1 Atk. 272, at 277.

23. Barbara Allen Babcock, Ann E. Freedman, Eleanor Holmes Norton, and Susan C. Ross, *Sex Discrimination and the Law: Causes and Remedies* (Boston: Little, Brown, 1975), 619–646; Banks McDowell, "Contracts in the Family," *Boston University Law Review* 45 (1965):43–62.

24. Durant v. Titley (1819), 7 Price 577, discussed in Chapter 6.

25. Moore v. Moore, 1 Atk. 272, at 276.
26. P. M. Bromley, *Family Law,* 5th ed. (London: Butterworth, 1976), 445. This rule was changed by the Married Women's Property Act, 1964, which provided that any property "derived from any allowance made by the husband for the expenses of the matrimonial home or for similar purposes" which came into dispute should "be treated as belonging to the husband and wife in equal shares." Cf. O. Kahn-Freund, "Inconsistencies and Injustices in the Law of Husband and Wife," *Modern Law Review* 16 (1953):34–49, 148–173; O. M. Stone, "Married Women's Property Act, 1964," *Modern Law Review* 27 (1964):576–580. In the United States the older rule has not been the subject of such sweeping statutory change. Comment, however, has been provoked by the case of a wife who, unbeknownst to her husband, saved enough money from her household allowance to create a portfolio of securities in her own name, securities which the court ruled belonged to her husband (Hardy v. Hardy, D.D.C., 1964), 235 F. Supp. 209, in Babcock et al., 626–627: "The court recognizes that such household allowances generally comprehend expenditures by the wife for personal needs such as clothes, entertainment and transportation. Such expenses are within the obligation of the husband to support and maintain his wife. Acquiescence in these expenditures does not indicate an acquiescence in the use of such funds for the creation of a portfolio of securities for the wife's sole account. To hold otherwise would be to invite disruptive influences in the home."
27. Sir Frederick Pollock and Frederic William Maitland, *The History of English Law before the Time of Edward I,* ed. S. F. C. Milsom, 2 vols. (Cambridge: Cambridge University Press, 1968), 2:26–27, 325–330; cf. J. H. Baker, *An Introduction to English Legal History* (London: Butterworth, 1979), 209–213.
28. Pollock and Maitland, 2:430.
29. Gore v. Knight (1705), 1 Eq. Ca. Abr. 66. Cf. the briefly reported Mangey and Hungerford, 2 Eq. Ca. Abr. 156, where Lord Chancellor King (Ch. 1725–1735) allowed a wife "a considerable Sum of Money out of Housekeeping."
30. Wilson v. Pack (1710), 2 Eq. Ca. Abr. 155.
31. Peacock v. Monk (1750–51), 2 Ves. Sen. 190, at 192.
32. Lady Tyrrell's Case (1674), Freem. Chy. 304. In Graham v. Londonderry (1746), 3 Atk. 393, Lord Chancellor Hardwicke decided that diamonds given to the wife by the husband's father on her marriage and subsequently pledged as security for her husband's debt were to be considered "a gift to her separate use," though as the husband's personal estate in this case had assets sufficient to redeem the diamonds, Hardwicke merely had to rule that she was entitled to reimbursement rather than to decide if her claim were to be satisfied in the absence of sufficient personal property in the husband's estate.
33. Tate v. Austin (1714), 2 Vern. 689. She is owed a debt from her husband's estate, "but all other debts shall be first paid."
34. "A Song. *The Tune,* Ye Commons and Peers," in *Love a la Mode; or, The Amours of Florella and Phillis: Being the Memoirs of Two Celebrated Ladies under Those Names, in Which the Whole Circle of Modern Gallantry Is Display'd* (London, 1732), [58].

35. Henry Fielding, *The History of Tom Jones, a Foundling,* ed. Martin C. Battestin and Fredson Bowers, 2 vols. (Middletown, Conn.: Wesleyan University Press, 1975), Bk. XI, chap. 7, 599–600. Fielding, of course, was a barrister as well as a novelist.
36. Grigby v. Cox (1750), 1 Ves. Sen. 518.
37. Fettiplace v. Gorges (1789), 3 Bro. C. C. 8, at 10.
38. Pybus v. Smith (1791), 3 Bro. C. C. 340, at 346.
39. Caverley v. Dudley and Bisco (1747), 3 Atk. 541, at 542.
40. Whistler v. Newman (1798), 4 Ves. Jun. 129, at 144. Happily for Mrs. Whistler, Lord Loughborough found himself able to distinguish her case from the ones he regretted on the ground that her trustees had made themselves party to the husband's act and had taken a bond of indemnity from him against any claims of her children, so the husband becoming insolvent, it was incumbent upon them to make up the fund. In a similar vein, Sir Richard Arden in Sockett v. Wray (1794), 4 Bro. C. C. 483, found for the trustees of a wife's separate estate who refused to permit her to dispose of her capital by deciding that the language of her marriage settlement allowing her to dispose of her estate "by any note or notes, instrument or instruments, writing or writings" had significantly and purposefully omitted reference to a power to dispose of the property by any "deed or deeds," thus showing that she was to dispose of it only by "a revocable act."
41. Pybus v. Smith, n. 1; Walter G. Hart, "The Origin of the Restraint upon Anticipation," *Law Quarterly Review* 40 (1924):221–226. Lord Chancellor Thurlow inserted the phrase "not to be paid by anticipation" into a settlement he drew up for one "Miss Watson," and equity subsequently allowed language of this kind to prohibit alienation of capital.
42. Tullet v. Armstrong (1839), 4 My. & Cr. 390, at 394, 405–406.
43. Earl Digby v. Howard (1831), 4 Sim. 588, at 605. Cf. Brodie v. Barry (1813), 2 V. & B. 36, an earlier case involving a lunatic wife.
44. Howard v. Digby (1834), 2 Cl. & Fin. 634, at 674.
45. 2 Cl. & Fin. 670.
46. 2 Cl. & Fin. 655, 657.
47. 2 Cl. & Fin. 677.
48. 2 Cl. & Fin. 679. Later Lord St. Leonards, who did not have the highest opinion of Brougham's legal learning, took a most critical view of Brougham's opinion in Howard, believing that although Shadwell should have allowed some account of the Duke's actual expenditure insofar as it was made for things the Duchess would presumably have bought with the pin money if sane, still her insanity might well have resulted in significant saving to which her personal representatives were entitled (Sugden, 170).
49. R. S. Donnison Roper, *A Treatise on the Revocation and Republication of Wills and Testaments: Together with Tracts upon the Law Concerning Baron and Feme* (London, 1800), 200; Roper, *A Treatise on the Law of Property Arising from the Relation between Husband and Wife,* 2 vols. (London, 1820), 2:131–150. Cf. *Baron and Feme: A Treatise of Law and Equity,* 3d ed. (Savoy, 1758), which offers no discussion of pin money, and Charles Viner, *A General Abridgment of Law and Equity,* 2d ed., 23 vols. (London, 1791–1795), 4:133–

134, which uses the term "pin money" and briefly reports several cases without attempting to derive any coherent doctrine.

50. Lawrence Stone, *The Family, Sex, and Marriage in England, 1500–1800* (New York: Harper and Row, 1977), 330.

51. *Spectator*, 3:51, 53.

52. Samuel Johnson, *Rambler* no. 97, in *The Yale Edition of the Works of Samuel Johnson: The Rambler*, ed. W. J. Bate and Albrecht Strauss, 3 vols. (New Haven: Yale University Press, 1969), 2:158.

53. [Mrs. Catherine Gore], *Pin Money, a Novel*, 3 vols. (London, 1831), 3:224, 293.

54. *The Complete Letters of Lady Mary Wortley Montagu*, ed. Robert Halsband, 3 vols. (Oxford: Clarendon Press, 1965–1967), 1:141.

55. Reginald Blunt, *Thomas, Lord Lyttleton: The Portrait of a Rake, with a Brief Memoir of His Sister Lucy Valentia* (London: Hutchinson, 1936), 92. I thank Edith Larson for calling Lord Lyndhurst's letter of July 22, 1772, to my attention. The manuscript is part of the Montagu Collection at the Huntington Library, MO 1370.

56. Slanning v. Style (1734), 3 P. Wms. 334.

6. Separate Maintenance Contracts

1. Arthur Friedman, ed., *Collected Works of Oliver Goldsmith*, 5 vols. (Oxford: Oxford University Press, 1966), 2:81–84, and cf. Friedman's notes on Goldsmith's sources.

2. Susan Staves, *Players' Scepters: Fictions of Authority in the Restoration* (Lincoln: University of Nebraska Press, 1979), 151–156, 187–188.

3. Manby v. Scott (1663), 1 Lev. 4; Moore v. Moore (1737), 1 Atk. 272. Neither of these cases involved a formal separate maintenance contract.

4. Manby v. Scott (1659), 1 Mod. 127.

5. 1 Atk. 273, 275.

6. Lawrence Stone, *The Family, Sex, and Marriage in England, 1500–1800* (New York: Harper and Row, 1977), 330. On separation, Stone observes, "although statistical proof is lacking, one gets a distinct impression that wives married to impossible husbands in the upper classes were increasingly seeking formal separation, accompanied by adequate financial provisions which allowed them to continue to live active and satisfying social lives" (333). Later he especially associates separations with the "highest court aristocracy," commenting, "in this class, separations were not uncommon, and they left the wife with considerable economic resources" (392).

7. Fletcher v. Fletcher (1788), 2 Cox 99, at 102.

8. E. M. Keate, *Nelson's Wife: The First Biography of Frances Herbert, Viscountess Nelson* (London: Cassell, 1939), gives Frances's allowance as £1,800 a year.

9. Ringstead v. Lady Lanesborough (1783), 3 Dougl. 197, at 199.

10. Sources for this account of John and Mary Wilkes are: Wilkes v. Wilkes (1757), Dickens 791; Rex v. Mary Mead (1758), 1 Burr. 541; John Almon,

ed., *The Correspondence of John Wilkes, with Memoirs of His Life,* 5 vols. (1805); Horace Bleakley, *Life of John Wilkes* (London: John Lane, 1917).

11. Bleakley, 42, citing manuscript correspondence of Wilkes and Dell.

12. Rex. v. Mary Mead, 1 Burr. 541, at 542.

13. Sources for this account of Sophia and Robert Baddeley are the following letters in David M. Little and George M. Kahrl, eds., *The Letters of David Garrick,* 3 vols. (Cambridge, Mass.: Harvard University Press, 1963): no. 605, "To George Garrick," August 30, 1770; no. 608, "To George Garrick," September 7, 1770; no. 653, "To Samuel Foote," September 24, [1771]; and *The Town and Country Magazine* 2 (March 1770), 157–158; Hatchett v. Baddeley (1776), 2 Black. W. 1079; Philip H. Highfill, Jr., Kalman A. Burnim, and Edward Langhans, *A Biographical Dictionary of Actors* (Carbondale: Southern Illinois University Press, 1973), s.v. "Robert Baddeley" and "Sophia Baddeley."

14. The reporter in *The Town and Country Magazine* affected some doubt as to which man she asked to spare the other: she "threw herself upon her knees, and, whilst she looked very languishing, *(but whether at her husband or her lover is not certain)* cried out, 'Oh! spare, spare him!' "

15. The creditors may not have been aware of the existence of a separate maintenance contract; Sophia's side would have had no incentive to make them aware of it.

16. 2 Black. W. 1079, at 1082.

17. Sources for this account of Hugh and Anne Percy are: *Trial for Adultery, &. the Rt. Hon. Hugh Baron Percy v. the Right Hon. Anne Baroness Percy, Libel Given in the 27th of May 1778* ([London? 1778?]); "An Act to Dissolve the Marriage between the Rt. Hon. Hugh Baron Percy . . . & the Rt. Hon. Anne Baroness Percy," Private Act, 19 Geo. 3, chap. 20 (1779); *Lords Journals* 35:529, 537, 548–549, 637; Corbett v. Poelnitz (1785), 1 T. R. 4; W. S. Lewis et al., eds., *Horace Walpole's Correspondence with Sir Horace Mann,* 11 vols. (New Haven, Conn.: Yale University Press, 1954–1971), 8:378; Poelnitz to James Iredell, February 20, 1788, in Griffith J. McCree, *Life and Correspondence of James Iredell,* 2 vols. (New York, 1858), 2:18–24; *Dictionary of National Biography,* s.v. "Hugh Percy"; *The New York Genealogical and Biographical Record* 80 (1949):130–141; Warren Hunting Smith, *Originals Abroad: The Foreign Careers of Some Eighteenth-Century Britons* (New Haven, Conn.: Yale University Press, 1952), 141–154.

18. Williams v. Callow (1717), 2 Vern. 752; the wife's portion was supposed to be £600, but her mother was able to give only £500, and various transactions concerning the £100 complicate the case.

19. 2 Vern. 753, n. 2.

20. Watkyns v. Watkyns (1740), 2 Atk. 96, at 98.

21. Cecil v. Juxon (1737), 1 Atk. 278. Cf. Oxenden v. Oxenden (1705), 2 Vern. 493, and Nicholls v. Danvers (1711), 2 Vern. 671.

22. Angier v. Angier (1718), Prec. Ch. 496, at 497.

23. Rex v. Mary Mead, 1 Burr. 541. Cf. Mr. Lister's Case (1721), 8 Mod. 22, and Lord Vane's Case (1748), 13 East 171 note a.

24. Todd v. Stoakes (c. 1695), Salk. 116, Ld. Raym. 444. Cf. 2 Str. 1214.

25. More v. Freeman (1725), Bunb. 205.

26. Guth v. Guth (1792), 3 Bro. C. C. 615, at 617.

27. Lean v. Shutz (1778), 2 Black. W. 1195, at 1199.

28. J. H. Baker, *An Introduction to English Legal History,* 2d ed. (London: Butterworth, 1979), 174, quoting Mansfield in Johnson v. Spiller (1784).

29. Ringstead v. Lady Lanesborough (1783), 3 Dougl. 197, at 204, 199, 203.

30. Barwell v. Anne Brooks (1784), 3 Dougl. 371.

31. Corbett v. Poelnitz (1785), 1 T. R. 5 at 7, 9.

32. Hyde v. Price (1797), 3 Ves. Jun. 437, at 444.

33. Legard v. Johnson (1797), 3 Ves. Jun. 352, at 360.

34. Beard and Arabella His Wife v. Webb and Another (1800), 2 Bos. & Pul. 93, at 107.

35. Marshall v. Rutton (1800), 8 T. R. 545, at 546–547.

36. Weedon v. Timbrell (1793), 5 T. R. 357.

37. [Henry Ballow], *A Treatise of Equity* (Dublin, 1756), 18–19.

38. John Fonblanque, *A Treatise of Equity,* 3 vols. (Dublin, 1793), Bk. I, chap. 2, s. 6, note p. Fonblanque apologizes: "It might be construed a want of that respect which is due to the high authority of those who decided the above cases, even to question the principles upon which they proceeded; an imputation to which I should seriously lament having subjected myself by any observation in the course of this work." In theory, it might be noted, the parish had some defenses against a wife's becoming chargeable, although it is certainly difficult to imagine the full range of remedies being used in practice to deal with an upper-class woman. Thus, by 5 Geo. 1, c. 8, when a wife was left a charge to the parish by the husband, the churchwardens or overseers of the poor could receive rents and profits of the husband's lands and seize his chattels to reimburse the parish for the wife's support. Also, by unrepealed Elizabethan poor law, poor women could be put to work or put into service.

39. Fitzer v. Fitzer (1742), 2 Atk. 511.

40. Jamil S. Zainaldin, "The Emergence of a Modern American Family Law: Child Custody, Adoption, and the Courts, 1796–1851," *Northwestern University Law Review* 73 (1979):1038, at 1060, n. 77, 1063, n. 97.

41. Wardell v. Gooch (1806), 7 East 582.

42. Chambers v. Caufield (1805), 6 East 244.

43. Lord St. John v. Lady St. John (1805), 11 Ves. Jun. 525, at 530, 532.

44. St. John, 11 Ves. Jun. 537.

45. R. S. Donnison Roper, *A Treatise on the Law of Property Arising from the Relation between Husband and Wife,* 2 vols. (London, 1820), 2:286; Appendices 19 and 20 contain two forms of deeds for separation.

46. Fitzer v. Fitzer, 2 Atk. 511; Guth v. Guth, 3 Bro. C. C. 615; Barwell v. Brooks (1784), 3 Dougl. 372. In Barwell, not only were there no trustees, there was no deed in evidence, yet Mansfield found that it was sufficient the wife had a competent separate maintenance duly paid to her and refused her plea of coverture as a defense against her creditor.

47. Worrall v. Jacob (1816, 1817), 3 Mer. 256, at 268. Cf. Eldon in Westmeath v. Westmeath, Jacob 126.

48. Logan v. Birkett (1833), 1 My. & K. 220, at 222, 225.
49. Hobbs v. Hull (1788), 1 Cox 446.
50. Westmeath v. Salisbury (1831), 5 Bligh N. S. 339, at 402; here Eldon is speaking as a peer hearing an appeal, not as a sitting judge.
51. Smith v. Smith (Consistory, 1781), cited 2 Hagg. Ecc. (Supp.) 42, note a.
52. Westmeath v. Westmeath (1827), 2 Hagg. Ecc. (Supp.) 61, at 115.
53. Wilson v. Wilson (1846–47), 1 H.L.C. 538, at 574.
54. Rodney v. Chambers (1802), 2 East 283, at 291.
55. Rodney v. Chambers, 2 East 297.
56. Durant v. Titley (1819), 7 Price 578.
57. Nurse v. Craig (1806), 2 Bos. & Pul. (N. R.), 148, at 165.
58. Hodgkinson v. Fletcher (1814), 4 Camp. 70.
59. S. M. Cretney, *Principles of Family Law,* 2d. ed. (London: Sweet and Maxwell, 1976), 233.
60. Hyde v. Price (1797), 3 Ves. 437.
61. Corbett v. Poelnitz (1785), 1 T. R. 10.

7. Conclusion

1. Simpson's statement made at the 1987 meeting of the American Society for Legal History. Philadelphia, Penn.
2. For some interesting suggestions about the English preference for medieval legal history, see Douglas Hay, "The Criminal Prosecution in England and Its Historians," *Modern Law Review* 47 (1984):23–27.
3. Morton Horwitz, "The History of the Public/Private Distinction," *University of Pennsylvania Law Review* 130 (1982):1423–28.
4. Cf. Duncan Kennedy, "The Stages of the Decline of the Public/Private Distinction," *University of Pennsylvania Law Review* 130 (1982):1352.
5. To list, in chronological order, only selected items in this debate, emphasizing recent entries and those which engage directly certain issues of married women's property:

   Christopher Clay, "Marriage, Inheritance, and the Rise of Large Estates," *Economic History Review,* 2d ser., 21 (1968):503–518.

   J. V. Beckett, "English Landownership in the Seventeenth and Eighteenth Centuries: The Debate and the Problems," *Economic History Review,* 2d ser., 30 (1977):567–581.

   Christopher Clay, "Property, Settlements, Financial Provisions for the Family, and Sale of Land by the Great Land Owners, 1660–1790," *Journal of British Studies* 21 (1981):18–38.

   Lloyd Bonfield, "Marriage, Property, and the Affective Family," *Law and History Review* 1 (1983):297–312.

   Eileen Spring, "The Family, Strict Settlement, and the Historians," *Canadian Journal of History* 18 (1983):379–398.

   Eileen Spring, "Law and the Theory of the Affective Family," *Albion* 16 (1984):1–20.

Lawrence Stone and Jeanne C. Fawtier Stone, *An Opin Elite? England, 1540–1880* (Oxford: Clarendon Press, 1984).

Eileen Spring and David Spring, "The English Landed Elite, 1540–1879: A Review," *Albion* 17 (1985):149–166.

Lawrence Stone, "Spring Back," *Albion* 17 (1985):167–180.

Eileen Spring and David Spring, "The English Landed Elite, 1540–1879: A Rejoinder," *Albion* 17 (1985):393–396.

Lawrence Stone, "A Non-Rebuttal," *Albion* 17 (1985):396.

Lloyd Bonfield, "Affective Families, Open Elites, and Strict Family Settlements in Early Modern England," *Economic History Review,* 2d ser., 39 (1986):355–370.

6. H. J. Habbakuk, "English Landownership, 1680–1740," *Economic History Review* 10 (1939–40):2–17; "Marriage Settlements in the Eighteenth Century," *Transactions of the Royal Historical Society,* 4th ser., 32 (1950):15–30.

7. On occasion, sons or other males who inherited through the female line changed their names to the patronymic the female had had before her marriage. This tactic gave particular satisfaction when an elder son could become his father's heir and a younger son could change his name to continue the line of his mother's family. Attention has recently been given to this practice in Stone and Stone, 126–142, and A. P. W. Malcomson, *The Pursuit of the Heiress: Aristocratic Marriage in Ireland, 1750–1820* (Antrim: Ulster Historical Foundation, 1982), 22.

8. Habbakuk, "English Landownership," 7–8.

9. Sir John Habbakuk, "The Rise and Fall of English Landed Families, 1600–1800," *Transactions of the Royal Historical Society,* 5th ser., 29 (1979):187–207; 30 (1980):199–221; 31 (1981):195–217; at 29 (1979):194, 192.

10. Lloyd Bonfield, "Marriage Settlements and the 'Rise of Great Estates': The Demographic Aspect," *Economic History Review,* 2d ser., 32 (1979):483–493. Cf. Barbara English and John Saville, "Family Settlement and the 'Rise of Great Estates,'" and Bonfield's reply, *Economic History Review,* 2d ser., 33 (1980):556–558, 559–563.

11. Lloyd Bonfield, *Marriage Settlements, 1601–1740: The Adoption of the Strict Settlement* (Cambridge: Cambridge University Press, 1983), 99.

12. Peter Roebuck, *Yorkshire Baronets, 1640–1760: Families, Estates, and Fortunes* (Oxford: Oxford University Press, 1980), 75. See also Malcomson, 48; David W. Howell, *Patriarchs and Parasites: The Gentry of South-West Wales in the Eighteenth Century* (Cardiff: University of Wales Press, 1986), 31–33.

13. Clay, "Marriage, Inheritance," 508.

14. Although the larger owners did attempt to consolidate, especially in the later part of our period, throughout this period the lands of individuals, particularly larger owners, were often scattered, not only through more than one county but even among England and other countries, including Wales, Ireland, and the West Indies. This fact can make economic conclusions from the sort of county studies now in vogue highly suspect.

15. Stone and Stone, 76.

16. Bonfield, "Affective Families," 352.

17. Malcomson, 2.

18. Judith Schneid Lewis, *In the Family Way: Childbearing in the British Aristocracy, 1760–1860* (New Brunswick, N.J.: Rutgers University Press, 1986), 61.

19. Ray A. Kelch, *Newcastle, a Duke without Money: Thomas Pelham-Holles, 1693–1768* (Berkeley: University of California Press, 1974); W. A. Maguire, "The 1822 Settlement of the Donegall Estates," *Irish Economic and Social History* 31 (1976):17–32.

20. J. R. Wordie, *Estate Management in Eighteenth-Century England: The Building of the Leveson-Gower Fortune* (London: Royal Historical Society, 1982).

21. Painless for whom? a female reader is apt to wonder. I imagine Professor Bonfield's unaccustomed levity in this passage was prompted by an understandable desire to liven up his exposition of what is usually thought to be a rather tedious subject, and I am confident that he has no personal wish to bring back suttee; nevertheless, the passage does illustrate the focus of many of these male writers on the interests of the male heir or the interests of the reified "estate." Bonfield, "Affective Families," 344.

22. A very useful corrective emphasis has recently been provided by Lewis's *In the Family Way*.

23. Stone and Stone, 73.

24. James Oldham, "Law Reporting in the London Newspapers: 1756–1786," *American Journal of Legal History* 31 (1987):197.

25. Maguire, 20–21.

26. Sybil Campbell, "Usury and Annuities of the Eighteenth Century," *Law Quarterly Review* 44 (1928):473–493.

27. Campbell, 486.

28. Roebuck, 60.

29. Malcomson, 37. And note also the third Duke of Devonshire's overcoming his Duchess's opposition to a proposed marriage for their son by having her locked up in a rectory in Hampshire (38).

30. Lawrence Stone, *The Family, Sex, and Marriage in England, 1500–1800* (New York: Harper and Row, 1977), 89.

31. Randolph Trumbach, *The Rise of the Egalitarian Family: Aristocratic Kinship and Domestic Relations in Eighteenth-Century England* (New York: Academic Press, 1978), 71.

32. Trumbach, 106, and note case of Lady Newport's daughter, Mod. Repts. 1, 309–314.

33. Cf. the sensible treatment of this subject in Lewis, chap. 1.

34. Stone and Stone, 122.

35. Stone and Stone, 142.

36. One common measure of celibacy rate counts persons not married by age 50 as celibate. T. H. Hollingsworth, "The Demography of the British Peerage," supplement to *Population Studies* 18, no. 2 (1964):20, gives the following data on females in the peerage:

Cohort born	Females not married at 50 (per 1,000)
1650–1674	163
1675–1699	238
1700–1724	267
1725–1749	218
1750–1774	239
1775–1799	234
1800–1824	202
1825–1849	238

My 1986 estimate is calculated from Table 2.6, "Marital condition of the resident population," in the *Annual Abstract of Statistics* (Central Statistical Office: Government Statistical Service, 1988). Taking the age cohort 45–55, I have added the total females (in England and Wales) reported as single, married, widowed, or divorced and calculated the percent of the total reported as single.

Since the overwhelming majority of aristocratic elder sons married, while the celibacy rates for male aristocrats were roughly as high as those of their sisters, and since a woman took on the class of the man she married, it appears that many aristocratic younger sons did not think they could afford aristocratic brides and that aristocratic women and/or their families resisted making marriages outside their own class.

37. Alice Clark, *Working Life of Women in the Seventeenth Century* (1919; reprint, New York: A. M. Kelley, 1968); Sheila Rowbotham, *Hidden from History: Three Hundred Years of Women's Oppression and the Fight against It* (London: Pluto Press, 1973); Roberta Hamilton, *The Liberation of Women: A Study of Patriarchy and Capitalism* (London: George Allen and Unwin, 1978).

38. Sara Heller Mendelson, "Stuart Women's Diaries and Occasional Memoirs," in *Women in English Society, 1500–1800*, ed. Mary Prior (London: Methuen, 1985), 190.

39. One exception is Eileen Spring, cited in n. 5.

40. Stone and Stone, 407.

41. 5 Eliz., c. 4.

42. M. Dorothy George, "The Combination Laws Reconsidered," *Economic History* 1 (1927):212–228.

43. John V. Orth, "English Combination Acts of the Eighteenth Century," *Law and History Review* 5 (1987):204, 207.

44. 5 Geo. 4, c. 95, s. 1 (1824); 6 Geo. 4, c. 129, s. 2 (1825), 5 Geo. 4, c. 96, s. 1 (1824). See also Patrick Park, "The Combination Acts in Ireland, 1727–1825," *Irish Jurist* 14, n.s. (1979):340–359. The acts (1727, 1743, 1780) passed in Ireland made combinations in all trades illegal; after the union between Ireland and England a special Combination Act for Ireland with heavier penalties and no arbitration clause was passed in 1803.

45. Mendelson, 194.

46. For a sophisticated and powerful analysis of the new public/commercial va-

riety of authoritative pronouncements on the family which claimed to be neither public nor authoritative, see Michael G. Ketcham, *Transparent Designs: Reading, Performance, and Form in the Spectator Papers* (Athens: University of Georgia Press, 1985).

47. Joseph Addison, *The Spectator,* ed. Donald Bond, 5 vols. (Oxford: Clarendon Press, 1965), 4:237.
48. Lenore Davidoff and Catherine Hall, *Family Fortunes: Men and Women of the English Middle Class, 1780–1850* (London: Hutchinson, 1987).
49. Davidoff and Hall, 279.
50. Davidoff and Hall, 209.
51. Davidoff and Hall, 275.
52. Susan Moller Okin, "Women and the Making of the Sentimental Family," *Philosophy and Public Affairs* 11 (1982):72.
53. Okin, 87.
54. John Cannon, *Aristocratic Century: The Peerage of Eighteenth-Century England* (Cambridge: Cambridge University Press, 1984), 128.
55. Malcomson, 24.
56. Fletcher v. Fletcher (1788), 2 Cox 99, at 102.

Case Index

General Index

Abbott, Charles (Lord Tenterden), 191
Act of Union. *See* Union with Ireland Act
Adams, J., 123
Addison, Joseph, 142–143, 145, 158–159, 269
Adequacy: problems of measuring, 126; of separate maintenance allowances, 182; of settlement provisions, 119–121, 129–130
Adultery, of husband, 224
Adultery, of wife, 3, 36–37, 83, 140–141, 162–163, 168–169, 173, 214
Alienability: as alleged public interest, 89–92, 198; arguments for, selectively applied, 94; contradictions in property law concerning, 213; and dower, 47–48, 49, 83; legal intellectuals and, 91; and liberal story, 32–33, 212–214; maximizing, 209; and newer conceptions of property, 147–148; promoting, insufficient explanation for separate property rules, 217–218
Alienation, wife's powers of, 136, 150–153, 193, 272n40. *See also* Restraint on anticipation
Alimony, 8, 37, 145, 191–192
Alvanley, Baron. *See* Arden, Richard Pepper
American law, 24–25, 49, 85, 92, 257n12
Annuities: granted, 110, 122, 188, 193; husband's attempt to get wife to surrender, 172; unusual contracts for, and usury, 207; used to bar, 102, 108; woman's purchase of, found revocable,

152–153; women's efforts to alienate, 152, 153
Arden, Richard Pepper (Baron Alvanley): on avoiding public scandal, 177; on election, 110, 113; on infant jointure, 119, 125; on law reports, 13; on recognizing separate maintenance contracts, 180; on testamentary devises and election, 110–111; on wife's power of alienation, 272n40; on wife's property in separate maintenance allowance, 193–194
Atherley, Edmond Gibson, 15, 125–126, 157–158
Austen, Jane, 60
Avoidance, 206–208, 229

Baddeley, Robert, 170, 172–173
Baddeley, Sophia, 170, 172–173, 274n14
Ballow, Henry, 15, 182
Bathurst, Henry (Lord Apsley, Earl Bathurst), 109–110, 123
Beckett, J. V., 199
Bentham, Jeremy, 226
Blackstone, Sir William: and archaic procedures, 210; and celebratory legal history, 9; on dower, 33, 257n12; as enlightenment treatise writer, 14–15, 15–16; prefers jointure to dower, 97, 113; on private acts, 87–88, 206; on public policy, 173, 212, 227–228; reverses Mansfield in *Perrin*, 73–74; settlement printed in *Commentaries*, 80
Board of Trade, 24